RECONSIDERING

THE DOCTRINE OF

GOD | Charles E. Gutenson

RECONSIDERING THE DOCTRINE OF

GOD | Charles E. Gutenson

London 4/1/16

t&t clark

NEW YORK • LONDON

T & T Clark International, Madison Square Park, 15 East 26th Street, New York, NY 10010

T & T Clark International, The Tower Building, 11 York Road, London SE1 7NX

T & T Clark International is a Continuum imprint.

Cover and interior design by Corey Kent

Library of Congress Cataloging-in-Publication Data

Gutenson, Charles E.
    Reconsidering the doctrine of God / Charles E. Gutenson.
        p.   cm.
    Includes bibliographical references and index.
    ISBN 0-567-02930-1 (pbk.) — ISBN 0-567-02920-4
    1. God.   2. Pannenberg, Wolfhart, 1928–   I. Title.
BT103.G88   2005
231'.092—dc22

                                                                        2005006665

Printed in the United States of America
05 06 07 08 09 10   10 9 8 7 6 5 4 3 2 1

CONTENTS

FOREWORD

IT IS A PLEASURE FOR ME to write a foreword to Charles Gutenson's book. For quite a number of years, I had the privilege of observing the growth of this work and of engaging in occasional exchange with the author on particular issues. I feel very satisfied with the final result of his investigations and with his presentation. Charles Gutenson not only provides an accurate presentation of my views with much detail and precision, but he also engages in critical discussions with their content, including the reactions of some of my critics. I agree with most of his conclusions.

A particularly helpful element of Gutenson's discussion centers on the concept of eternity and its relevance to issues such as divine omniscience, especially to his extensive treatment of my proposal to interpret the biblical idea of God as spirit in terms of a field of power as suggested by the root meaning of the biblical term. Gutenson's treatment of this issue offers the best commentary presently available. He is correct that I use the term "field" in an analogical sense as compared to the various field concepts of the physicists. This should be clear already from the fact that the "field" of the divine spirit does not have waves that can be counted, as I repeatedly emphasize. Of course the divine spirit is not identical with any field of physics, not even with the universal fields of space-time and energy. The divine spirit is understood to be the ultimate source and comprehensive condition of all physical field effects. Furthermore, the divine spirit (as a concept of the divine essence) is concrete only in the three persons: Father, Son, and Holy Spirit. The divine essence as such is not personal (that would amount to a fourth person), but it is realized only in the three persons manifesting the one "field" of the divine spirit.

Such a theological use of the field concept is not simply a metaphorical use transferred from the language of physics, but rather a reclamation of the philosophical and metaphysical roots of field language used by the physicists, roots that are evident from the history of the scientific terminology. It is therefore that I refer often to the field concept of Michael Faraday, although I know very well that current field concepts of physicists are quite different in many respects. Still, the attempt to recapture the philosophical roots of the field concept in theological language about God should be appreciated as a contribution to a new awareness of a close proximity between science and theology; a proximity closer than many have considered possible.

The issue of talking about God as spirit in terms of field language is just one example of the many intellectual challenges issuing from the traditional Christian doctrine of God, and I hope that many readers not only use this book as an introduction to my personal thought, but also as a gateway to the fascinating adventure of systematic theology.

Wolfhart Pannenberg

CHAPTER 1

Introduction

HOW DOES ONE PREDICT the significance that a theologian's career will have when his first few publications begin to appear? Interestingly, with the publication of *Revelation as History* (German: *Offenbarung als Geschichte*) in 1961, many suspected that one or more significant theological careers had been launched. The work was authored by a group of seven young German philosophers and theologians, sometimes referred to as the "Heidelberg Circle."[1] The group had undertaken inquiry into a broad range of theological issues, as suggested by the different theses identified and defended in the final form of the work. At the time that the work started, all in the original group were in the midst of doctoral programs at the University of Heidelberg, and ten years would pass before *Revelation as History* would be published. The members of the group represented various fields and initially included Rolf Rendtorff (Old Testament), Klaus Koch (Old Testament), Ulrich Wilkens (New Testament), and Dietrich Roessler (New Testament). Added somewhat after the initial formation of the group were Trutz Rendtorff (systematic theology) and Martin Elze (church history).[2] The other systematic theologian of the group, considered by many its leader, was Wolfhart Pannenberg. It was a fitting first step for Pannenberg, whose work would continually delight, challenge, and frustrate (depending

---

1. Later it would often be referred to as the Pannenberg Circle.
2. This information is from W. Pannenberg, *Theology and the Kingdom of God* (ed. R. J. Neuhaus; Philadelphia: Westminster, 1977), 16.

---

upon one's perspective) the theological and philosophical communities for the next thirty-five years.

An early indication of the significance of Pannenberg's work, as well as something of a prediction of what would follow, is evident in the comments made by James M. Robinson in 1967: "A new school has been launched," and it is "the first theological school to emerge in Germany within recent years that is not in one form or the other a development of the dialectic theology of the twenties."[3] Similar comments were made on the other side of his academic career when, in a series of lectures honoring Pannenberg upon his retirement from the University of Munich, one lecturer applauded Pannenberg for delivering theology from the subjectivism so evident in the theology of the first half of the twentieth century. While there might be some discussion concerning the precise characterization of Pannenberg's contribution to the theological enterprise, there is little doubt that he will be considered one of the most significant theologians of the twentieth century.

Returning for a moment to *Revelation as History*, it is now reasonably clear that Pannenberg's contribution, an essay entitled "Dogmatic Theses in the Doctrine of Revelation,"[4] was something of a programmatic essay that both anticipated and guided much of his subsequent work. If one examines the seven theses laid out in this piece, one will see already the importance of the concept of history for his theological reflection. Reality, Pannenberg believes, is fundamentally historically structured. Consequently, the theologian, who seeks to investigate and understand matters that are themselves historical in nature, must be prepared to use the historian's tools to lay bare the content of those historical events. Not surprisingly, some have gone so far as to consider Pannenberg as much historian as theologian. Pannenberg was once asked how he structured his studies during the early part of his academic career—that is, did he dedicate some number of years to the Fathers, so many to the Reformers?[5] He responded that, as it turned out, his early studies were largely determined by his need to respond to questions and objections raised in response to the theses presented in this early essay. While it would be simplistic to propose that all of Pannenberg's contributions to theology are suggested in one early essay, it is not unreasonable to suggest that a good deal of Pannenberg's work can be understood as working out the consequences of the particular view of the theological enterprise first advanced there. In a sense, then, Pannenberg's work has

---

3. J. M. Robinson, "Revelation as Word and as History," in *Theology as History* (ed. J. M. Robinson and J. B. Cobb Jr.; New York: Harper & Row, 1967), 12–13.

4. W. Pannenberg, "Dogmatic Theses in the Doctrine of Revelation," in W. Pannenberg et al., *Revelation as History* (trans. D. Granskou; London: Macmillan, 1968), 123ff. Pannenberg also wrote the introduction to this volume.

5. From private discussions with the author between December 1993 and February 1994.

been guided by remarkable faithfulness to a vision of theology already present at the outset of his academic career.

Now standing at the other end of Pannenberg's career, we are able to examine what must be seen as the culmination of his theological vision: his three-volume *Systematic Theology*. We may now evaluate Pannenberg's mature proposals in light of the theological system they imply. There are undoubtedly a number of perspectives one might take in evaluation of Pannenberg's theology, but perhaps the best is the one most consistent with his own indicated intentions. While it has not been unusual for modern theology to make primary the human response to God (or otherwise to move God from the very center of theology), Pannenberg refuses to go this way. In fact, in *An Introduction to Systematic Theology*, he writes, "Everything in theology is concerned with God, so that God is the one and only subject of theology."[6] As to the content of systematic theology, he writes, "Dogmatics as presentation of Christian doctrine, then, has to be systematic theology, namely a systematic doctrine of God and nothing else."[7] Certainly in his systematic presentation of Christian doctrine, Pannenberg deals with the issues traditionally handled, issues such as soteriology, eschatology, and the like. However, when he says that systematic theology is nothing other than a systematic doctrine of God, he is arguing that all other doctrines and doctrinal claims are the working out of the implications of the doctrine of God in those respective areas.

For this examination of the theology of Wolfhart Pannenberg, I will focus my attention according to Pannenberg's own prioritization, that is, on his proposed doctrine of God. My examination, however, will not extend to the implications of the doctrine of God as worked out in, say, soteriology or eschatology, but rather will focus more narrowly upon the set of issues related to the concept of God itself. The suitability of this approach is suggested by the fact that, first, Pannenberg has written that "the concept of God which was developed by medieval and early modern theology in close contact with classical metaphysics is in need of rather radical revision."[8] Further, as one might expect, Pannenberg's *Systematic Theology* presents and defends those revisions he believes necessary. In short, it is Pannenberg's doctrine of God that drives his mature theological system, and so the purpose of my examination is to present and assess the proposals Pannenberg advances for revising the Christian concept of God. Before turning directly to the examination of Pannenberg's doctrine of God, however, I will briefly discuss two other issues. First, I will outline the historical

---

6. W. Pannenberg, *An Introduction to Systematic Theology* (Grand Rapids: Eerdmans, 1991), 13.

7. W. Pannenberg, *Systematic Theology* (vol. 1; trans. G. W. Bromiley; Grand Rapids: Eerdmans, 1991), 59.

8. Pannenberg, *Introduction to Systematic Theology*, 23.

context of Pannenberg's work. Second, I will reflect upon the underlying reasons for the significance of Pannenberg's work for the broader theological enterprise.

Biographical Sketch

Wolfhart Pannenberg was born on October 2, 1928, in the city of Stettin, which was at the time part of Germany but now is part of Poland. His father was a middle-class civil servant, and as Olive reports, "From all accounts, his home did not profess a devotional type of Christianity."[9] In fact, Pannenberg points out that his family left the church in the 1930s.[10] Pannenberg was early interested in music, and he began to study the piano at age seven. Upon his family's relocation to Aachen, where they lived from 1936 to 1942, he reports that music was his primary interest. In 1942 the family moved from Aachen to Berlin, and in the summer of 1944 the Pannenberg home was lost to an Allied bombing mission, the family barely escaping with their lives.

For the next few months, the Pannenbergs lived with relatives in Pomerania. As fate would have it, the young Wolfhart, still enamored with music, found a book at the local library entitled *The Birth of Tragedy from the Spirit of Music*. It turned out to be a philosophical work by Nietzsche, and over the next few months, Pannenberg reports that he "devoured everything written by Nietzsche that [he] could get hold of."[11] As one would expect, this led Pannenberg to a negative assessment of Christianity, an assessment he was to hold until later influenced by a German literature teacher who was a Christian but who did not live according to the expectations Pannenberg developed from reading Nietzsche. This opened the door for Pannenberg's reassessment of Christianity and his eventual embrace of it. It is one of the serendipitous tensions of Pannenberg's life that the theologian many would consider to be the consummate rationalist can trace God's initial call upon his life to what must be considered a mystical experience. Here is how he describes it:

> On the sixth of January, while I was walking back home from school (instead of using the train)—a somewhat lengthy walk of several hours—an extraordinary event occurred in which I found myself absorbed into the light surround-

---

9. D. Olive, *Wolfhart Pannenberg* (Makers of the Modern Theological Mind; ed. B. E. Patterson; Waco, TX: Word Books, 1973), 17.

10. W. Pannenberg, "An Autobiographical Sketch," in *The Theology of Wolfhart Pannenberg* (ed. C. E. Braatan and P. Clayton; Minneapolis: Augsburg, 1988), 11–18. Many of the details in the following are taken from this autobiographical essay.

11. Ibid., 12.

ing me. When I became aware again of my finite existence, I did not know what had happened but certainly knew that it was the most important event of my life; I spent many years afterwards to find out what it meant to me.[12]

Pannenberg believes this "visionary" experience was the initial claim of Christ upon his life, and the theological work he has undertaken must be seen as his response to that claim.

Toward the latter part of World War II, when he was sixteen, Pannenberg was forced into military service. He was soon captured by the British and held prisoner for a short time, after which he was released. During this period (1945–1947), Pannenberg became more serious about his studies and made his first foray into the writings of Kant. In the spring of 1947, Pannenberg enrolled at Humboldt University; soon thereafter, he knew that he "was to be a theologian for the rest of [his] life."[13] In the fall of 1948, Pannenberg transferred to Göttingen, where he studied under Gogarten and Hartmann. Following this period, he studied for a term at Basel under Barth and Jaspers. While Pannenberg admits Barth exerted an important influence on his thought, he quickly became disappointed with what he perceived to be the lack of philosophical rigor in Barth's theology. Pannenberg moved on to Heidelberg in the fall of 1950, where he was influenced by von Rad, particularly his commitment to theology as an interpretation of history, and Lowith's work in the philosophy of history.

In 1953 Pannenberg submitted his dissertation on the doctrine of predestination in the thought of Duns Scotus. Two years later, he submitted his *Habilitationsschrift*, which dealt with the doctrine of analogy in medieval thought. In 1955 Pannenberg was ordained a Lutheran minister at the Heidelberg University chapel. During the same year, he became a docent at Heidelberg and began to teach his first classes in theology. In 1958 Pannenberg was called to Wuppertal, where he taught with Jürgen Moltmann. In 1961 Pannenberg moved to the University of Mainz, where he remained until he became professor of systematic theology at the University of Munich. He remained there until his retirement in early 1994.

Pannenberg and the Development of the Doctrine of God

While Pannenberg believes that systematic theology is primarily concerned with articulating an adequate doctrine of God, he treats the actual presentation of this subject matter with a great deal of caution. For example, in 1988 he wrote:

---

12. Ibid.
13. Ibid., 13.

In my experience, the most difficult subject to deal with was the doctrine of God. I soon became persuaded that one first has to acquire a systematic account of every other field, not only theology, but also philosophy and the dialogue with the natural and social sciences before with sufficient confidence one can dare to develop the doctrine of God. In fact, not until the early 1980s did I begin to feel solid ground under my feet in this area.[14]

He goes on to admit that he had written on the idea of God prior to the early 1980s, but those writings should be seen as precursors to the full-orbed doctrine of God advanced in his *Systematic Theology.*

It is reasonable at this point to ask for a more precise statement of what Pannenberg intends by saying that "one has first to acquire a systematic account of every other field" and why he thinks this a necessary prerequisite. It is not likely, for example, that Pannenberg intends by his claim that before one can embark upon the task of presenting a doctrine of God, one must have expertise in veterinary medicine or marine biology. Rather, his claim flows out of his commitment to the absolute centrality of the concept of God to all knowledge and truth. This commitment is clearly articulated when he writes:

If the God of the Bible is the creator of the universe, then it is not possible to understand fully or even appropriately the processes of nature without any reference to that God. If, on the contrary, nature can be appropriately understood without reference to the God of the Bible, then that God cannot be the creator of the universe, and consequently he cannot truly be God and be trusted as a source of moral teaching either.[15]

It is Pannenberg's position that if God is the Creator of all reality, then all reality must bear traces of its creatureliness. The only state of affairs in which this would not be the case is that in which God is not the Creator of all reality. Consequently, if God is the Creator, no object of reality can be fully understood without reference to God.[16]

It is from this context that Pannenberg makes the claim that the development of an adequate doctrine of God requires one to gain expertise in "every other field." If one were to undertake an exhaustive, "unsurpassable" doctrine of God, one might be inclined to take Pannenberg very liter-

---

14. Ibid., 16.

15. W. Pannenberg, "Theological Questions to Scientists," in *Toward a Theology of Nature* (ed. T. Peters; Louisville, KY: Westminster/John Knox, 1993), 16.

16. Obviously, then, there is a close connection between ontology and epistemology in Pannenberg's thought. I shall say much more about this in chapter 2, where I deal with the influence of Dilthey's work on Pannenberg.

ally. However, there are three reasons not to do so. First, there is a subset of "every other field" that gives one access to the central issues regarding the world's processes, which, in turn, bring to the fore those matters relating to God's interactions with the world. These would include, besides philosophy and theology, certain areas from the natural and social sciences. Second, it is clear from other writings that what Pannenberg really has in mind is an interaction with other fields *at the level of philosophical reflection.* In speaking of the dialogue between scientists and theologians, for example, he writes that "theologians should address their questions to scientists . . . on the level of philosophical reflection on the work of science."[17] Consequently, one need not gain a "systematic account," for example, of anthropology and cosmology in their fine details, but rather at the level of philosophical reflection upon these topics. Subjects such as the philosophy of science provide coverage for a range of scientific fields. Finally, if one examines the writings of Pannenberg, one finds this to be just the course of study he has undertaken. In addition to his numerous methodological, programmatic, and topical writings on purely theological matters, he has undertaken major works on the philosophy of science and anthropology. Consequently, one must understand Pannenberg's caution toward development of the doctrine of God in relation to his belief that to affirm God as Creator is to recognize the dependent relation of all reality upon God. However, one need not exhaustively examine all aspects of created reality or all scientific theories, since God's free creative act makes it clear that the doctrine of God is not dependent upon any particular created process or scientific theory. Rather, it is at the level of philosophical reflection abstracted from these processes and theories that one may develop the knowledge that, Pannenberg believes, makes it possible to undertake development of the doctrine of God.

If one examines closely Pannenberg's various publications and the course of research suggested by them, one can see how they have led to his *Systematic Theology,* which, as we have seen, he considers to be the systematic presentation of his doctrine of God. His contribution to *Revelation as History* set forth the framework for the historical element of his method. *Jesus: God and Man* represented a specific application and further development of this method. In *Theology and the Kingdom of God,* Pannenberg made an initial foray into a cluster of issues relating to the doctrine of God. The two-volume set (three in Germany and Britain) entitled *Basic Questions in Theology* dealt with both methodological issues and certain aspects of the concept of God. In the 1970s, he wrote his major works on the philosophy of science (*Theology and the Philosophy of Science*) and on

---

17. Pannenberg, "Theological Questions to Scientists," 17.

anthropology (*Anthropology in Theological Perspective*). In addition, two volumes relate the concept of God to specific sets of issues: *Metaphysics and the Idea of God* and *The Idea of God and Human Freedom*. This is by no means an exhaustive listing of Pannenberg's publications, but it does show something of the wide-ranging preparation he felt was necessary before proceeding to his more formal articulation of the doctrine of God.

In this brief recounting of the course of research that led to the development of his three-volume *Systematic Theology*, I have already outlined one of the reasons to believe an inquiry into the doctrine of God, specifically as articulated by Pannenberg, would be fruitful. The breadth of research represented by Pannenberg's range of publications is virtually unparalleled in contemporary theology. In addition to the breadth of work, it is not uncommon for him to give a rather thorough presentation of the history of ideas leading to the position that he intends to analyze. In short, there are very few indeed who can match Pannenberg's research in both its breadth and its depth.

A second reason is directly related to his intense commitment to the discovery of truth.[18] He laments the extent to which theology has both allowed and participated in the redefinition of the Christian faith so that the question of its truth has become secondary, if not ignored altogether. Pannenberg is clear in stating his belief that a failure to attend to the truth of Christianity has far-reaching implications:

> If theology properly faces [the task of confirming the truth of Christian doctrine], it can be of invaluable help in encouraging the preacher and in strengthening the good conscience of every individual Christian that the teaching of the church is true. If theology does not properly face its particular task regarding the truth claims of the Christian tradition, then it easily happens that the clergy of the church are the first to become insecure and evasive about the message they are supposed to preach. When they become doubtful about the truth of the gospel, they will tend to replace it by other "causes," and the believers will be disturbed, because they no longer get to hear in church what they rightfully expect to be taught there.[19]

Such statements raise a number of questions, some of the more important of which deal with Pannenberg's epistemology and, of course, his theory of truth, since even highly subjectivist interpretations generally claim the Christian faith to be true in some sense. These matters will be taken up in the next chapter as we examine Pannenberg's methodology.

---

18. Consider, for example, his foreword in F. LeRon Shults, *The Postfoundationalist Task of Theology* (Grand Rapids: Eerdmans, 1999), ix–x.

19. Pannenberg, *Introduction to Systematic Theology*, 6.

At this point, it is appropriate to expand briefly upon one aspect of Pannenberg's commitment to the truth of Christian claims, namely, his defense of their historical foundations. He makes this concern explicit when he writes that we "cannot honestly go on to identify ourselves as Christians if the story of Jesus Christ and of his God is merely a story (in the sense of a fairy tale)—fiction, but not history. . . . The story of Jesus Christ has to be history, not in all its details, but in its core, if the Christian faith is to continue."[20] Pannenberg believes, for example, that existentialist interpretations, which make the Gospels primarily about the human search for meaning, are inadequate because they fail to take seriously Christianity's truth claims, especially those concerning the historicity of God's presence in Jesus and his historical acts of redemption and reconciliation. In this, Pannenberg resists modern trends on these matters, and as one might expect, his position is often hotly contested. Nevertheless, the fact that he seeks to articulate the historicity of the faith in a manner consistent with the bulk of the Christian tradition makes his proposals worth evaluating. We must be careful, however, not to overemphasize this point to suggest that Pannenberg embraces a facile literalism. Notice that he readily admits that not all the details of the Gospel accounts must be historical, but rather its core.

Another concern that Pannenberg frequently raises is the tendency of Christian theologians not to take seriously atheistic criticisms. In fact, he argues that these challenges have often simply been ignored. It is not, Pannenberg believes, that the criticisms advanced by, for example, Fichte, Feuerbach, and Marx are by any means decisive, but rather that the failure of Christian theology to engage and refute these positions has tended to give them more credibility and to create the impression that Christianity has no adequate response. Pannenberg's criticism extends beyond claiming that theologians have not provided an adequate refutation to atheistic criticisms. He also believes that some atheistic criticisms have elements of truth from which Christian theologians should learn.[21] That Pannenberg engages these challenges seriously, whether by seeking to refute them or by showing what might be learned from them, further supports using Pannenberg's proposals as a point of access to the doctrine of God.

A good many of the points raised above can be characterized as expressions of Pannenberg's determination to restore what he believes to be the damaged intellectual credibility of the Christian faith. When the intellectual credibility of the faith is called into question, the question of the *truthful-*

---

20. Ibid., 5.

21. Consider Merold Westphal's essay "Taking Suspicion Seriously: The Religious Uses of Modern Atheism," *Faith and Philosophy* 4, no. 1 (October 1987): 26–43, for examples of areas where Christians might better admit the validity of aspects of certain criticisms. See also Merold Westphal, *Suspicion and Faith* (New York: Fordham University Press, 1998).

ness of Christian claims is often dismissed as unworthy of debate. Other matters, then, become primary. In the following quotation, Pannenberg is sympathetic to Bartley's critique of those such as Braithwaste who argue that the biblical narratives are not about truth claims but rather are intended to reinforce particular personal decisions or commitments:

> Theology was now conceived as the explication of the content of personal or communal faith, the truth of which had to be presupposed as a matter of personal decision. William W. Bartley pointedly characterized and attacked this attitude as a "retreat to commitment": It actually represents a retreat from the arena of public critical discourse of truth claims of all sorts, a retreat into some sheltered corner of personal preference. The impact of this attitude on Christian thought did a great deal of damage to the righteous claim of Christian teaching to be taken seriously as a candidate of rational discourse.[22]

One of Pannenberg's primary goals, then, has been to show that Christianity does indeed deserve a place at the table of rational discourse.

Pannenberg's theology, broadly taken, has proven to resist facile categorization. Those who favor a more liberal theological perspective often find solace in his embrace of the historical-critical method and the attendant willingness, for example, to dismiss certain aspects of the Gospel accounts as nonhistorical. Similarly, his deep commitment to rationality may be taken by some as an exaltation of reason over revelation. On the other hand, more conservative theologians look with favor upon Pannenberg's affirmation of the historicity of the resurrection of Jesus. They also agree with his opposition to abortion and homosexual practice, and his refusal to fall back to a "Bible merely as story" position. However, he has also been roundly criticized by both camps. For example, conservatives object to his reference to the term "resurrection" as metaphorical, while liberals object to his arguments for the historicity of the resurrection. There is, however, no doubt that Pannenberg must be considered a major player in contemporary theology, and it is reasonable to predict that the path to theology's future will pass through, rather than around, Pannenberg's work.

Outline of This Examination

This examination of the being and nature of God in the theology of Pannenberg is divided into two sections, with the bulk of the work comprising the second section. The first section (dealt with primarily in chapter 2) is a critical presentation of Pannenberg's method. Chapter 2 includes an exami-

---

22. Pannenberg, *Introduction to Systematic Theology*, 16.

nation of his epistemology and theory of truth as well as his understanding of the tasks and norms of systematic theology. I will consider the structure Pannenberg proposes for a systematic presentation of Christian doctrine and identify the central issues he believes a systematic theology must address. In the course of discussing Pannenberg's method, I will address what he sees as a fundamental question: In the light of the debatability of God's existence, how does one justify talk of God in the first place?

The second section (consisting of chapters 3 through 7) analyzes five of the substantive proposals advanced in Pannenberg's theology. Chapter 3 considers Pannenberg's appropriation of the concept of infinity (which he proposes be elevated to primacy within the Christian doctrine of God) and his deployment of it. As we shall see, Pannenberg's analysis of the concept of infinity borrows meaningfully from Descartes and Hegel, and there he sees his assertion of the primacy of the concept of infinity in the doctrine of God in line with the much earlier work of Gregory of Nyssa.

One of the proposals Pannenberg advances, which has generated a good deal of debate, is that the future has an ontological priority over the present and the past. The phrase that is often associated with Pannenberg's work and that captures this proposal is his description of God as the "power of the future which determines everything." Chapter 4 deals with this interesting proposal, which Pannenberg believes opens the door to the solution of a number of problems that have historically plagued the tradition.

In a private discussion, Pannenberg once told a colleague that volume 1 of his *Systematic Theology* would be primarily about the Father and the Son and the Holy Spirit—and so would volumes 2 and 3. During the second half of the twentieth century, there was a resurgence of interest in the doctrine of the Trinity, and Pannenberg's name has often appeared as one of several at the leading edge of the development of Trinitarian doctrine. Chapter 5 outlines and assesses his proposed doctrine of the Trinity.

Perhaps the most controversial and provocative proposal that Pannenberg makes with regard to the development of the doctrine of God involves a fundamental reconceptualization. He proposes that we appropriate the field concept from modern physics and conceive God as an infinite field of power. His proposal is intended to provide an answer to the question of what it means to say that God is Spirit—that is, what is the nature of Spirit? Numerous difficulties have been raised with this proposal, not the least of which is how one maintains God's personhood with such a reconceptualization. These issues, and related ones, are addressed in chapter 6.

In chapter 7, I examine the impact of these proposals upon the doctrine of the divine attributes. As it turns out, Pannenberg's proposal to draw on the concept of infinity as the central aspect of the doctrine of God has implications for the manner in which the divine attributes are understood.

Finally, chapter 8 summarizes the findings of the various assessments and draws summary conclusions regarding Pannenberg's proposed doctrine of God. Additionally, where it has been discovered that various modifications of one degree or another have the potential for resolving difficulties, these will be outlined and summarized.

CHAPTER 2

Pannenberg and Theological Method

ONE OF PANNENBERG'S OBJECTIVES is to reestablish the intellectual credibility of the Christian faith. He believes that its credibility has suffered at the hands of Christian believers (theologians, pastors) who, though well intentioned, have often failed to adequately engage atheistic (or other) challenges to Christian truth claims. In fact, he has sometimes argued that Christian philosophers and theologians who do not take with adequate seriousness the criticisms of, for example, Fichte and Feuerbach are still operating in a precritical mode.[23] As one might expect, then, a fundamental element of Pannenberg's method involves demonstrating that the Christian faith has the intellectual resources to secure a place in the marketplace of public debate by facing directly the challenges raised to it. Of course, in order to join the public intellectual marketplace, one must be willing to be guided in debate by some minimal set of shared, reasonably neutral presuppositions. Pannenberg believes that appropriate presuppositions are those that can be derived from reflections, at the philosophical level, concerning the sciences. Consequently, Pannenberg argues in some detail in *Theology and the Philosophy of Science* that theology is a science, specifically the science of God.

Coupled with, and perhaps exacerbating, these matters is a datum of human existence that Pannenberg takes as fundamental: the debatability of

---

23. Related in personal conversation between December 1993 and February 1994.

God's existence. It seems we live in a state of affairs such that one cannot decisively prove (or disprove either, for that matter) the existence of God. Theological inquiry, then, may not bypass this question, but rather must begin with it. Does God exist? If so, which one? The God of Abraham, Isaac, and Jacob? Or perhaps the One of certain Eastern religions? Pannenberg argues that Christian truth claims, even the mere claim that God exists, must be understood as fundamentally hypothetical in nature, which means of course that they stand in need of confirmation. The confirmation of these truth claims, according to Pannenberg, is being worked out in the course of human history. This suggests that Christian doctrinal claims, as embodied in a particular systematic theology, might best be understood as a theory aimed to provide the best explanation of the world of shared human experience. Consequently, one may accept as true a systematic presentation of Christian doctrine to the extent that it coheres internally and corresponds to human experience. Already, from only this brief introduction, a host of methodological issues arises: the nature of Pannenberg's underlying epistemic commitments, his understanding of the nature of truth, the nature and weight of various evidence, and the factors that make believing some systematic presentation of Christian doctrine rational. Each will receive attention in due course.

Since in modern secular cultures the presuppositions regarding the reality of the God whom Jesus called Father are in question, Pannenberg holds that one can no longer engage in a systematic presentation of Christian doctrine without first taking steps to justify that presentation. He recognizes the changed cultural situation when he writes, "In earlier cultures the words 'God' and 'gods' had a more or less clearly defined place in the cultural world and human vocabulary. . . . In modern secular cultures the word 'God' has increasingly lost" its function.[24] He continues:

> In the public mind statements about God are mere assertions which are ascribed to the subjectivity of the speaker and the truth claim of which not only needs to be generally tested before it can be accepted but is for the most part set aside in advance, the belief being that the testing will lead nowhere and that the truth claims of statements about God are not even worth discussing publicly.[25]

While it may have been true in the past that the theologian could launch directly into a systematic presentation of the truth claims of the Christian faith, Pannenberg believes that in the present situation one must justify

---

24. W. Pannenberg, *Systematic Theology* (vol. 1; trans. G. W. Bromiley; Grand Rapids: Eerdmans, 1991), 63.
25. Ibid., 1:64.

such an endeavor by recognizing the debatability of God's existence and winning a starting point for such a presentation.

If this is correct, then the questions mentioned above (epistemic commitments, theory of truth, and the like) become crucial, for the answers to these questions in turn provide the grounds for determining the manner in which religious assertions are to be justified. As one would expect, these matters are handled primarily within the scope of Pannenberg's methodological proposals, and a good deal of Pannenberg's work prior to about 1980 focused upon methodology. Perhaps the most significant of these works was the 1973 volume *Theology and the Philosophy of Science*. Here Pannenberg makes his argument for treating theology as the science of God. In this chapter, I will turn my attention to the methodological proposals Pannenberg advances to support the claim that theology is the science of God. My aim will be to assess critically the extent to which these proposals satisfy the requirement for establishing a starting point for developing a systematic presentation of the Christian faith. First, I will consider Pannenberg's position vis-à-vis the purpose, content, and structure of systematic theology. Next, before examining Pannenberg's own constructive proposal, I will review his rationale for rejecting certain alternative proposals for establishing a grounding for systematic theology. Third, given its importance in Pannenberg's theological method, I will undertake a somewhat extended discussion of his understanding of the nature of truth. These discussions will prepare us for an examination of Pannenberg's attempt to win a launching point for systematic theology. I will conclude with a critique of Pannenberg's methodological proposals.

The Purpose, Content, and Structure of Systematic Theology

Purpose

A careful examination of Pannenberg's work reveals at least three distinct purposes that drive the task of the systematic theologian. All three are closely related, though the first two are so intimately related that they will be discussed together. One of the purposes of systematic theology is to show the interrelation of the various elements of Christian doctrine, and the second is to demonstrate the plausibility of the truth claims implied by those doctrines. Hence, the systematic theologian must make a presentation of the various Christian doctrines that is thorough in scope and systematic in presentation. In other words, the first goal of a systematic presentation of the Christian faith is to show, in some detail, the manner in which the various doctrines relate and give support to each other. Since the concept of coherence is a central element of Pannenberg's concept of truth, one sees immediately that to engage in such a systematic presentation of Christian doctrine is to engage, at least in a preliminary fashion, the question of each doctrine's truth. If a given theological system were to contain contradictions, the truth of at least a portion of that system would be suspect. Hence, the very presentation of a theological system makes an initial foray into the question of the truth content of Christian doctrine, and thus, the close relation between systematic presentation and initial plausibility of the implied system is evident.

Early in the first volume of *Systematic Theology*, Pannenberg himself makes these matters explicit when he cites with approval Buddeus on systematic theology: "A presentation of theology can be called systematic if it meets two conditions: 1) it deals with its subject matter comprehensively, which means, for Buddeus, that it takes into consideration all that is necessary to salvation; 2) it also explains, proves, and confirms . . . its content in detail."[26] Buddeus's second point relates closely to what was said above about systematic theology demonstrating the interrelation between doctrines and the establishment of their mutual interdependency and support. As for engaging the question of truth, Pannenberg writes: "If truth can only be one, the things that are regarded as true will not contradict one another, and they can be united with one another. To this extent a systematic presentation of the articles of faith directly involves their truth and the ascertainment of their truth."[27] It is, of course, the absence of contradiction and the ability to unite the various doctrinal claims into a unified whole that demonstrate the coherence of the elements of a systematic theology. Caution is appropriate at this point, however, for some have taken what Pannenberg says in this context to imply that his concept of truth is simply coherentist. However, such a conclusion would be unwarranted.

I mentioned three purposes above, and the third, according to Pannenberg, is to support the church in its task of proclaiming the gospel. The goal of the church's proclamation, of course, is to bring individuals into the kingdom of God through faith in Jesus Christ. In *An Introduction to Systematic Theology*, Pannenberg examines the motivations that determine why individuals choose to become adherents of particular religions. With regard to Christianity, he argues that one chooses to confess Christ because one believes the story of Christ to be true.[28] He writes, "We cannot honestly go on to identify ourselves as Christians if the story of Jesus Christ and of his God is merely a story (in the sense of fairy tale)—fiction, but not

---

26. Ibid., 1:18.

27. Ibid., 1:19.

28. Of course, there are individuals who consider themselves Christian while denying the historicity of Christ or the essential historicity of the Gospel narratives. It is precisely such a position that Pannenberg challenges.

history."[29] It is the primary task of the systematic theologian to take up the defense of the truth of Christianity, and in so doing, systematic theology provides an invaluable service to the church. Notice what Pannenberg believes is at stake:

> If the theologian properly faces [the task of defending the truth of Christian assertions], it can be of invaluable help in encouraging the preacher and in strengthening the good conscience of every individual Christian that the teaching of the church is true. If theology does not properly face its particular task regarding the truth claims of the Christian tradition, then it easily happens that the clergy of the church are the first to become insecure and evasive about the message they are supposed to preach. When they become doubtful about the truth of the gospel, they will tend to replace it by other "causes," and the believers will be disturbed because they no longer get to hear in church what they rightfully expect to be taught there.[30]

In short, when the systematic theologian fails to fulfill his or her unique responsibilities to the church, a crisis of confidence in the gospel itself can easily arise. As far as Pannenberg is concerned, of those responsibilities undertaken by the systematic theologian, the central one is to demonstrate the plausibility of the truth claims of Christian doctrine. In fact, Pannenberg entitles the last section of chapter 1 of *Systematic Theology* "The Truth of Christian Doctrine as the Theme of Systematic Theology."[31] Throughout, Pannenberg makes clear the connection between the question of truth and the responsibility of the systematic theologian to engage that question.

Content

According to Pannenberg, the content of systematic theology is the "doctrinal content of scripture and the articles of faith."[32] Of course, the church's proclamation also engages in presentation of Christian doctrine. Pannenberg acknowledges this, arguing that they differ only in that systematic theology undertakes its inquiry into and presentation of Christian doctrine in a scientific manner.[33] Pannenberg unites these issues regarding the purposes of systematic theology and those concerning its content when he writes that "[systematic theology] has as its task, then, the comprehensive and coherent presentation of the doctrinal content of scripture and the articles of

---

29. W. Pannenberg, *An Introduction to Systematic Theology* (Grand Rapids: Eerdmans, 1991), 5.
30. Ibid., 6.
31. Pannenberg, *Systematic Theology*, 1:v.
32. Ibid., 1:18.
33. Ibid.

faith."[34] So far, these definitions are relatively straightforward. However, Pannenberg makes important modifications to the manner in which systematic theology is structured.

Structure

The first thing one notices about Pannenberg's *Systematic Theology* is the absence of a formal prolegomenon. To understand the significance of this departure from the manner in which systematic theologians have oft proceeded, one has to consider the reason for the development of prolegomena to systematics. Pannenberg, in a section entitled "The Development and Problem of So-Called Prolegomena to Dogmatics,"[35] presents a rather detailed analysis of the use of prolegomena in earlier dogmatic works. First of all, he has no objection in principle to preparing the reader for the presentation of a given subject: "In the presentation of a theme there is nothing unusual about postponing the actual treatment in favor of a few preliminary remarks on the theme itself and the mode of presentation."[36] The difficulty, as Pannenberg sees it, is that the prolegomenon, over time, "widened considerably in scope and had increasing thematic ramifications."[37] In other words, the so-called prolegomenon came more and more to deal with issues that were not merely introductory, but rather were issues of substance to the presentation of Christian doctrine itself. Pannenberg argues that the "fully developed form [of] the older Protestant prolegomena thus includes the following themes: (1) the concept of theology; (2) the Christian religion as the general object of theology; (3) scripture as the guiding principle of theology; (4) the articles of faith; and (5) the use of reason."[38]

In his critical assessment of the historical development of the prolegomenon to systematic theology, Pannenberg draws the following conclusion. While prolegomena were initially intended merely to be an introduction to systematic theology, the manner in which they came to be expanded led to a separation between the question of the truth of Christian doctrines and their systematic presentation. The prolegomenon, then, according to Pannenberg, dealt with the issue of truth, while the body of systematics focused upon the interrelations of various doctrines. However, Pannenberg believes that it is precisely the task of systematic theology, *as it engages in its presentation*, to inquire into the truth of Christian doctrine. Hence, one should not separate the question of truth from the systematic presentation of

---

34. Ibid.
35. Ibid., 1:26.
36. Ibid.
37. Ibid., 1:27.
38. Ibid., 1:28.

Christian doctrine, nor should one seek a guarantee of truth prior to the presentation of doctrine, but rather one should undertake the matter of truth in the course of the systematic presentation itself. Philip Clayton suggests the divergence of Pannenberg's method at this point from other systematicians: "Readers often find it difficult to believe that his theology does not separate theology and criticism at some point. Yet Pannenberg insists that there is no separate prolegomena to decide the truth question, no natural theology to serve as foundation for a 'science of faith.'"[39]

At the end of Pannenberg's analysis of the development of prolegomena, he summarizes his position, making it clear in the process that to give up the quest for a prior guarantee of truth is not to surrender the issue: "What, then, does it mean for the Christian faith consciousness and for dogmatics if it renounces the claim to a prior guarantee of its truth? What it does not mean, at all events, is that it must abandon the truth claim of Christian doctrine itself. On the contrary, *it means making the claim a theme of systematic theology*."[40]

We can now draw these discussions together in order to indicate what is, perhaps, Pannenberg's most fundamental methodological commitment. To begin with, he believes it is the special task of systematic theology to inquire into the truth content of Christian doctrine. However, this is not to be undertaken by dealing with the question of truth apart from the systematic presentation of that doctrine. Rather, it is precisely in the presenting of Christian doctrine in a systematic fashion that the question of its truth is addressed. Since "the fact that the reality and revelation of God are debatable is part of the reality of the world which dogmatics has to consider as God's world,"[41] and since Christian theology must defend itself in that world, the question of truth, Pannenberg argues, may not be avoided by prior guarantees, but must be addressed directly as the doctrines themselves are presented. This raises two important questions. In the first place, why does Pannenberg object to the attempt to resolve the issue of truth in the prolegomenon? Would it not seem reasonable, if possible, to settle the truth question at the outset so that one need only be concerned with presenting Christian doctrines and their interrelations? Second, these matters again raise the question of Pannenberg's concept of truth. Just what are the criteria for being able to say that a given doctrine may be taken as true? And in working that out, how does plausibility relate to all this?

The short answer to why Pannenberg rejects attempts to obtain a guarantee of truth prior to the systematic presentation of Christian doctrine is

---

39. P. Clayton, "Anticipation and Theological Method," in *The Theology of Wolfhart Pannenberg* (ed. C. E. Braaten and P. Clayton; Minneapolis: Augsburg, 1988), 125.
40. Pannenberg, *Systematic Theology*, 1:48 (emphasis added).
41. Ibid., 1:49.

that he does not believe one is available. Recall that Pannenberg has argued that the debatability of God's existence is part of the human condition that will continue throughout the march of human history. This means that there exists between God and humans a certain epistemic distance, which the majority of the Christian tradition has tended to affirm by speaking of the hiddenness of God. To provide a successful guarantee of the truth of Christian doctrine prior to its presentation would be, in principle, to overcome the debatability of God's existence, a thing Pannenberg believes cannot be done. This raises important questions about the status of religious assertions, questions that can be adequately addressed only in a subsequent discussion dealing with his concept of truth. Nevertheless, it is appropriate to anticipate our discussion by observing that Pannenberg, consistent with his intent to defend the scientific nature of theology, holds that religious assertions, such as those that comprise Christian doctrine, have the status of explanatory hypotheses about the world of human experience. In other words, the sum total of Christian doctrine constitutes a theory aimed to provide the best explanation of the totality of the experienced world.

The Unacceptability of Prior Guarantees

There is only one way that the truth content of explanatory hypotheses can be defended: by testing the hypotheses that purport to explain against the phenomena purported to be explained. Before considering Pannenberg's constructive proposals, it is instructive to consider briefly the manner in which theologians have attempted to provide a guarantee of the truth of Christian doctrine *prior to* its systematic presentation. Pannenberg argues that these attempts fall into at least three broad categories: (1) appeal to the magesterium of the church, (2) appeal to the doctrine of the inspiration of Scripture, and (3) appeal to the faith consciousness of the believer.[42]

The Magesterium of the Church

While the emphasis within Protestantism has been upon the perspicuity of Scripture and, thus, the ability of individuals to interpret the Scriptures for themselves, Roman Catholicism has tended to question these commitments and seeks, rather, to emphasize the teaching office of the church. The church authoritatively passes on acceptable interpretations of the Scriptures and, therefore, of their doctrinal content. This raises a question: How does

---

42. In what follows, my intent is to consider briefly Pannenberg's concerns with these attempts to gain a prior guarantee of truth.

the church determine what constitutes acceptable interpretations? The answer is that the teaching office of the church expresses doctrinal determinations made by certain conciliar decrees as well as the teaching authority vested in the bishops and the pope. In each case, however, Pannenberg argues that the teaching office of the church is intended to express the *consensus* of the church regarding particular issues of Christian faith. This suggests a consensus theory of truth. However, the problem with a consensus theory of truth is that while "consensus can express and denote the universality of truth . . . it can also express mere conventionality among the members of a group, society, or culture."[43] Pannenberg cites the geocentric model of the solar system as an example in which the consensus of the church actually passed on error rather than truth. In light of this possibility, Pannenberg argues, using the teaching office of the church as a means to obtain a prior guarantee of the truthfulness of Christian doctrine must be seen as problematic. As noted, Protestantism tended to move away from the authority of the teaching office of the church in favor of the authority of Scripture itself.

The Doctrine of Inspiration

As early as 1963, in a series of lectures delivered in the United States, Pannenberg raised a number of issues related to the authority and inspiration of Scripture. These lectures were published in volume 1 (English version) of *Basic Questions in Theology*, and one was titled "The Crisis of the Scripture Principle."[44] I will not review this essay in detail here; however, there are a couple of points worth mentioning. In the first place, Pannenberg claims that the development of the historical-critical method was a direct consequence of the Reformation doctrine of the perspicuity of Scripture: "The doctrine of the clarity of Scripture necessarily led to the demand that each theological statement should be based on the historical-critical exposition of Scripture."[45] If the Scriptures are clear, then surely a scientific analysis would make evident their unity and truth. However, it was just this method of exposition that challenged their literal accuracy.

> Scrutiny of the various tendencies among the New Testament writers threw the differences between the individual writings into bold relief. Thus, the old conception of the biblical canon, involving a material agreement among the biblical writings free from contradiction, collapsed. It was found necessary

---

43. Pannenberg, *Systematic Theology*, 1:12.
44. W. Pannenberg, "The Crisis of the Scripture Principle," in *Basic Questions in Theology* (vol. 1; trans. G. H. Kehm; Philadelphia: Westminster, 1983), 1–14.
45. Ibid., 1:6.

to distinguish between the attested events themselves and the tendencies in
the reporting of the individual biblical writers.[46]

While scholars might reasonably question whether Pannenberg has stated
the problem too strongly, it seems that the challenges raised by historical-
critical exegesis accentuate the hypothetical nature of doctrinal claims and
the need for testing their truth. Consequently, presupposing their truthfulness will necessarily seem inadequate to many, and thus Pannenberg's argument against the doctrine of inspiration as a prior guarantee of truth seems
a reasonable position. Again, the claim is not that these challenges decisively disprove the veracity of the Scriptures, but rather that they make the
testing of their truth claims necessary.

While Pannenberg has often been criticized for his position concerning
the inspiration of Scripture, he does not deny the inspiration of Scripture.[47]
His objection, as one would expect, is to advancing the doctrine of inspiration as a means of settling the question of the truth content of Scripture prior
to engaging the task of systematic theology. Rather, Pannenberg would say,
since Scripture is to be understood as making assertions that are to be taken
as true, those assertions can be subjected to testing to determine their truthfulness. For example, where claims are made regarding historical fact, one
may use the relevant tools from the historian's repertoire in order to render
judgment upon the historical veracity of these claims. Pannenberg argues that
the *result* of this process of testing, which is precisely the task that the systematic theologian undertakes, is a demonstration of the plausibility (or
implausibility) of claiming that Scripture is true. In this way, Pannenberg
reverses the normal way of thinking about inspiration. Rather than presupposing the inspiration of Scripture at the beginning as a way of establishing
the truthfulness of Christian doctrine *prior to* its systematic presentation, he
believes that one should instead argue for the inspiration on the grounds that
its truthfulness has been demonstrated *through* its systematic presentation.
To do otherwise, according to Pannenberg, is to fail to recognize properly the
hypothetical status of Christian truth claims. Likewise, it fails to recognize
the sorts of reasonable challenges that can be and have been raised.[48]

---

46. Ibid., 1:7.

47. What follows is a summary of comments made by Pannenberg in private conversation. Further, it
should be noted that Pannenberg readily admits that the construal of inspiration implied by this position
would be rather different than normally taken. He argues that one goes in the opposite direction from what
is generally presumed; rather than moving from inspiration to truth, one first tries to show Scripture true
and from there affirm inspiration.

48. The issue here, of course, is not that the sorts of challenges represented by historical-critical exegesis
are decisive, but rather that they require response. Consequently, it seems Pannenberg's rejection of using
the doctrine of inspiration as a means to circumvent the need to engage the question of truth is eminently
reasonable. For more details, in addition to "The Crisis of the Scripture Principle" mentioned above, see
Systematic Theology, 1:26–48.

The Faith Consciousness of the Believer

Interestingly, Pannenberg argues that the move to secure the truth claims of Christianity by appealing to the faith consciousness of the believer is closely related to the position just considered. The first move, he believes, was a transition from an objective appeal to the authority of Scripture to a more subjective one, by appealing to the inner witness of the Holy Spirit. The following outlines Pannenberg's view:

> With the weakening of the doctrine of the divine authority of scripture as something that precedes all human judgment, the doctrine of the internal testimony of the Spirit took on the sense of an *additional* principle of subjective experience and certainty which supplements the external Word and evaluates the truth claim and truth content of scripture. . . . [T]he doctrine of the Spirit's inner witness became the turning point in a major shift away from the Reformation thesis of the precedence of God's truth over human judgment to the modern Neo-Protestant conviction that subjective experience is the basis of faith and Christian doctrine.[49]

After some discussion, Pannenberg considers the theology of Schleiermacher, which aimed to ground systematic theology in the "expression of the religious subjectivity of the theologian."[50] In fact, according to Schleiermacher, "Christian doctrines are accounts of the Christian religious affections set forth in speech."[51] Or as Pannenberg puts it, "For Schleiermacher, then, the sole criterion of dogmatic presentation was the faith consciousness, and he understood church doctrine as its expression."[52]

Pannenberg believes that Barth, notwithstanding efforts to the contrary and in spite of Barth's specific criticism of Schleiermacher's subjectivism, fell prey to the same error. In Barth's case, claims Pannenberg, the move was expressed by his grounding confidence in the truth of Christian doctrine in the existential, and therefore subjective, encounter between God and the individual believer.[53] In every case, the fundamental problem Pannenberg sees is the necessarily subjective nature of all appeals to the mental states (faith consciousness) of individual believers. Such a subjective experience

---

49. Pannenberg, *Systematic Theology*, 1:34.

50. Ibid., 1:41. Some recent studies question the adequacy of this construal of Schleiermacher's position. Consider, for example, W. J. Abraham, *Canon and Criteria* (Oxford: Clarendon, 1998).

51. F. D. E. Schleiermacher, *The Christian Faith* (ed. H. P. Mackintosh and J. S. Stewart; Edinburgh: T&T Clark, 1989), 76.

52. Pannenberg, *Systematic Theology*, 1:42.

53. Of course, Barth scholars might disagree with Pannenberg's assessment of Barth at this point. That need not detain us, however, since the denial of the subjectivism of Barth's work would support Pannenberg's broader point denying the appropriateness of seeking a prior guarantee in this manner.

cannot supply absolute certainty, nor can it provide intersubjective certainty. As Pannenberg notes, "To claim unconditional, independent certainty is forcibly to make oneself, the believing I, the locus of absolute truth. Any occurrence of this phenomenon, among Christians or others, is justifiably regarded as irrational fanaticism."[54] What some have called the "atheism of suspicion," that form of atheism which found perhaps its clearest expression in the work of Feuerbach, Nitzsche, Freud, and Marx and which focuses upon the motivations for and function of religion, is taken quite seriously by Pannenberg. These writers drew attention to the possibility of, or as they believed the virtual certainty of, the self-deception that arises in the religious life as a consequence of self-interest. When the appeal is to the inner religious consciousness, Pannenberg believes that the possibility of self-deception is particularly acute and without appropriate counterbalances. Consequently, the need for the testing of truth claims cannot be avoided by appealing to the faith consciousness of the individual believer. Further, even if one is unwilling to agree completely with Pannenberg on this point, it seems he is correct that assertions based in an individual's faith consciousness cannot serve to provide intersubjective certainty.[55] So, Pannenberg concludes, they cannot provide the desired prior guarantee of truth.

Pannenberg's Epistemic Proposals

Since Pannenberg concludes that neither appeals to the teaching office of the church, nor appeals to the doctrine of the inspiration of Scripture, nor appeals to the faith commitment of the individual believer can provide a guarantee of the truth of Christian doctrine prior to the testing of that doctrine, we can see why he argues that the truth content of the Christian faith must be a primary theme of the systematic presentation of Christian doctrine. It follows, then, that we must ask, what criteria can be used to assess whether a given doctrine has been reasonably demonstrated as true? There are three specific points we must address: (1) the role of notions of correspondence and coherence, (2) the status and nature of religious assertions, and (3) the place of anticipation, or provisionality.

Correspondence and Coherence

Some have taken Pannenberg's emphasis upon the notion of coherence to indicate that he holds a coherentist epistemology. Certain passages lend initial credence to this view:

---

54. Pannenberg, *Systematic Theology*, 1:47.

55. It should be noted that Swinburne argues in some detail that testimony, even of this sort, should be given *prima facie* credibility. See R. Swinburne, *The Existence of God* (Oxford: Clarendon, 1979).

> The systematic investigation and presentation itself entails a very specific understanding of truth, namely, *truth as coherence*, as the mutual agreement of all that is true.[56]

> Coherence provides the final criterion of truth, and it can serve as such a criterion because it also belongs to the nature of truth.[57]

While these statements reflect the importance of coherence to Pannenberg's epistemology, it is a mistake to suppose that his position can be simply categorized as coherentist. Pannenberg references coherence as "the *final* criterion of truth" (emphasis added), but he does not indicate that he believes coherence is the *only* criterion of truth. His reference to coherence as the final criterion of truth is rooted in the ultimate unity of truth and, thus, the centrality of the law of noncontradiction. If one could list exhaustively all true propositions, they would be mutually supportive and none would stand in contradiction to another. Consequently, as Pannenberg mentions, it belongs to the nature of all truth ultimately to stand in mutual coherence.

In *Theology and the Philosophy of Science*, Pannenberg appropriates certain insights from the work of Karl Popper. Popper argues that we gain knowledge by conjectures, models, and/or hypotheses, which we then test to determine whether conceivable experiments falsify them.[58] One of the key points here is that the notion of falsification implies testing the hypothesis against what one actually experiences in the world. Pannenberg cites a passage from Popper's *The Logic of Scientific Discovery* that identifies four ways of testing a hypothesis:

> We may . . . distinguish four different lines along which the testing of the theory could be carried out. First, there is the logical comparison of the conclusions among themselves, by which the internal consistency of the system is tested. Secondly there is the investigation of the logical form of the theory, with the object of determining whether it has the character of an empirical or scientific theory, or whether it is, for example, tautological. Thirdly, there is the comparison with other theories, chiefly with the aim of determining whether the theory would constitute a scientific advance. . . . And finally, there is the testing of the theory by way of empirical applications of the conclusions which can be derived from it.[59]

---

56. Pannenberg, *Systematic Theology*, 1:21.

57. Pannenberg, *Introduction to Systematic Theology*, 6.

58. Popper argues for falsification as a means of assessing hypotheses rather than verification because, in principle, it would take an infinite number of tests to verify a hypothesis, while only one counterinstance serves to falsify a hypothesis. See K. Popper, *Conjectures and Refutations* (New York: Routledge, 1992), 228ff.

59. W. Pannenberg, *Theology and the Philosophy of Science* (trans. F. McDonagh; Philadelphia: Westminster, 1976), 37.

Obviously, the first of Popper's four points, dealing as it does with the issue of internal consistency, expresses the concept of coherence, which we have already seen is an important part of Pannenberg's concept of truth. Points two and three deal with the form and novelty of scientific theories, and as such, do not require our attention. However, the last point expands our discussion, and it turns out to be an essential, but often underemphasized, element of Pannenberg's position.

It is the fourth point Popper raises concerning testing hypotheses that deals specifically with making sure that the proposed hypotheses make contact with the world. In other words, the fourth test that Popper proposes is the test of *correspondence*. While a fair amount of attention has been given to the place of coherence in Pannenberg's work, there can be little doubt that correspondence is at least as significant. Shortly after citing the previous passage from Popper, Pannenberg observes, "It is fundamental to the semantic structure of assertions that they claim to be true in the sense of agreeing with the state of affairs to which they relate."[60] It is Pannenberg's contention that to assert something is to make a claim about the nature of some state of affairs. Consequently, assertions about the world can be tested to determine whether the assertions correspond to the world of human experience. So, for example, if one were to hypothesize that two atoms of hydrogen combine with one of oxygen to form water, one may perform the appropriate tests to determine whether the world conforms to this hypothesis. This example deals with a scientific assertion; the question for us is whether theological statements can be expected to meet the standard of truth as correspondence.

The answer depends upon the manner in which one understands theological statements. Are they cognitive? Expressive? Emotive? Without delving into the various positions concerning the status of religious assertions, Pannenberg holds that they are cognitive: "There is no getting round the fact that people who express their religious convictions are in so doing referring to a specific—usually divine and divinely instituted—reality and intend to assert something as true of it."[61] Consequently, as long as "it can be assumed that theological propositions have a cognitive content,"[62] an appropriate test of their truthfulness is the correspondence between the assertion and the referenced state of affairs. So to make the simple claim

---

60. Ibid., 41. Pannenberg is not merely playing a semantic game here. Rather, he is recognizing that the very structure of truth claims implies correspondence between the claimed state of affairs and what occurs in the world. So to claim that "*X* is a *Y*" is to say that there is a state of affairs in the world such that an *X* is seen to be a *Y*.

61. Ibid., 327. Pannenberg, of course, recognizes the objections raised to this claim by, for example, the positivists. For Pannenberg's arguments against positivism and noncognitivist responses to it, see *Theology and the Philosophy of Science*, 1–70.

62. Ibid., 327.

that "God exists" or the somewhat more complicated claim that "Jesus was raised from the dead," according to Pannenberg, is to make a factual assertion about an actual state of affairs that corresponds to "the way things really are."

Obviously, much more needs to be said; however, let us pause momentarily to summarize before proceeding. Two important criteria of Pannenberg's epistemology have been identified: (1) the test of coherence, which is constituted by the law of noncontradiction, and (2) the test of correspondence, which assures that the claims to truth make contact with the world. Pannenberg sees theological assertions as cognitive in nature and as having the status of hypotheses that are intended to explain certain phenomena.

The Status and Nature of Religious Assertions

Let me begin by clarifying what "explanatory" and "hypothesis" mean in their more generic senses. Perhaps the meaning of "explanatory" is the most straightforward: To say that a given assertion is explanatory is simply to say that the assertion provides an explanation, in some sense, of its referents. Explanations come in a variety of types. For example, an assertion might provide a causal explanation of something, or an explanation might provide an interpretation or clarify the meaning of some thing or event. Further, regarding the acts of human agents, an explanation might clarify the reasons for the selection of a particular act or the means by which it is to be accomplished. So to make the claim that an assertion provides an explanation of some thing or event is to claim that the assertion provides insights into the thing or event. One might, for example, explain the occurrence of war by assertions that incorporate the relevant antecedent events.

A hypothesis is "an assumption or set of assumptions provisionally accepted," or referring specifically to science, "a hypothesis is a proposition advanced as possibly true, and consistent with known data, but requiring further investigation."[63] For Pannenberg's epistemology, the point of significance is the claim that a hypothesis is provisional and, thus, stands in need of further testing and confirmation. Pannenberg also draws attention to the predictive aspect of hypotheses: They predict what one might expect when further testing is conducted. Explanation by hypotheses also has a descriptive function, which is to say that there is correspondence between the hypotheses and the states of affairs to which they refer. By combining these points, one arrives at the following definition: An explanatory hypothesis is a proposition or set of propositions that provides a provisional explanation of a given thing or state of affairs. In so

---

63. *Funk and Wagnalls Standard Desk Dictionary* (New York: Harper & Row, 1984), 317.

doing, the explanatory hypothesis incorporates the known data about the thing or state of affairs so as to be descriptive (in the sense of reality depiction) as well as predictive. Now let us consider how Pannenberg deploys the notion of an explanatory hypothesis with regard to the sorts of theological assertions that he wishes to advance.

A theological assertion that functions as an explanatory hypothesis is one that provides an explanation, in one or more of the senses noted, of the matters to which the assertion refers. This explanation must satisfactorily deal with the known data and describes accurately the referenced state of affairs. To the extent a theological explanatory hypothesis accurately reflects that state of affairs, it would meet the requirement of correspondence. Also, such an explanatory hypothesis would be provisional as noted above. More specifically, it would be accepted provisionally as true but would be open to further investigation.[64] Pannenberg summarizes as follows:

> We should not think it strange if epistemologically the statements of dogmatics and the theses of the Christian doctrine which it presents are given the status of hypotheses. In both cases we have propositions which are not self-evident and which do not follow with logical necessity from self-evident propositions. They are assertions which formally might be either true or false, so that we can meaningfully ask whether they are right and true.[65]

Pannenberg insists upon the hypothetical nature of theological assertions and, therefore, of systematic theology itself. We must now consider why he makes this claim.

In the last citation, we see one reason why Pannenberg argues for the hypothetical nature of theological assertions and systematic theology: Theological assertions are not self-evident, nor do they follow from self-evident propositions. Consider an example Pannenberg discusses in the paragraph immediately following the preceding citation: the assertion that Jesus was raised from the dead. First, such an assertion is certainly not self-evident, nor does it follow from self-evident propositions. Second, the claim is a historical one and, therefore, must be assessed using the considerations a historian would normally bring to bear in determining the accuracy of historical claims. Third, since resurrections are hardly a normal part of human experience, this claim would be subject to challenge in ways that less extraordinary assertions would not be. Any of these considerations

---

64. The question arises here concerning the degree of certainty one must have to make rational the acceptance of such a provisional, explanatory hypothesis. According to Pannenberg, the standard of certainty is plausibility. Of course, our description of plausibility can only proceed so far since the worldview that each of us holds will set parameters for what we see as plausible—that is, there is a person-relative aspect of plausibility.

65. Pannenberg, *Systematic Theology*, 1:56.

would be adequate, according to Pannenberg, to establish the debatability of the assertion that Jesus was raised from the dead, thus rendering it a hypothesis about a certain state of affairs after the death of Jesus.

According to Pannenberg, when a plausible objection is raised to a truth claim, those embracing that assertion must provide a plausible response or give up the claim to rationality. Who bears the burden of proof in establishing the plausibility of a given explanatory hypothesis?[66] The answer to this question is of some significance given that Pannenberg's strongly rationalist commitments make it possible to construe his position as evidentialist. W. K. Clifford represents, perhaps, the paradigm case of strong evidentialism when he argues in his essay "The Ethics of Belief"[67] that it is at all times wrong to believe anything on inadequate evidence. So the evidentialist position may be characterized as that position which holds that it is rational to believe some proposition P only if one has adequate evidence. Thus, the burden is always on the believer of P to have such evidence. Is Pannenberg's position evidentialist, such that believers always have the burden of proof?

Reformed epistemologists—for example, Alston, Plantinga, and Wolterstorff—have argued at length against evidentialism. Let us consider Wolterstorff's essay "Can Belief in God Be Rational If It Has No Foundations?"[68] wherein he distinguishes between two ways, broadly speaking, of construing epistemologies: (1) obligations epistemologies, which focus upon the positive requirements of the knower to exercise appropriate epistemic duties, and (2) permissions epistemologies, which focus upon the right of the knower to believe propositions in the absence of counterevidence. The evidentialist position would be an obligation epistemology since the obligation for rationally believing P is adequate evidence. So is Pannenberg's epistemology obligations oriented?

I believe the answer to this question is no. In the first place, Pannenberg has mentioned that in the past, theologians were able to launch immediately into a presentation of Christian doctrine, but present circumstances render this approach inappropriate. What caused this change? The fact that plausible, and in some cases valid, objections have been raised to certain Christian beliefs. Consequently, though Pannenberg is sometimes cast as an evidentialist, his position is closer to Wolterstorff's notion of a permissions epistemology. The primary difference is that, in light of reasonable objections, Pannenberg believes the necessity of response has already been

---

66. Note again that the standard of certainty is plausibility, not demonstration.

67. W. K. Clifford, "The Ethics of Belief," in *Philosophy of Religion* (ed. L. Pojman; Belmont, CA: Wadsworth, 1987), 383.

68. N. Wolterstorff, "Can Belief in God Be Rational If It Has No Foundations?" in *Faith and Rationality* (ed. A. Plantinga and N. Wolterstorff; Notre Dame, IN: University of Notre Dame Press, 1983), 135–86.

established. Of course, this tends to clarify further his rationale for arguing that theological assertions have the status of explanatory hypotheses.[69]

Provisionality and the Science of God

The issues that were identified at the outset of my discussion of Pannenberg's epistemology were (1) the roles of coherence and correspondence, (2) the status of theological assertions, and (3) the place of provisionality. I have examined in adequate detail items 1 and 2, and my discussion concerning the hypothetical nature of theological assertions has introduced the third. Until now, I have considered provisionality to the extent it is a consequence of the hypothetical nature of theological assertions. However, provisionality, understood as anticipation, is a very important part of Pannenberg's epistemology apart from the issues cited. Specifically, Pannenberg, under the influence of the German philosopher of history Wilhelm Dilthey, believes that truth has an anticipatory, or provisional, structure. During the last lectures that Pannenberg delivered prior to his retirement from the University of Munich, he named Dilthey as the philosopher who had most influenced his position on these matters. And it is precisely the anticipatory structure of truth and meaning that Pannenberg had in mind when speaking of Dilthey's influence.

For Dilthey, events that occur within human history are given their meaning by their relation to the historical context in which they occur. The problem is that history continues to march forward, and therefore, the historical context (or "horizon") changes, making it possible that the meaning/truth of events will also change as their horizon of meaning changes. If this is correct, it follows that the more universal the horizon within which given events can be placed, the more likely one is to understand the meaning/truth of those events.[70] It also follows immediately that, given the ever-continuing march of history, our grasp of the truth at any given point in history can

---

69. That this is a reasonably accurate construal of Pannenberg's position was confirmed in personal conversation in late 1999. We briefly discussed Wolterstorff's position, and he relayed information from a discussion he had had with Alvin Plantinga regarding Plantinga's proposal that belief in God could be a properly basic belief. Pannenberg reported that he had asked if, in Plantinga's proposal, the burden of response shifted back to the religious believer once plausible objection to religious belief was raised. Plantinga reportedly responded that it did, and thus Pannenberg felt that some of the substantive differences between their respective positions were thereby minimized.

70. Two things must be clarified at this point. First, notice that the focus here is upon events. Epistemologically speaking, then, Pannenberg and Dilthey intend propositions that deal with events and their meaning. So, for example, Pannenberg is not particularly concerned to argue that propositions dealing with objects/artifacts ("A dog has four legs," for example) need await confirmation in light of some final, all-encompassing historical horizon. This would tend to exclude analytic statements. Rather, the focus is more upon synthetic statements that deal with meanings of events and states of affairs. Second, of course, Pannenberg does not argue that every expanded historical context or horizon will provide relevant additional material, but rather that as relevant additional material is available, one gains additional insight into the meaning of a given proposition.

only be an anticipation of what we will find to be true in light of the final, most universal horizon. What would constitute the final, most universal horizon of meaning? According to Dilthey, "One would have to wait for the end of a life and, in the hour of death, survey the whole and ascertain the relation between the whole and its parts. One would have to wait for the end of history to have all the material necessary to determine its meaning."[71]

Observe that the ever-expanding horizon of meaning makes it necessary to gain a vantage point beyond all possible changes before one occupies a position that allows the final resolution of the question of truth.[72] Pannenberg draws on these notions to argue that truth is an eschatological concept: "Only God's final revelation at the end of history will bring with it final knowledge of the content and truth of the act of God in Jesus of Nazareth. God alone has the competence to speak the final word about God's work in history."[73] It is only, Pannenberg believes, as one looks back from the end of history that one has the perspective to see the final truth of all matters. No further discoveries will allow an expansion of the horizon of meaning beyond that point; consequently, the relation of the various events that is evident from that perspective will, for eternity, resolve all open issues.

In light of these considerations, Pannenberg believes that all systematic presentations of Christian doctrine remain provisional during the course of human history. We cannot know in advance what new discoveries or new challenges will require modification of the hypotheses that systematic theology proposes. Consequently, Pannenberg affirms that our statements about God must generally retain the status of hypotheses and must be examined continually in the light of any new and relevant data that may arise in the world of human experience. Philip Clayton captures something of the centrality of the concept of anticipation in Pannenberg's work by observing that "virtually every author to write on his theology has drawn attention to his use of this concept."[74]

With these elements in place, it is now possible to summarize the primary contours of Pannenberg's epistemology and how that relates to the propositions set forth in a systematic presentation of Christian doctrine. Truth claims that comprise a given systematic theology are to be understood as hypotheses intended to give the best explanation of the world of

---

71. W. Dilthey, *Selected Writings* (ed. and trans. H. P. Rickman; Cambridge: Cambridge University Press, 1976), 236. The original German is as follows: "Man müsste das Ende des Lebenslaufes abwarten und könnte in der Todesstunde erst das Ganze überschauen, von dem aus die Beziehung seiner Teile feststellbar wäre. Man müsste das Ende der Geschichte erst abwarten, um für die Bestimmung ihrer Bedeutung das vollständige Material zu besitzen." W. Dilthey, *Gasammelte Schriften*, vol. 7 (Stuttgart: Vandenhoeck & Ruprecht, 1965), 233.

72. Of course, the claim that there will be a final resolution is itself a provisional claim.

73. Pannenberg, *Systematic Theology*, 1:16.

74. P. Clayton, "Anticipation and Theological Method," in Braaten and Clayton, *Theology of Wolfhart Pannenberg*, 128.

shared human experience. A given proposition from a given systematic theology may be rationally taken to be true[75] if it (1) contains no internal contradictions and is therefore coherent and (2) can be shown to make contact with the world by correspondence between the proposition and the world of shared human experience. Even though such propositions may be rationally accepted as true, they may never be taken as more than provisionally true during the march of human history; therefore, the truth content of these theological assertions/propositions must be subject to ongoing testing in the light of ever-expanding horizons of meaning. Consequently, Pannenberg argues that such assertions/propositions are anticipated to be true in light of their present plausibility.[76]

As we might expect, the methodology that Pannenberg lays out matches rather closely, at the level of philosophical reflection, his construal of the methodology of science.[77] This is no accident, as Pannenberg's *Theology and the Philosophy of Science* can largely be understood as his attempt to justify viewing theology as a science. Further, the concern to avoid dogmatic guarantees of truth prior to engaging the task of systematic theology, the attention to the notion of correspondence, and the judgment that theological assertions are hypothetical in nature all combine to demonstrate the degree to which Pannenberg intends to assert the scientific nature of theology. In fact, after a discussion of the nature of critical assessment, Pannenberg observes that "if the idea of critical examination is taken in such a general sense, however, it can no longer be used as a criterion for excluding philosophy (or metaphysics) from the class of scientifically meaningful statements."[78] The question this observation suggests is this: How is theology to be understood as a science? Is it a science of Christian thought? Is it the science of religion in general? Pannenberg gives an initial answer by considering the scope of the explanatory hypothesis that systematic theology is intended to provide. According to Pannenberg, what separates philosophy from the natural sciences is precisely the scope of philosophy: "[The] concern with reality as a whole in all its aspects distinguishes philosophical hypotheses not only from the hypothetical laws of the natural and social sciences, but also from historical hypotheses."[79]

---

75. The claim here is that if the following criteria are met, then the given systematic theology may be taken to be true. This does not set aside the issue of provisionality or anticipation. Therefore, to say that one may rationally hold as true a set of propositions, according to Pannenberg, is not to say that the question of their truth has been settled.

76. This is why plausibility is the appropriate standard rather than, say, demonstrable certainty.

77. Of course, there are rather deeply divided intuitions about the precise nature of science, and the purview of this book does not permit detailed analysis of Pannenberg's philosophy of science. I believe he provides a plausible account of science. My point here is that Pannenberg's method assumes that theology is a form of scientific inquiry, with a plausible account of science underlying the discussion.

78. Pannenberg, *Theology and the Philosophy of Science*, 68.

79. Ibid., 69.

Later, Pannenberg broadens this to include theological statements: "Like philosophical statements, theological statements are offered as hypotheses about the total meaning of experience."[80] However, as we have already seen, the totality of the meaning/truth of human experience is dependent upon having a universal context from which to assess that experience. So how are we as theologians to make truth claims, even anticipatory ones, regarding the totality of the meaning of human experience *from within* the march of human history? This could only be done, says Pannenberg, if there were a unifying ground underlying the totality of reality that could serve as the basis for theological anticipations of the totality of meaning. According to Pannenberg, the Christian concept of God is such a unifying ground. In fact, it is the concept of God as the necessary entity *upon whom all finite reality depends* that provides the unifying ground from which one may develop anticipations of the totality of meaning. Pannenberg often refers to God as "the all determining reality." Thus, Pannenberg concludes, theology must be the science of God as the all-determining reality and nothing else.

This means that God as the all-determining reality upon whom everything depends is the unifying ground of the totality of reality. Consequently, this claim becomes the centerpiece of Pannenberg's systematic theology as its explanatory hypothesis. A problem remains, however: If the hiddenness of God is a real aspect of the human experience of God, as is affirmed by the biblical claim that no one has ever seen God, how can one obtain adequate information from experience of the world to make the sort of hypothetical assertions that theology wishes to make? Pannenberg's answer is clear: "only on the assumption that the reality of God is *co-given* to experience in other objects."[81] In other words, the only way that we may come to know this hidden God is if the reality of God is inextricably bound up with the experiences humans have of other, nonhidden objects. As Pannenberg continues, *"In what objects of experience* is God—as a problem—indirectly co-given, and what objects of experience can therefore be considered as possible traces of God? The only possible answer is: *all objects.*"[82]

It now becomes obvious why Pannenberg has said that it must be "plausible that all finite reality depends on [God], not only human beings and the course of their history, but also the world of nature."[83] If God is to be the unifying ground of the world of shared human experience so that God as the all-determining reality can be the central thesis of Pannenberg's science of God, then God must be related to all aspects of the world. Further, consistent with the very notion of God, that relation must be one of

---

80. Ibid., 341.
81. Ibid., 301.
82. Ibid., 302.
83. Pannenberg, *Introduction to Systematic Theology*, 10.

dependence. In his interaction with the scientific community, Pannenberg puts this claim in the strongest of terms: "If the God of the Bible is the creator of the universe, then it is not possible to understand fully or even appropriately the processes of nature without any reference to that God."[84] The central hypothesis, then, in the set of hypotheses that is Christian systematic theology is this: God, as the all-determining reality, is the unifying ground of the totality of the world of shared human experience.

To summarize Pannenberg's epistemic proposals: In the first place, Pannenberg proposes that theology is to be understood as a science (the science of God) and that the epistemology deployed by the theologian ought to be acceptable to theologian and scientist alike *at the level of philosophical reflection*.[85] Three specific aspects of his concept of truth are (1) coherence, (2) correspondence, and (3) the provisional or anticipatory structure of assertions. Additionally, the form of theological assertions, in light particularly of their provisionality, is that of explanatory hypotheses. Finally, theological assertions, consistent with their relation to the one God upon whom all finite reality depends, are intended to provide anticipatory explanation of the *meanings* of the totality of reality. Consequently, a systematic presentation of Christian doctrine must be seen as a theory aimed to provide the best explanation of the totality of the world of shared human experience. Further, to the extent plausible, objection can be raised to the various parts of this explanatory hypothesis, and testing of the various truth claims must be undertaken on an ongoing basis. Only upon the completion of human history will the hypothetical nature of theological assertions be forever resolved as the light of God's eternity reveals the final and decisive truth of that history.

Justification of God-Talk

While my discussion so far has provided the necessary framework, I have not yet undertaken the question of how one justifies a systematic presentation of Christian doctrine. In other words, how does one establish the plausibility of the existence of the God of Abraham, Isaac, and Jacob and as affirmed in the Christian tradition[86] so that one might rationally engage in the presentation of Christian doctrine? This is a particularly important

---

84. W. Pannenberg, *Toward a Theology of Nature* (ed. T. Peters; Louisville, KY: Westminster/John Knox, 1993), 16.

85. A perusal of *Theology and the Philosophy of Science* would reveal that the affirmation of the scientific nature of theology does not mean a corresponding affirmation of a crass empiricism or positivism.

86. I use this language somewhat advisedly, for Pannenberg is very concerned with writing as if there were more than one God. There is only one God—the one God upon whom all depends—and to engage in terminology that suggests otherwise, according to Pannenberg, is to regress "to a situation of a plurality of gods in which Christian talk about God has reference to the specific biblical God as one God among others." Pannenberg, *Systematic Theology*, 1:68.

question for someone like Pannenberg, who begins the theological enterprise by admitting the debatability of God's existence and the provisional character of truth claims. Pannenberg's answer to this challenge involves analysis of (1) the place of rational argumentation, in particular the traditional arguments for God's existence; (2) the claim that a religious nature is a constitutive element of the human self; (3) the observation that humans have an innate awareness of God; and (4) the significance of the history of the world's religious traditions.

The Role of the Classical Arguments

Early in *Systematic Theology*, Pannenberg points to the inevitable importance of rational argumentation in the development of a systematic theology guided by the epistemic commitments laid out above:

> If, however, the truth of Christian teaching is not presupposed in dogmatics as its coherent presentation; if this truth is made a theme of discussion which includes also its debatability, does not rational argumentation become a court which decides for (or against) the truth of faith? Does not this truth then depend on the criteria of rational evaluation and therefore finally on human beings themselves as the subjects of their thinking?[87]

One must read this with a bit of caution to avoid mishearing an unwarranted exaltation of human reason. What Pannenberg intends here is to emphasize the importance of rationality in undergirding our beliefs. For example, it would be very difficult to believe that some proposition *P* is both true and irrational. It is, of course, altogether possible that one might defend *as rational* a particular, cherished belief that is, in fact, quite irrational. But that is rather different from saying that whether something is rational or not does not matter. Even if one thinks Pannenberg goes too far in assigning significance to the "criteria of rational evaluation," it is hard to object to the more general claim that rational argument plays a profound role in the sorts of propositions one believes.[88] One of the forms that

---

87. Ibid., 1:52.

88. I recognize that this pushes to the side a good many issues. For example, Alvin Plantinga has argued that much of our believing is outside of our control. Instead, we merely find ourselves, upon reflection of a proposition under certain circumstances, drawn to believe it. So, for example, I do not, says Plantinga, have rational arguments to support the belief that I ate popcorn at the game tonight. Upon reflecting on the game and my actions while there, I simply find myself believing that I ate popcorn. Many beliefs like this, Plantinga believes, are properly basic. In fact, as I have already noted, Plantinga believes that the proposition "God exists" might, in the right circumstances, be properly basic. However, Pannenberg argues that once plausible objection is raised, the properly basic status (if it is properly basic in the first place) is lost, and then, so it seems, the need for rational assessment and argument arises. Since this is the condition in which Pannenberg believes that we always find ourselves, rational assessment and argument are of central importance from the start.

rational argumentation takes in theology is the arguments for God's existence. Consequently, if rational arguments are to have a place in establishing the plausibility of Christian theology, the so-called proofs of God's existence will require attention.

In exploring the historical development of these arguments, Pannenberg observes, "If knowledge of God is to be a matter of natural theology in the sense of being achieved by rational reflection and arguments, then it will finally rest on proofs of God."[89] Of course, the question that immediately arises is, just what do these so-called proofs establish? It is generally accepted, even within conservative Christian circles, that plausible objection can be raised to each of the families of argument. Even Richard Swinburne's very well researched and argued book *The Existence of God* concludes only that the cumulative force of the various arguments makes it more probable than not that God exists.[90] It is hard, then, to see how anyone could rationally hold that the so-called arguments for God's existence could be treated as anything even remotely comparable to a decisive proof. That Pannenberg would concur is no surprise, given his assertion that the reality of God's existence remains debatable throughout the march of human history. So what gives? If these arguments are not proofs, how does Pannenberg see them contributing to the justification of God-talk?

Even though these arguments are not proofs per se, Pannenberg believes that the manner in which they have evolved provides an invaluable insight. The important point is that the arguments have shifted over time from a cosmological basis to a more anthropological basis. By this he means that initially the arguments were grounded in analysis of certain concrete aspects of the human encounter with the cosmos: the need for a Prime Mover to ground movement, the need for a Creator to explain the existence of the cosmos, and the need for an Orderer to make sense of the order we experience in the cosmos. However, Pannenberg argues that the march of scientific discovery has systematically eroded the persuasiveness of these cosmologically based arguments, and this has resulted in the transition to arguments that are based upon the "need of reason to conceive of the unity of empirical reality" and to conceptualize it as such.[91] We need not explore in great detail the sorts of scientific discoveries Pannenberg has in mind, but one example is the discovery of inertia as a *vis insita*. While William of Occam argued that a first cause is needed not to produce fur-

---

89. Pannenberg, *Systematic Theology*, 1:82.

90. It should be noted further that Swinburne goes beyond the traditional arguments by adding other, persuasive, arguments of his own and finally adding what he thinks to be the evidential force of religious experiences.

91. Pannenberg, *Systematic Theology*, 1:90.

ther effects but rather to uphold or sustain motion, the discovery of inertia did away with any such need:

> This assumption of the existence of God as the principle of the ongoing existence of finite things became superfluous when with the introduction of the principle of inertia by Descartes and its refinement by Isaac Newton . . . there was ascribed to all things a tendency to remain as they are, whether their state be one of rest or one of movement. In a mechanistic worldview the concept of God was no longer needed to explain natural events.[92]

Pannenberg argues that the transition to anthropologically based arguments is evident already in Descartes, who argued for the reality of God on the basis of the "idea of God which is native to the human mind."[93] This was exacerbated by Leibniz's contingency form of the cosmological argument, which argued from the principle of sufficient reason rather than from experiences of the cosmos. The trend reached its zenith in Kant, who believed that the constructive role the mind plays in acquisition of knowledge is the unification of the manifold of sense experience. We search for ever-broader horizons to serve as the ground for the unity of ever-broader manifolds of sense experience. The idea of God that serves as the most encompassing horizon is precisely that which serves to ground the attempt to unify the totality of all possible experiences. Pannenberg suggests that while many remember Kant's critique of the arguments for God's existence, "it is easily overlooked that he also maintained the necessity of the rational ideal of such a being on which all empirical reality bases its supreme and necessary unity and which we can think of only after the analogy of a real substance that by the laws of reason is the cause of all things."[94] Additionally, in *Critique of Practical Reason*, Kant adds a moral argument for God's existence. This is not so much a proof of God's existence as a demonstration that the concept of God is needed to maintain the ultimate rationality of the world, particularly as regards moral acts and consequences. Once again we see how Kant construes the concept of God as the necessary presupposition of the human psyche that seeks to establish the highest degree of rational synthesis of the world. One can see why Pannenberg claims that Kant's work is the high point in the transition to anthropologically based arguments for God's existence.

Toward the end of this discussion, Pannenberg explicitly states what he believes are the limits of anthropologically based arguments: "No anthropological argument can prove God's existence in the strict sense. In most

---

92. Ibid., 1:88.
93. Ibid., 1:84.
94. Ibid., 1:90.

cases no such claim is made. All that is maintained is that we are referred to an unfathomable reality that transcends us and the world, so that the God of religious tradition is given a secure place in the reality of human self-experience."[95] So even though the debatability of God's existence remains a part of the human condition, these arguments "at least make the talk of God intelligible."[96] In other words, what has been demonstrated so far is the necessity of the *concept* of God to human reason and, therefore, that it is an essential part of the world of human experience. From this Pannenberg reasons that if the concept of God is an essential part of human experience, then it seems clear that a religious disposition is a constitutive part of human nature.

Religious Disposition

At various points throughout Pannenberg's writings, he comments upon the idea that a religious disposition is constitutive for human nature. He cites with approval the thesis developed by Schleiermacher that religion is not superfluous to human existence but rather is part of everyday reality.[97] Similarly, he appeals to the notion of basic trust as articulated by Erikson and given theological interpretation by Küng, and then builds upon it by way of human "ec-centricity," the human need to place trust in something beyond themselves: "Here is what we might now call the ec-centric form of human life. We have to rest upon something outside ourselves. We have no choice. We can choose only on what to rest."[98] This is further emphasized when, in another place, he refers to the "hidden idolatry" of modern secular culture.[99] We must define ourselves in relation to something else, and this "something else" may be God, or it may be an idol or a false god. Of course, modern culture does not readily admit the notion of idols, but Pannenberg believes that our pursuit of wealth, pleasures, and the like makes them "hidden idols" and thus shows that we do not easily avoid the question of ec-centricity or the idea of god that Pannenberg believes it implies.

Whether one initially calls this a "religious disposition" is debatable. However, if Küng, Erikson, Pannenberg, and others are correct in claiming that humans inevitably ground their existence beyond themselves, then it seems clear that the ultimate ground for human existence would be an absolute ground of being. Of course, many religious traditions believe that an absolute ground of being corresponds to the concept of God. While

---

95. Ibid., 1:93.
96. Ibid., 1:94.
97. Ibid., 1:139.
98. Ibid., 1:113.
99. Pannenberg, *Introduction to Systematic Theology*, 22.

humans may seek satisfaction in less absolute terms, Pannenberg believes this is a mere stopgap measure. In this, one is reminded of Augustine's observation that humans remain restless until they find their rest in God. One need merely couple these observations with the ubiquitous nature of religion and the corresponding longing for meaning to sense the force of the claim that a religious disposition is constitutive of human nature.

We must be careful, however, what conclusions we draw from this piece of evidence. Pannenberg concludes cautiously that a religious disposition is a *necessary but insufficient* evidence for God's existence:

> Radical criticism of religion stands or falls with the claim that religion is not a constitutive part of human nature, that in spite of its persistent influence on humanity and its history we must view it as an aberration, or at best as an immature form of the human understanding of reality which has been overcome in principle by the secular culture of the modern West, or by a new society that is still in process of creation, so that it will finally wither away. If, however, religion is constitutive, then there can be no fully rounded and complete human life without it.[100]

A religious disposition is insufficient evidence of God's existence because one cannot be sure, Pannenberg argues, that human nature is not profoundly entangled in illusion. Herein lies the truth of the atheistic criticisms of Fichte and Feuerbach, who argued that religion might merely be a projection or might be falsely grounded in wish fulfillment of humanity's deepest desires and insecurities. This is not to accept, for example, Feuerbach's claim that belief in God is merely projection of desire, but rather to accept its *plausibility*. For example, as Westphal argues, while Christians need not accept the claim that all religious belief is merely the expression of self-interest, we ought to admit that all too often self-interest does corrupt religious belief and behavior.[101] However, as with the anthropologically based "proofs," to the extent the concept of religion implies the concept of God, the concept of God is again shown to be firmly ensconced in human experience.

Innate Knowledge of God

The next step in the argument begins the transition from the necessity of the *concept* of God to a defense of the claim that the concept has objective content, that is, that God exists. Initially this involves combining the eccen-

---

100. Pannenberg, *Systematic Theology*, 1:155.
101. M. Westphal, "Taking Suspicion Seriously: The Religious Uses of Modern Atheism," *Faith and Philosophy* 4, no. 1 (October 1987): 29–30.

tricity of human existence with Descartes' observations concerning innate knowledge of God. In *Meditations*, specifically the third meditation, after having doubted everything but his own existence, Descartes comes to consider the idea of perfection that he finds within himself. He quickly connects this idea of perfection with the idea of the infinite and proceeds to argue, on the principle that the cause of a thing must have as much objective reality as the effect, that he could not have been the source of this idea. He writes:

> Nor should I think that I do not perceive the infinite by means of a true idea, but only through a negation of the finite, just as I perceive rest and darkness by means of a negation of motion and light. On the contrary, I clearly understand that there is more reality in an infinite substance than there is in a finite one. Thus the perception of the infinite is somehow prior in me to the perception of the finite, that is, my perception of God is prior to my perception of myself.[102]

There are two very important points that Pannenberg makes here. First, he affirms Descartes in correctly identifying the relationship between the infinite and the finite: The infinite has priority over the finite, since the finite is derived by negation of the infinite and not vice versa. Pannenberg cites Schleiermacher, who makes the same point: "All that is finite exists only through the determination of its limits, which must, as it were, be 'cut out' from the infinite."[103] The key here is the ordering of the relationship between the finite and the infinite.

We recognize finite objects only to the extent that we become aware of their boundaries; yet in the awareness of the boundaries, we become aware, even if only by implication, of the "others" from which the finite objects before us are distinguished. Pannenberg credits Hegel with showing convincingly in the *Science of Logic* that "we cannot think the border [of some object] without thinking the other that lies on the far side of the border."[104] For example, in perceiving the pencil that lies on my desk, I perceive it as I become aware of its boundaries and as, at the boundaries, I distinguish it from the "other" that lies beneath it.

My awareness of the "other" that lies beneath the pencil may be only implicit; I may not recognize it as a desk but only as "something" that is distinguished from the pencil. To be explicitly aware that it is a desk, then, I

---

102. R. Descartes, *Meditations on First Philosophy* (3rd ed.; trans. D. A. Cress; Indianapolis: Hackett, 1993), 77.

103. F. D. E. Schleiermacher, *On Religion: Speeches to Its Cultured Despisers* (trans. R. Crouter; Cambridge: Cambridge University Press, 1988), 103; quoted in W. Pannenberg, *Metaphysics and the Idea of God* (trans. P. Clayton; Grand Rapids: Eerdmans, 1990), 25.

104. Pannenberg, *Metaphysics and the Idea of God*, 24.

must be aware of the boundaries by which it is delimited from what under-lies it. In this way, every perception of a finite object requires an "other" from which the object can be delimited and against which the object is dis-tinguished and that must be logically prior to our distinguishing the object at hand. In the most general terms, there are only two possibilities for the "other(s)" from which a given finite object is distinguished; either it is another finite object, or it is the other of the finite as such, that is, the infi-nite. Accordingly, both the finite other and the infinite other are implied by the boundary of any finite object. Pannenberg summarizes by saying that "the notion of the finite as such can therefore not be thought without already thinking the infinite at the same time—at least by connotation."[105] Hence, explicit reflection upon the concept of finitude reveals that aware-ness of finitude and all finite objects implies a prior intuition of the infinite. It seems clear that these considerations establish the conceptual priority of the infinite, so that an intuition of the infinite underlies all finite experiences.

The second point that Pannenberg raises concerning the quotation from Descartes is an objection to Descartes' facile connection between the intu-ition of the infinite and God. Recall that Descartes writes, "The perception of the infinite is somehow prior in me to the perception of the finite, that is, my perception of God is prior to my perception of myself." Descartes moves, with no intervening argument, to equate the idea of God with the infinite. While the underlying point is the same, Pannenberg's objection has two elements. First, neither in his third meditation nor in subsequent writ-ings on the intuition of the infinite did Descartes adequately recognize the vague, fuzzy nature of that initial awareness of the infinite. Pannenberg writes: "The intuition that precedes all finite representations is not present as an explicit thought but only in an *unthematized* fashion within all repre-sentations of the finite. By contrast, the explicit treatment of the infinite no longer precedes all finite subjects."[106] These comments clarify Pannenberg's use of the unthematized intuition of the infinite. The original intuition is not actually an explicit awareness of the infinite but is rather a vague and confused awareness of an implied totality that underlies all experiences of finitude. In fact, it is only later, with explicit reflection upon the initial con-ditions of human perception, that the vague intuition is recognized as the infinite (hence, "explicit treatment . . . no longer precedes . . ."). So the ini-tial intuition (which upon reflection turns out to correspond to the infinite) has no specific content.

Pannenberg draws the following conclusion: "The general, confused, and pre-thematic idea of the infinite does not explicitly connote identity

---

105. Ibid., 25.
106. Ibid., 27.

with the idea of God."[107] Here Pannenberg states directly the second concern with Descartes' treatment: The concept of God, which has considerable specificity, cannot merely be equated with the concept of infinity without intervening justification. In the final analysis, "the idea of God cannot be separated from the elements of personality (however we are to understand it) and of a will (whatever form it takes)."[108] Yet these notions are not explicit in the pre-thematized notion of the infinite, and therefore whatever reality turns out to correspond to the infinite shall have to import its specificity from elsewhere. Pannenberg makes the point explicit when he comments that nothing so far discussed (neither the concept of absolute perfection nor the concept of necessary existence, which some have attempted to derive from the concept of infinity) "yet entails the idea of an *existing being*."[109] However, if a concept of God, which can be shown to correspond to the idea of the infinite, is discovered in the world of human experience, then it may yet turn out that this vague awareness of the infinite was, in fact, a pre-thematic awareness of God.

The Role of the History of Religious Traditions

If Pannenberg is correct that one cannot justifiably move directly from the initial intuition of the infinite to the concept of God (or the concept of a maximally perfect being, which, more accurately speaking, Descartes attempted to derive from the concept of infinity) because it implies such things as personality, will, and intellect that cannot be inferred directly from the intuition of the infinite, what recourse do we have? The things listed (personality, will, etc.) cannot be derived directly from the intuition of the infinite. Nor was Descartes correct to try to derive the concept of a maximally perfect being from the concept of infinity. Most of the historical religious traditions have concepts of God that have a good deal of specificity and that, it can be plausibly argued, have been developed in an effort to account for the mysterious, transcendent reality that humanity finds active in its midst. These concepts of God, then, arise as a consequence of religious experiences, which are experiences of that mysterious reality as it interacts with the world.

Pannenberg suggests that these concepts of God can be examined to determine if any properly comprise a reflective account of the intuition of the infinite. If so, then one may argue that the intuition of the infinite was, after all, an awareness of God, and such a concept of God may provide specificity and content for that intuition. Religious traditions that con-

---

107. Ibid., 29. See also Pannenberg, *Systematic Theology*, 1:350ff.
108. Pannenberg, *Metaphysics and the Idea of God*, 28.
109. Ibid., 37.

nect the idea of God with notions that are implied by the concept of infinity offer the most promise for correlation with the pre-thematic awareness of the infinite. Because Pannenberg conceives "infinity" as a positive category implying totality, wholeness, and the like, he argues that correlation between the idea of infinity and the idea of God is most likely in traditions that conceive God in monotheistic terms. He writes, "Only when we see later on the basis of experience and reflection that the infinite in the true sense is one, and is identical with the one God, can we say that the nonthematic awareness of the infinite was an awareness of God."[110] Without the religious traditions and their robust articulations of the mysterious, transcendent One, the intuition of the infinite would be but an interesting aspect of human experience.

Given the conflicting claims of the various religious traditions, the next question is, which concept of God, if any, corresponds to an actual existent entity? Throughout the course of human history, the existence of God remains debatable, both whether he exists and, if he does, his proper identification. However, in the conflicting truth claims of the different religious traditions as they engage each other in the public marketplace of debate, the truth is being worked out. Pannenberg writes that this "testing of the truth claims which religions make with their statements about the existence and work of the gods does not take place primarily in the form of academic investigation and evaluation but in the process of religious life itself."[111] That is to say that only God, by the demonstration of his deity over the world, is finally able to bring to resolution all questions concerning his existence.

Summary of Pannenberg's Justification of God-Talk

I have covered a number of important points in Pannenberg's argument for the justification of a systematic presentation of Christian doctrine. First, Pannenberg argues that the fundamental manner in which the traditional arguments for God's existence have developed leads us no longer to see them as proofs for God's existence, but, he argues, they do establish the importance of the concept of God. Second, Pannenberg argues that religion is constitutive for human nature. In so doing, he draws attention to the fact that humans find themselves referred beyond themselves in their quest for meaning, which is what one would expect if God were, in fact, the source of meaning for human lives. In reflecting upon the nature of human perception, Pannenberg advanced the thesis that all perception of finitude is preconditioned by an unthematized awareness of the infinite.

---

110. Pannenberg, *Systematic Theology*, 1:114.
111. Ibid., 1:159.

Since, conceptually, all experience of finitude arises by limitation of the infinite, the finite is dependent upon the infinite for its being. While this intuition of the infinite cannot be directly connected with the idea of God, it is suggestive and invites further analysis. Third, in the religious traditions, one finds specific and detailed conceptions of a transcendent entity who has attributes that correspond to the notion of infinity and upon whom all finite reality is said to depend. While not a decisive proof of God's existence, Pannenberg concludes that it is at least plausible to speak of an actually existing being who is rightly the object of humanity's religious urges and who is the infinite One. Consequently, if the Christian religious tradition's concept of God proves coherent, belief in the God of the Christian tradition would be plausible. At this point, Pannenberg believes that he has established a starting point for the systematic presentation of Christian doctrine.

Critical Assessment

It would take a monograph to examine thoroughly Pannenberg's theological method. However, since our narrower concern is Pannenberg's doctrine of God, we need not undertake such a detailed examination. So we shall restrict our attention to issues that would tend to undermine Pannenberg's attempt to justify religious assertions and thereby to undermine his attempt to establish successfully a point of departure for systematic theology. Three separate issues require our attention: First, we shall consider whether such a high-powered epistemic apparatus must be deployed merely for the sake of beginning the task of systematic theology. Second, it has been objected that Pannenberg's methodology fails to appropriately appreciate the noetic condition of humanity. More specifically, objectors argue that he underestimates the noetic effects of the fall and that he does not adequately account for the noetic role of the Holy Spirit in our coming to belief. Finally, the question has been asked whether "eschatological verification" is adequate for the level of confidence needed to engage in the theological enterprise today. In other words, is it adequate to see doctrinal statements as hypothetical in nature?

Pannenberg's Methodology as Point of Departure

To address properly whether such a sophisticated and complex methodological proposal is necessary merely to begin the task of systematic theology, one must remember how Pannenberg understands the theological enterprise. Pannenberg argues strongly against what he sees as the widespread privatization of Christianity. Stanley Grenz summarizes:

In Pannenberg's view, 20th century existentialist theologies have tended to compartmentalize reason and faith into separate spheres, thereby shielding faith from the potentially critical findings of reason. . . . Pannenberg decries this compartmentalization as an illegitimate privatization of theology. For him faith is not a separate way of knowing truth not open to the scientific method but rather is a personal commitment to God who can be indirectly seen in history and therefore whose acts are open to scientific confirmation.[112]

If theology is to have intersubjective validity, it must not withdraw from the arena of public debate but instead must engage that debate to defend the truth of Christian doctrine. To engage in subjectifying Christianity is, in effect, to withdraw from that arena and to surrender before the challenge to show the objective validity of Christian truth claims. In other words, to engage in the presentation of truth claims is not merely to assert that some proposition *p* is true *for me*, but rather to claim that it is objectively true and thus intersubjectively true.

Since Pannenberg sees theology as a science, he argues that theologians must engage the task with a methodology appropriate to theology's scientific status. First, and perhaps foremost, this means that truth claims advanced by the systematic theologian must be critically examined and appropriately defended. When plausible objections are raised to a given scientific theory, the adherents of the theory must respond to those objections. If a response is not forthcoming or if the response is inadequate, the credibility of the theory appropriately suffers. Pannenberg does not believe that the constructive theories atheists have advanced to disprove theism are particularly strong. Nevertheless, he does believe they have validly identified problems that require response. Summarizing, then, under Pannenberg's construal of the task of the systematic theologian, there are three reasons why one must justify presentation of a systematic theology:

1. because the fundamental issue is whether the Christian message is true;
2. because during the course of human history, the existence of God is debatable; and
3. because overly subjectivist understandings of truth are inadequate.

One might respond by arguing that the systematic theologian seeking to do theology specifically for the church need not be concerned with the pub-

---

112. S. Grenz, "The Appraisal of Pannenberg: A Survey of the Literature," in Braaten and Clayton, *Theology of Wolfhart Pannenberg*, 21. Of course, one can debate Pannenberg's portrayal of these theologies. However, the widespread tendency to see religion as dealing with personal beliefs and commitments, which are fundamentally subjective in nature, and to see science as the epitome of objectivity suggests that this portrayal has a good deal of validity.

lic arena and thus may launch into a systematic presentation of Christian doctrine that aims merely to show that the Christian doctrines are self-referentially coherent. However, one wonders whether such a view of the task of systematic theology does not collapse into the position that every community has its own "truth." As Neuhaus notes:

> The question is whether the Christian message is *true*. And the testing of the truth of the matter must be in conversation with the ways in which we test the truth of other matters. Self-referentiality is not enough. Christian truth claims cannot be interpreted and vindicated simply by reference to Christian truth claims.[113]

There must be more to the claim that some proposition is true than that it is merely consistent with one's own worldview. The issue of whether, for example, Hinduism is true is not simply a matter of whether Hindu truth claims are internally consistent. Those truth claims must also make contact with the world in that they accurately describe (i.e., correspond to) what one finds in the world.

Alvin Plantinga's proposal that belief in the existence of God is a properly basic belief could be taken as an alternative way to justify presentation of a system of Christian doctrine. According to Plantinga, a belief is warranted[114] if formed by an individual whose epistemic faculties

1. are functioning properly,
2. have been well-designed,
3. are operating in a congenial epistemic environment
4. are aimed at the production of truth, and
5. have a high objective probability of arriving at truth.[115]

If these conditions are met under the right circumstances and if one finds oneself inclined to believe some proposition *p*, then *p* is properly basic for that person. Plantinga argues, "There are . . . many conditions and circumstances that call forth belief in God: guilt, gratitude, danger, a sense of God's presence, a sense that he speaks, perceptions of various parts of the universe."[116] Space does not permit a lengthy examination of Plantinga's proposal. Nor is it required, as our primary question is, does it provide an acceptable alternative to Pannenberg's proposal? It seems not because it

---

113. R. J. Neuhaus, "Reason Public and Private: The Pannenberg Project," *First Things* (March 1992), 59.

114. *Warrant* is the term Plantinga uses that is roughly equivalent to the more usual epistemic term: *justification*.

115. For more detail, see Alvin Plantinga, *Warrant and Proper Function* (New York: Oxford University Press, 1993).

116. Alvin Plantinga, "Reason and Belief in God," *Faith and Rationality*, 81.

falls prey precisely to the difficulties mentioned above. If, on Plantinga's account, belief in God is properly basic for the Christian, then it seems that belief in Krishna could be properly basic for the Hindu, provided the stated conditions are met. It is hard to see, then, how a position that leads to such a conclusion could be viewed as providing an adequate point of departure for a specific systematic theology.[117] Further, Pannenberg would argue that the debatability of God's existence leads to plausible challenge to religious belief, thus placing Plantinga in the position of needing to provide rational defense of those beliefs, even if they might have been, at some point in the past, properly basic beliefs.[118]

So far, then, it seems that Pannenberg's insistence that the state of affairs that exists in philosophy and theology today requires justification of systematic theology is eminently reasonable. Yet, even granting Pannenberg's claim that such a systematic presentation must be justified, one still may ask whether he has provided the only reasonable alternative. For example, could one appeal to some form of the doctrine of the authority/inspiration of Scripture as justifying a point of departure for systematic theology? The question is whether there is an argument for the authority of Scripture that can serve the same purpose as Pannenberg's methodological proposals, not in the form of a prior guarantee of truth so that one might circumvent the need for testing Christian truth claims, but rather merely to justify their presentation. Let us consider one possible argument that might be presented in a manner consistent with Pannenberg's broader set of concerns, one that Pannenberg should find acceptable.

The first question that requires consideration is, precisely what do we intend to gain from the claim that the Scriptures are inspired or authoritative?[119] For example, some theories intend to vouchsafe the veracity of the Scriptures on all matters, whether they are historical, scientific, geographical, or the like. Others more modestly seek to protect the veracity of all that the Scriptures affirm as necessary for the salvation of humans. The latter position, for example, allows recognition that differing genres are intended to communicate differently. For example, a poetic genre may be deployed to communicate truth while using metaphorical language that is not literally true. Let us consider this more modest position as merely seeking to

---

117. This is not, by the way, to denigrate the important contribution Plantinga has made by emphasizing the importance of proper function and the related issues to epistemology in general—an emphasis sorely lacking in the antecedent epistemic tradition. Likewise, we must readily admit that there is no indication that Plantinga intends his proposal to satisfy the requirements for a starting point for a systematic presentation of Christian doctrine along the lines laid out herein.

118. Charles Gutenson, "Can Belief in the Christian God Be Properly Basic? A Pannenbergian Perspective on Plantiga and Basic Beliefs," *Christian Scholar's Review* (Fall 1999), 49–72.

119. Henceforth, I will use the term "authoritative" in an attempt to avoid some of the negative connotations connected to the term "inspired."

defend the doctrinal content of the Scriptures, and further, that the doctrinal content corresponds to that which is necessary for human salvation. Consider the language from the United Methodist Book of Discipline in the confession of faith dealing with the Holy Bible:

> We believe the Holy Bible, Old and New Testaments, reveals the Word of God so far as it is necessary for our salvation. It is to be received through the Holy Spirit as the true rule and guide for faith and practice. Whatever is not revealed in or established by the Holy Scriptures is not to be made an article of faith nor is it to be taught as essential to salvation.[120]

Here the focus is clearly upon those aspects of the Scriptures relating to human salvation, which is taken as equivalent to the claim that the Scriptures are authoritative as regards their doctrinal content, or the "articles of faith." If it can be shown that this claim is *prima facie* plausible, then it seems that one has what one needs to provide *prima facie* justification for presenting a systematic account of Christian doctrine. Remember, we are only seeking to *justify the engagement* of the task of systematic theology; we are not seeking a definitive guarantee of the truthfulness of the Scriptures.

So how might one proceed to establish the *prima facie* plausibility of the claim that the Scriptures are true as regards their doctrinal content? We might begin with the idea of power that is implied by the very concept of God (Pannenberg calls it the "semantic minimum" for the concept of God[121]). We need not defend the divine omnipotence at this point but rather note that if God exists, he surely would have the power to communicate successfully with humans. Consequently, if God exists and had so willed, it seems he could have communicated with the appropriate subjects in such a manner as to assure the truthfulness of the doctrinal content of the Scriptures. So any argument concerning the claim that God has or has not done this must arise from the evidence itself and not from presuppositions about the nature of God's power. Then the question becomes whether or not there are reasons to believe that God, if he exists, has assured the doctrinal content of the Scriptures. One way to address this question is to consider historical evidence.

Over the years, Pannenberg has been one of the staunchest supporters of the historicity of the resurrection. His analysis in *Jesus—God and Man* leads him to believe that the historian must conclude that "Jesus was raised from the dead" is a proposition that has adequate evidence to justify its embrace. He has also written extensively on the implications of the resur-

---

120. United Methodist Book of Discipline, 64. (As this citation is from the confession of faith, it does not generally change from year to year. So one might consult any post-1968 Book of Discipline.)

121. Pannenberg, *Introduction to Systematic Theology*, 8.

rection, not the least of which would be establishing the plausibility of the existence of God. Further, Pannenberg sees the event of Jesus' resurrection as having a retroactive power in establishing the Sonship of Christ. He frequently cites Rom 1:1–4:

> Paul, a servant of Jesus Christ, called to be an apostle, set apart for the gospel of God, which he promised beforehand through his prophets in the holy scriptures, the gospel concerning his Son, who was descended from David according to the flesh and was declared to be the Son of God with power according to the spirit of holiness by resurrection from the dead.

For Pannenberg, it is the reality of the resurrection that serves to confirm the pre-Easter ministry of Christ. He argues that prior to the Easter event, the divine Sonship of Christ was not evident, nor was the authorization of his ministry clearly settled. However, in the light of Easter morning, not only the divine Sonship but also the claims advanced in the course of his ministry (pre- and post-Easter) are settled as authoritative and spoken with the Father's approval.[122]

Once the authority of Christ has been plausibly established, one has a variety of claims to examine. Relevant to this matter is Acts 1:8, wherein Jesus tells his disciples that when the Holy Spirit comes upon them, they will become his witnesses. Oscar Cullmann is one theologian who has referenced this verse as a means of establishing the authority of the Scriptures to the extent they bear witness to Christ. In other words, if the Spirit empowers the disciples to be witnesses of Christ, surely the Spirit would lead them to valid testimony of Christ and his teachings. Since Pannenberg argues that Christ is the hermeneutical center of the Scriptures, it seems reasonable to argue that if the scriptural witness to Christ is a faithful witness, it is entirely plausible to argue that the doctrinal content of Scripture may be taken as authoritative.[123]

When one notes that arguments for the authority of Scripture are well attested within the tradition, it seems one has reasonable grounds for utilizing the doctrine of the authority of Scripture as a means for establishing a starting point for theology. Pannenberg objected to using the doctrine of the authority of Scripture as a means of avoiding the necessary task of engaging the question of the truthfulness of Christian doctrine. Emphasizing the point, we need not argue that one can set aside the hypothetical nature of theology or the need to inquire systematically into the truth of the doctrinal claims of the Christian faith. On the contrary, rather than use the

---

122. W. Pannenberg, *Jesus—God and Man* (trans. L. L. Wilkins and D. A. Priebe; Philadelphia: Westminster, 1977), 135.

123. Of course, one may debate whether these words from Acts 1:8 are rightly attributable to Jesus.

complex methodological apparatus Pannenberg deploys to establish a point of departure for theology, one might instead employ the line of argument advanced above. After all, we are merely at the beginning, not the end of the inquiry.[124]

Noetic Effects of the Fall

The objection that Pannenberg's methodology does not adequately address the noetic effects of the fall frequently shows up in a couple of different forms. On the one hand, the objection is that he is inadequately sensitive to human spiritual blindness, or as Grenz reports:

> Pannenberg has repeatedly been described as a rationalist. Several conservative critics have found aspects of his rationalistic approach problematic for the relation between faith and reason. For them, Pannenberg has failed to see that the human problem of spiritual blindness goes deeper than merely a lack of historical evidence. Rather, there is in humans a moral bias toward evil that interferes with the rational process and makes the task of reading revelation in history difficult.[125]

The challenge is quite serious, for it asks whether Pannenberg's method, which admittedly hangs much on reason, can be trusted in light of fallen human nature. On the other hand, the issue is whether Pannenberg's method leaves space for the active involvement of the Holy Spirit in our coming to knowledge of religious matters. Grenz writes:

> The working of the Spirit was the missing element, Fuller maintains against Pannenberg, in whose system no such supernatural element must be added to the historical event carrying its own inherent meaning. In a similar assessment Hamilton charges Pannenberg with substituting proper methodology for the Spirit.[126]

The question, of course, is whether these criticisms accurately reflect the content of Pannenberg's proposal.

---

124. The issue here is not to show that Pannenberg's methodology is inadequate or even inappropriate, but rather to show that there are alternate possibilities for justifying a systematic presentation of Christian doctrine. This particular alternative, if acceptable, shows that a path more consistent with what many evangelicals might propose is also plausible. Pannenberg is clearly interested in starting from "neutral propositions," and he likely would argue that his method does this in a way that the alternative outlined above could not. And, hence, Pannenberg would rightly prefer his own method in light of his perception of the theological task.

125. Grenz, "The Appraisal of Pannenberg," 23.

126. Ibid.

On the first issue, one is immediately inclined to point out that whatever the effects of the fall actually were, they could not extend beyond the bounds that God chose to allow. Consequently, one must keep in mind the scriptural claim that God is willing that none should perish but that all should come to faith, no matter what effects the fall had upon human rationality and upon human epistemic faculties in general. In other words, those effects must not be conceived so severely as to make coming to the knowledge of God impossible. If we take seriously God's love for humanity, it is exceedingly hard to imagine that he would allow the fall to render human epistemic faculties impotent in their ability to come to know God. However, one might respond that, while he or she concurs that God intends to make himself known, human reason alone is not adequate. Further, the hypothetical objector might continue, it is precisely such a confidence in reason that Pannenberg exhibits. Consider Pannenberg's comments on these issues at the outset of volume 1 of *Systematic Theology*:

> [T]he knowledge of God that is made possible by God, and therefore by revelation, is one of the basic conditions of the concept of theology as such. Otherwise the possibility of the knowledge of God is logically inconceivable, it would contradict the very idea of God.[127]

Note the strong language Pannenberg employs here when he writes that the very possibility of knowledge of God is contingent upon God's giving himself to be known through revelation. Only a few lines farther, Pannenberg writes:

> But in any case, whether inside the Christian church or outside it, and even in the so-called natural knowledge of God, *no knowledge of God and no theology are conceivable that do not proceed from God and are not due to the working of his Spirit.*[128]

So in Pannenberg's most mature thought, as exemplified in his three-volume *Systematic Theology*, he explicitly states that humans are utterly dependent upon God for knowledge of God. How, then, do we make sense of Pannenberg's admitted rationalist tendencies in light of these explicit comments? Before we attempt to answer this question, it is necessary to consider the objection that Pannenberg ignores the epistemic role of the Holy Spirit.

Let us begin with an examination of certain scriptural passages that suggest that the Holy Spirit plays a role in our coming to knowledge of one sort or another. First, consider Rom 8:14–16:

---

127. Pannenberg, *Systematic Theology*, 1:2.
128. Ibid (emphasis added).

For all who are led by the Spirit of God are children of God. For you did not receive a spirit of slavery to fall back into fear, but you have received a spirit of adoption. When we cry, "Abba! Father!" it is the very Spirit bearing witness with our spirit that we are children of God.

Consider also 1 Cor 2:12–14:

Now we have received not the spirit of the world, but the Spirit that is from God, so that we may understand the gifts bestowed on us by God. And we speak of these things in words not taught by human wisdom but taught by the Spirit, interpreting spiritual things to those who are spiritual.

Those who are unspiritual do not receive the gifts of God's Spirit, for they are foolishness to them, and they are unable to understand them because they are spiritually discerned.

And 1 Cor 12:3:

Therefore I want you to understand that no one speaking by the Spirit of God ever says "Let Jesus be cursed!" and no one can say "Jesus is Lord" except by the Holy Spirit.

One might add Matt 16:17 or other references, but the point will be the same: There are sufficient grounds for arguing that the Holy Spirit plays an important role in our coming to knowledge on matters of faith. So how would Pannenberg respond to the challenge that he does not adequately consider the relationship between the Spirit's action and human knowledge?

One might simply respond to the objection by pointing out the similarities between Pannenberg's claim that no knowledge of God is possible apart from the working of the Spirit and the citation from 1 Cor 2. Additionally, Pannenberg's commitment to the involvement of the Holy Spirit in all aspects of human life permeates his writings; consider, for example, his works dealing with the interconnections between theology and the natural sciences. One of Pannenberg's more controversial proposals is that we conceive God along the lines of an infinite field of power.[129] As he presents his arguments for this proposal, it becomes increasingly clear that he thinks of God's Spirit as pervasively present and active in all of creation. In fact, the Spirit constantly interacts with and guides the development of the creatures. Within the context of evolution, Pannenberg thinks that the biogenetic field in which humans evolve is a partial manifestation of the presence of the Spirit of God with the creatures. In this way, Pannenberg

---

129. A proposal that shall receive attention in due course in chapter 6.

forges a profoundly intimate relationship between God's Spirit and all of creation. *No act whatsoever* occurs outside the presence of the Spirit. Even sin, which represents the creature's rejection of the Spirit, cannot happen outside the active presence of the Spirit since he wills a level of autonomy to the creatures. When one combines this understanding of the presence of the divine Spirit with the claim that no knowledge of God comes apart from the interaction of the Spirit, it seems clear that Pannenberg does indeed have a strong sense of the epistemic role of the Holy Spirit, though admittedly he seldom puts the matter in these terms. This, then, raises one more question: What warrants Pannenberg's confidence in reason so that all may read the significance of events off the events themselves, while still affirming a strong sense of the need of the Spirit to come to the knowledge of God?

In the Wesleyan tradition the tension between human depravity and human free will is bridged by means of the concept of God's prevenient grace. This gift of grace from God is imparted by the Holy Spirit to all humans so that the effects of original sin and the consequent human depravity are overcome just to the degree that humans may make free choices. Obviously, the goal of prevenient grace is to make it possible for humans to freely embrace a relationship with God and to escape their slavery to sin. The key point is that Wesley understood prevenient grace to be given to all, prior to exercise of belief in God, and therefore, prior to their becoming believers. All are recipients of prevenient grace, and therefore, all may freely respond to God's gracious offer of reconciliation through Christ. One might draw a parallel between Wesley's concept of prevenient grace and Pannenberg's confidence in reason as follows.

As we have seen, Pannenberg readily affirms that no knowledge of God is possible apart from God's self-revelation and the work of the Holy Spirit. At the same time, Pannenberg is convinced that no "supernatural element"[130] needs to be added to the historical events for individuals to read off their meaning. How else can this be understood than that God, through the working of the Spirit in a prevenient fashion, makes it possible for all to come to knowledge about God? In fact, the passage that Wesley cites in defense of the doctrine of prevenient grace is John 1:9. The term used in the passage ("enlightens") generally carries epistemic weight, and here it seems eminently plausible to argue that this enlightenment is mediated through the Holy Spirit and that it aims to counterbalance, to some degree, the noetic effects of the fall.

---

130. Of course, the prevenient grace I speak of here is a "supernatural" gift in that it comes from God. However, here, consistent with Wesley, the intent is to point out the pervasive nature of prevenient grace so that it is present in all human lives at all times and, therefore, is not something beyond what all bring to the task of grasping the meaning of historical events.

To Pannenberg, then, God's Spirit enables reason to grasp the divine reality in a fashion similar to Wesley's conception of prevenient grace that enlightens all. This, of course, does not mean that all will use the free will given by God's grace to come to know God. In fact, humans may not come to the knowledge of God for a variety of reasons, all of which, under this construal, must be understood as related to sin in some way. This will undoubtedly sound harsh to the unbeliever, for it inevitably connects unbelief with perversity. However, this is no more harsh than Paul's claim in Rom 2 that, due to natural revelation, those who do not respond to God's offer of redemption are without excuse. Consequently, one must see even Pannenberg's rationalism as grounded in the power of God's Spirit to make God known to all humans. Pannenberg's methodology provides a description of how he understands the outworking of human knowledge in light of the Holy Spirit's epistemic role. Since this initial restoration of reason is provided to all humans, Pannenberg's position here further supports his concern to avoid the privatization of faith.

Eschatological Verification

The last objection we shall consider is whether the provisional nature of all truth claims and eschatological verification, as it is often called, provide the necessary level of confidence for the theologian who engages the task of systematic theology prior to the eschaton. David Holwerda expresses this concern as follows:

> A basic problem in Pannenberg's theology is the transition from the probabilities of historical reason to the certainty of faith. By agreeing that historical reason produces only judgments of probability while affirming that faith requires absolute trust, Pannenberg creates a dilemma in his theological system.[131]

According to Holwerda, the problem is that Pannenberg's view of the provisional nature of truth does not correlate with his claim that the believer must trust absolutely. A good deal hinges, however, on precisely what Pannenberg intends when he uses the phrase "certainty of faith,"[132] and it is not at all clear that Pannenberg intends it in the sense that Holwerda believes. If one considers the broader scope of Pannenberg's writings, important parts of which were not available when Holwerda wrote, a somewhat weaker view of the "certainty of faith" becomes evident. In

---

131. D. Holwerda, "Faith, Reason, and the Resurrection," *Faith and Rationality*, 306.
132. Which he admittedly uses in his response to the criticisms presented in *Theology as History*.

Introduction to Systematic Theology, Pannenberg reminds us that "the scriptures themselves tell us that the universal recognition of God's glory will not occur before the eschaton" and that this is consistent with Paul's affirmations in 1 Cor 13:9.[133] He then goes on to say that

> [t]he results [of systematic reconstructions of Christian doctrine] will remain provisional, but that is in keeping not only with the spirit of modern science but also with Paul's understanding of the provisional form of our knowledge, due to the incompleteness of salvation history itself. To engage in systematic theology in this way is quite compatible with personal confidence in the ultimate truth of the Christian doctrine, even more so than on the basis of a prior commitment to authority.[134]

Perhaps the reference to modern science combined with Pannenberg's understanding of theology as science can help here. Consider, for example, scientific theories about the nature of the universe. In the last fifty years, a great deal of research in the philosophy of science has reasonably demonstrated that scientific theories themselves must be understood as provisional.[135] Nevertheless, scientists are not prevented from making technological advances based upon a particular provisional hypothesis about the nature of the world. Similarly, the systematic theologian advances provisional hypotheses about the ultimate meaning of the cosmos. These hypotheses are subject to testing for their ability to explain the world of shared human experience, and they are subject to reformulation in the face of appropriate challenges and counterevidences. This does not mean, however, that the systematician proceeds without confidence in the ultimate truthfulness of the overarching hypotheses comprised by those doctrinal truth claims any more than the scientist would with regard to scientific hypotheses. Perhaps one may correlate this to Paul's notion that we now see through a glass darkly but then (eschatologcially) face-to-face. In the end, it seems Holwerda's criticism rests on an interpretation of "certainty of faith" not intended by Pannenberg.

In *The Doctrine of Revelation*, Gabriel Fackre draws comparisons between the work of Pannenberg and Ronald Thiemann. According to Fackre, Pannenberg is more the rationalist than Thiemann because Pannenberg is more concerned to advance the rational arguments that give substance to his position. However, Fackre offers an insightful summary of Thiemann:

---

133. Pannenberg, *Introduction to Systematic Theology*, 17.
134. Ibid., 18.
135. Consider, for example, Pannenberg's own *Philosophy of Science*, Thomas Kuhn's *The Structure of Scientific Revolution*, and Karl Popper's *Conjectures and Refutations*.

Revelation is the continuing reality of God's active presence among his people. Since it is a reality "not seen" and not fully experienced, it must be expressed by a confession of faith, i.e., an "assurance of things hoped for, a conviction of things not seen." . . . The justifiability of one's faith and hope in the trustworthiness of a promiser is never fully confirmed (or disconfirmed) until the promiser actually fulfills (or fails to fulfill) his/her promises. Until the moment of fulfillment the recipient must justify faith and hope on the basis of a judgment concerning the character of the promiser. . . . Consequently we live in a situation in which there can be no indubitable foundation for knowledge and thus in which both belief and refusal to believe can appear to be justified.[136]

It is enlightening that Thiemann draws attention to the personal character of Christian faith. Christian faith is ultimately faith in a person and not simply faith in a set of propositions. According to both Pannenberg and Thiemann, faith must be seen as trust and thus depends ultimately upon the trustworthiness of the One trusted. As Fackre notes, "both [Pannenberg and Thiemann] reflect the accent on faith short of its ultimate homecoming, and thus epistemologically understood as *trust* not 'sight,' as the risk and insecurity of a revelatory Not Yet."[137] Consider the personal nature of the trust involved in a marriage commitment. Each person makes an ultimate commitment at the time of marriage ("Till death do us part"), while neither has ultimate certainty that the other will keep that promise. Such uncertainty, however, does not justify a less than ultimate commitment. Likewise, it is not necessary that absolute trust in God be mediated by absolute certainty of the truthfulness of Christian doctrine.

Interestingly, however, Fackre identifies what he believes is an inconsistency in the way that Pannenberg relates the working of God's Spirit and the provisionality of Christian truth claims:

Pannenberg also appears to make assertions inconsistent with his major premise of Christian truth-claims as "hypotheses" awaiting eschatological confirmation, by speaking of our adherence to them as "provisionally made in human hearts by the convicting ministry of the Spirit of God."[138]

Fackre's concern becomes evident when he argues that if we are confident that the witness born within is from the Spirit of God, then surely we must see the truth communicated thereby not as merely provisionally true, but rather as actually true, since "a conviction born of the third Person of the

---

136. Gabriel Fackre, *The Doctrine of Revelation* (Grand Rapids: Eerdmans, 1997), 218.
137. Ibid., 220.
138. Ibid., 221.

Trinity must be trustworthy knowledge."[139] It seems Pannenberg's response to this objection is quite straightforward. Whenever we believe ourselves to be recipients of a direct communication from the Holy Spirit, there are actually two propositions that come bound closely together: (1) the item of knowledge communicated to us—let us for simplicity's sake call it some proposition p; and (2) a belief about the source of the knowledge, say, "P is communicated to me by the Holy Spirit."

Now, we must remember that the provisionality of Christian truth claims, as Pannenberg sees it, is tied up with the debatability of God's existence. Consequently, it is the belief about the source of the knowledge, that p is communicated by the Holy Spirit, that would render both beliefs provisional. If one could be certain that the item of knowledge had been communicated by God, then I believe Pannenberg would have to agree that such knowledge would not be provisional. However, according to Pannenberg, we cannot have absolute certainty that we are not engaging in self-deception when we believe ourselves direct recipients of knowledge from God. Consequently, given Pannenberg's sensitivity to the criticisms that flow from the tradition of Feuerbach, Freud, and Marx concerning false consciousness, we can see how Pannenberg has both theoretical (the provisional nature of truth) and pragmatic (the possibility of self-deception) reasons to question the source of, to use our earlier designation, p. So it seems that Fackre's objection does not adequately appreciate the reasons underlying Pannenberg's claim that Christian truth claims remain provisional prior to the eschaton. Further, in consideration of these discussions, it does not seem that Pannenberg's notion of the provisionality of truth claims presents much of an obstacle to the ability of the systematic theologian to carry out his or her task.

In this chapter, we have examined the various aspects of Pannenberg's methodology with a particular focus on the manner in which he justifies the development of systematic theology. We have seen that the debatability of God's existence, which is a continuing part of human experience, leads Pannenberg to provide justification prior to engaging in a systematic presentation of the truth claims of Christianity. Afterward, we considered several distinct objections to his methodology. While we have argued that one might proceed in other ways, Pannenberg's method succeeds in establishing the beginning point for theology as he intends. Consequently, it is appropriate that we now proceed to examine the details of his doctrine of God. In the next chapter, we undertake an examination of the manner in which Pannenberg appropriates and deploys the concept of infinity, a concept that he seeks to make central to the overall Christian doctrine of God.

---

139. Ibid.

CHAPTER 3

The Role of the Infinite in
Pannenberg's Doctrine of God

IN THE PRECEDING CHAPTER, we saw how Pannenberg deployed the concept of the infinite as part of his justification of religious belief. However, given that Pannenberg is proposing to elevate the importance of the category of the infinite within the Christian doctrine of God and, hence, in his theology, we must attend to several of the concerns that arise with deployment of this notion in theological/philosophical contexts. It is not my intent to develop the concept of the infinite in exhaustive detail[140] or to examine all of the implications for Pannenberg's theology. Rather, the fundamental questions relate whether the concept of the infinite can reasonably be applied to God, and if so, how. Intuitions on these questions are deeply divided.

The Christian tradition has not had a single voice on the relation of infinity to the doctrine of God. For example, Origen wrote: "We must maintain that even the power of God is finite, and we must not, under the pretext of praising him, lose sight of his limitations. For if the divine power were infinite, of necessity it could not even understand itself, since the infinite is by its nature incomprehensible."[141]

---

140. For a more thorough examination of these issues, see A. W. Moore, *The Infinite* (London: Routledge, 1990).

141. Origen, *On First Principles* (trans. G. W. Butterworth; Gloucester: Peter Smith, 1973), 129. We ought not immediately assume that Origen is seeking to "finitize" God; rather, what we see here is the tendency to conceive infinity as a negative category within the philosophical tradition to which Origen was heir.

While Origen, for reasons yet to be examined, tended to deny the divine infinity, Gregory of Nyssa was one of the first in the Christian tradition to make the concept of infinity central to the Christian doctrine of God. Hanson writes of Gregory's position:

> In place of God's ingenerateness Gregory presented God's infinity, which is his master-thought. The conviction that the being of Christ is the same as that of God demanded a rethinking of the traditional concept of God; unoriginatedness cannot simply be ingeneratedness. Gregory found the answer in the concept of God's infinity which Greek philosophy had tended to avoid.[142]

Whereas Origen found fundamental absurdities in using the concept of infinity with regard to certain aspects of the doctrine of God, Gregory found that the concept gave him a way of resolving difficulties related to the common nature of the Father and the Son. Already in the early period, the question of whether the concept of infinity can be properly applied to God found disagreement.

In *The History of Western Philosophy*, W. T. Jones occasionally refers to what he calls "fundamental partings of the way" within the philosophical tradition. By this phrase, he means that from time to time, philosophers come upon an issue that allows two (or more) plausible explanations, neither of which can be decisively proven by its supporters nor decisively refuted by its opponents. In these cases, one must simply take the path that seems most plausible to him or her while recognizing that a degree of uncertainty will attend the position chosen. Regarding the concept of infinity, there are at least two of these "fundamental partings of the way." The first concerns whether the infinite is primarily a mathematical or a metaphysical concept. The second has to do with whether the infinite is a regulative, limit concept that is always potential and never actual, or whether it can ever be actual. From what we have seen so far, we may conclude that Pannenberg focuses primarily upon a metaphysical rather than a mathematical notion of the infinite, and since he holds that God is the infinite One, he believes that the infinite is actual.

Pannenberg proposes to elevate the concept of infinity to a central place within the Christian doctrine of God. Consequently, in addition to examining the two issues noted above, I will consider Pannenberg's rationale for making this proposal and evaluate his supporting arguments for applying the concept of infinity to God. I will proceed as follows in this chapter. First, I will undertake an examination of the history of ideas regarding the

---

142. R. P. C. Hanson, *The Search for the Christian Doctrine of God* (Edinburgh: T&T Clark, 1988), 721 n. 161.

concept of infinity. Of course, this examination will reveal those "fundamental partings of the way" mentioned above. Second, I will give detailed consideration to Pannenberg's proposal for elevating the concept of infinity within his theology. Third, since Hegel's analysis of the infinite, primarily as contained in *Science of Logic*, plays an important role in Pannenberg's thought, I will examine those aspects of Hegel's philosophy that Pannenberg appropriates. Fourth, I will consider the philosophical and theological arguments regarding the application of the concept of infinity to God. Finally, I will assess the persuasiveness of Pannenberg's position. Let us now turn our attention to a brief historical sketch of the development and deployment of the concept of infinity, keeping particularly in mind the issues identified above.[143]

The Concept of the Infinite in Historical Context

The Pre-Socratics

When considering the historical development of the concept of infinity, it is customary to begin with the pre-Socratics. These philosophers tended to conceive of infinity in predominantly negative terms. For them, the infinite was identified with that which is indeterminate, unbounded, and without form. The pre-Socratics, as a general rule, saw perfection in determinate forms—those things that had clear and well-defined boundaries. Writing about the Pythagoreans, Moore comments, "The regular cycles of the planets, the recurring patterns in nature, the finely proportioned structures in the physical world—these all betokened, for the Pythagoreans, rhyme and reason; that which is comprehensible and good; that which has a *peras*."[144] Since the infinite is, by definition, that which is without limits, without center, without boundaries, it could only be seen as imperfect precisely as a consequence of its very nature. The earlier quote from Origen, in which he denies the divine infinity, suggests a similar line of reasoning. Origen certainly would have argued that all perfections had to be applied to God maximally, so he could only argue that it was "a pretext of praise" to apply the concept of infinity to God, since Origen saw infinity as an imperfection.

However, the pre-Socratics were not uniform in their assessment of the concept of infinity. In fact, philosophizing with regard to the origin of all that is real, Anaximander proposed conceiving of the infinite (or in Greek terms, *to aperion*, which literally means "the unbounded") as the ultimate

---

143. While this work focuses upon Pannenberg's theology, in this chapter, Pannenberg will be in the background in various places as we seek development of an adequate grasp of these difficult concepts. This will allow us more ably to consider Pannenberg's proposals.

144. Moore, *Infinite*, 19.

source of everything. Anaximander held that all that is bounded and determinate has its source in that which is indeterminate and unbounded. Further, Anaximander argued that everything bounded and determinate will finally return to *to aperion*: "The principle and origin of existing things is *to aperion*. And into that from which existing things come to be they also pass away according to necessity; for they suffer punishment and make amends to one another for their injustice, in accordance with the ordinance of time."[145] While this position conceives of the infinite somewhat differently than the position generally held during this period, it would perhaps be an exaggeration of the importance of Anaximander's position to suggest that he significantly and systematically presented an alternative to the prevailing view. Nevertheless, it does demonstrate that intuitions regarding the infinite were somewhat divided even at this early date.

Plato/Aristotle

What can be called the Platonic tradition (broadly speaking) generally continued the tendency to conceive of the infinite in negative terms, preserving more positive assessments for that which had determinate form. Plato himself seemed to have adopted elements from the positions of a number of those who preceded him, though his position tended to be more abstract.[146] According to Plato, the finite, through the principle of universal reason, imposed order upon the infinite. In a sense, the infinite, conceived as the boundless and indeterminate, underlay reality but became manifest only as it was given form. Given the role that the form of the good plays in unifying the forms, Moore could write, "The unity of the Ideas, encapsulated in the supremacy of the Idea of the good, meant that there was an element of the metaphysically infinite in reality."[147] Moore recognizes here Plato's attention, albeit somewhat superficial, to what I will refer to as the "metaphysical infinite." There is little of consequence in Plato's thoughts concerning what I will refer to as the "mathematical infinite." Overall, the concept of the infinite continued to be evaluated negatively, as it was held to be imperfect on account of its indeterminate, formless nature.

While continuing to think of the infinite in similar fashion to those who preceded him, Aristotle made important contributions to the conceptualization of the infinite. In the first place, Aristotle held that the infinite is, in fact, real and not merely an abstraction. However, he went on to say that the infinite is never anywhere actualized; rather, the infinite is real only as

---

145. Anaximander, as cited in Moore, *Infinite*, 19.
146. Moore, *Infinite*, 27.
147. Ibid., 28.

potentiality. By this, Aristotle meant that the infinite is real in the sense of a limit concept (one can pile item upon item, ever striving for the infinite), but since more can always be added, one can never actually reach infinity. Consistent with his more empirical focus, one sees immediately that Aristotle's concept of the infinite was more mathematical than was Plato's more idealistically grounded notion.

Aristotle used the analogy of traversing a distance to make his point concerning the potential, rather than actual, nature of the infinite. He argued that to say that some actual infinite exists would be like saying that one had traversed an infinite interval in arriving at an actually infinite value. However, as Aristotle pointed out, one could always add more to the interval. Thus, to say that one had arrived at the infinite would be, according to Aristotle, absurd. Moore cites a lecture by Wittgenstein to make the point: "Wittgenstein in a lecture once asked his audience to imagine coming across a man who is saying, '. . . 5, 1, 4, 1, 3—finished!', and, when asked what he has been doing, replies that he has just finished reciting the complete decimal expansion of pi backwards—something he has been doing at a steady rate for all of past eternity."[148] Since pi is an irrational number that may be calculated forever without either repeating or terminating, the gentleman in this hypothetical account would have completed an infinite task. But, claimed Wittgenstein, this cannot be done, since more decimal places can always be added. In this way, Wittgenstein seemed to show that the concept of an actual infinite was absurd in a way that surely Aristotle would have embraced. In summary, then, Aristotle's conception of the infinite is primarily a mathematical one. Given that, he made the important distinction between the infinite as actual and as potential, using his analogy from traversal to argue against the possibility of the former. While these are important contributions to the development of thought about the infinite, since Pannenberg's use of the concept is primarily metaphysical, Aristotle provides little help for Pannenberg. However, all of that changes with our next figure.

Plotinus

Three distinct strands of Platonism can be identified within the broader philosophical tradition. First is the Platonism of the Old Academy, with Plato as its immediate founder. In roughly the last two hundred years before the time of Christ, there arose a revival of Platonism that came to be known as Middle Platonism. The third movement is known as Neoplatonism, and its founding is generally attributed to the influential figure Ploti-

---

148. Ibid., 44.

nus. While Plotinus's form of Platonism was informed by important strands within Aristotelianism, he reemphasized a number of Plato's themes, some of which ultimately impacted his conception of the infinite. First, as Moore notes, Plotinus resurrected the strong distinction between appearances and reality that was so prevalent in Plato's own work.[149] It was, of course, this distinction that Aristotle tended to deny and that may well have enabled him to conceive of the infinite as primarily a mathematical concept. With this distinction restored, "Plotinus was in a position to upturn much of what Aristotle had argued for and to rehabilitate the metaphysically infinite."[150] There can be no doubt but that the infinite was a metaphysical rather than mathematical concept for Plotinus.

By emphasizing the metaphysical infinite, Plotinus made a major contribution to reconceptualizing the infinite in positive rather than negative terms. In fact, Moore writes: "In this his thinking marked something of a turning point. No longer in the history of philosophy would there be, as there had been among the Greeks, a tendency to hear 'infinite' as a derogatory term. Henceforth, quite the opposite."[151] For Plotinus, the infinite in the metaphysical sense was to be understood primarily in terms of wholeness, completeness, self-sufficiency, and the like. Plotinus emphasized the unifying nature of the infinite by perhaps most frequently referring to it as "the One," though he sometimes used the Platonic term "the Good" and sometimes the term "God." Regardless, the utterly transcendent nature of the infinite did not escape Plotinus, who recognized that the ineffability of the One meant that mystical union would be the primary means of coming to knowledge of the One. While Plotinus was generally sympathetic to Aristotle's claim that the infinite was never actualized in the *sensible* world, Plotinus's affirmation of something like an *intelligible* realm opened up the possibility of affirming the actualization of the infinite there.

Plotinus made at least three important contributions to the developing thought about the infinite. First, he emphasized the importance of the metaphysical infinite over against the mathematical infinite. Second, he succeeded in recasting the infinite in a positive sense using notions such as wholeness, completeness, totality, and self-sufficiency. Third, Plotinus's affirmation of the utterly transcendent nature of the One presented an excellent opportunity to identify the One/the infinite with God, an opportunity the Christian thinkers of the day were not slow to take. In light of the position outlined by Plotinus, it should come as no surprise that Pannenberg is particularly sympathetic to his work.

---

149. Ibid., 45.
150. Ibid.
151. Ibid., 46.

Gregory of Nyssa

Working approximately a century after Plotinus, Gregory was the first major Christian thinker to make the concept of the infinite central to the overall doctrine of God. Pannenberg calls this move by Gregory an "epochal contribution" to the Christian tradition.[152] Interestingly, Gregory based his argument for the infinity of God upon the divine perfection, which was one of the relatively few things that Gregory thought could be rationally known about God.[153] The essence of Gregory's argument is that since God is himself the Good, the divine perfection requires that he be the perfect Good. However, a perfect Good would have nothing within it that stands in contradiction to its Goodness. Consequently, that Good which is itself God must be unlimited, and as Gregory wrote in *Contra Eunomius*, "the unlimited is the same as the infinite."[154] Therefore, according to Gregory, God is himself the infinite.

As one might expect, there are important similarities between the positions taken by Gregory and Plotinus. First, as with Plotinus, Gregory emphasized the infinite in its metaphysical sense and had virtually nothing to say about the mathematical sense. Second, Gregory continued Plotinus's use of positive conceptions of the infinite. In fact, the idea of perfection, which Gregory used, seems to align very well with the concepts deployed by Plotinus, such as wholeness, completeness, and self-sufficiency. Perhaps Gregory's major contribution was to make explicit the connection between the concept of infinity and the Christian doctrine of God. From what we have discovered about Gregory's position combined with what we have learned of Pannenberg's use of the concept of infinity, it is obvious that Pannenberg's proposal is dependent upon an understanding of infinity similar to that of Gregory.

Thomas Aquinas and Nicholas of Cusa

Next we will consider briefly the positions of two medieval thinkers: Thomas Aquinas and Nicholas of Cusa. Aquinas is particularly interesting for our study since he was a Christian theologian in the tradition of Gregory, but he was particularly influenced by Aristotelianism. As a Christian,

---

152. Pannenberg references the work of his student Ekkehard Mühlenberg on certain of these points. See Mühlenberg, *Die Unendlichkeit Gottes bei Gregor von Nyssa* (Göttingen: Vandenhoeck & Ruprecht, 1966), for further detail.

153. W. Pannenberg, *Systematic Theology* (vol. 1; trans. G. W. Bromiley; Grand Rapids: Eerdmans, 1991), 347.

154. Gregory of Nyssa, *Contra Eunomius* (Nicene and Post-Nicene Fathers; series 2, vol. 5; ed. P. Schaff; Albany, NY: AGES Software, 1996–1997), 107.

he had a natural tendency to conceive God as possessing what have been called the "omni-attributes," each of which expresses aspects of the divine infinity. However, because Aquinas was sympathetic to the work of Aristotle, who tended to ignore or deny the metaphysical infinite, we have to ask how Aquinas brought these disparate tendencies together. Moore summarizes Aquinas's position:

> Because of his commitment to Christianity, he parted company with Aristotle on the same fundamental issue as the Neoplatonists. He believed in a metaphysical infinitude, the metaphysical infinitude of God, Whom he held to be self-subsistent and perfect. He did not believe that God was *mathematically* infinite, since this would have meant His having parts and therefore being imperfect.[155]

Apart from his views on the metaphysical infinite, which are similar to the position of Plotinus and the Neoplatonists, Aquinas generally accepted the Aristotelian treatment of the infinite. Nothing in creation, so he said, is either metaphysically or mathematically infinite. Further, Aquinas also accepted Aristotle's distinction between the actual and potential infinite generally as outlined by Aristotle.

Almost two hundred years later, Nicholas of Cusa articulated a position on the infinite that is similar in a number of ways to that of Plotinus. As with Plotinus, the infinite as described by Nicholas was predominantly a metaphysical concept, which he often called God. Nicholas also seemed to embrace the ineffability of the infinite, which suggested that knowledge of the infinite came through mystical union. There are some ways in which Nicholas's view is suggestive of the position taken later by Hegel. First, Nicholas was not overly concerned with the apparent contradictions that relate to the infinite. He argued that the infinite is beyond our finite categories and, therefore, that contradictions are taken up within the infinite. Second, to the question of how one knows that the infinite exists, Nicholas seemed to hold that "our own finitude only made sense in terms of, and in contrast with, the infinite."[156] More specifically, all appearances of the finite are really only partial expressions of the infinite; consequently, the existence of the finite is itself proof of the existence of the infinite. This latter point seems particularly suggestive of Hegel, a point we must consider when we examine Hegel's thoughts on the infinite. The reader will likely notice the correspondence with my discussion of Pannenberg's theological method.

---

155. Moore, *Infinite*, 48.
156. Ibid., 56.

Locke and Hume

Our examination of the historical development of the concept of the infinite moves now to the fifteenth and sixteenth centuries, a time when the debates between the empiricist and rationalist/idealist strands of the philosophical tradition were at their peak. As is well known, the empiricists held that experience plays the primary role in the acquisition of knowledge, while the rationalists/idealists held that reason plays the primary role. As one might expect, the positions taken by these two strands were quite different with regard to the concept of the infinite. Let us begin by considering the positions generally taken by the empiricists.

We will consider the work of John Locke and David Hume as representative of the empiricist tradition on the proper construal of the infinite. Before we delve into their respective positions, however, one problem for empiricist accounts of the infinite relates directly to the empiricist's most basic commitment: Whatever is to be affirmed as real and accessible to human knowledge is only that which can be experienced directly. Even those who have affirmed the metaphysical infinite have not held that the infinite could be directly and exhaustively experienced; consequently, one would expect the denial of the infinite in its metaphysical sense by the empiricist tradition.

Of the two, Locke took a somewhat softer position, arguing that while we can never experience the infinite, we can imagine what it would be like to continue quantity without end. This means that we can have a *negative* concept of the infinite. By this, Locke meant that while we can never grasp the infinite, as it were, all at once, we can always add more to any finite quantity that we can imagine. This would, however, go on without end so that the infinite would never be actualized even though it could be conceived. In this, Locke is reminiscent of Aristotle. Locke went on to explain that the paradoxes of the infinite, such as those Zeno and others had presented, arise when we mistakenly treat our negative concept of the infinite as if it were positive.

With Hume we can be more brief. In essence, Hume's position was that anything that cannot be experienced cannot be real, and any discussion of it must be based upon confusion and error. Moore cleverly captures Hume's point when he suggests that he would respond to those who argued, on *a priori* grounds, that space and time must be infinite by saying, "On the contrary, space and time must be capable of being how they struck us as being in experience."[157]

---

157. Ibid., 82.

Descartes and Spinoza

We will now consider the work of Descartes and Spinoza as exemplars of rationalism's treatment of the concept of the infinite. Of course, one of the fundamental differences between the empiricists and the rationalists concerning the infinite is that while the rationalists agreed with the empiricists that experience could not access the infinite, they affirmed the ability of *reason* to make contact with the infinite. Even if reason could not exhaustively grasp the infinite, it could provide positive knowledge about it. Throughout the history of thought on the concept of infinity, one of the things that has given rise to the very concept itself is its contrast with our own finitude. Some have argued that we conceive the infinite precisely as a negation of our finitude, which implies that the finite has priority over the infinite. However, the rationalists reverse this relationship by arguing that the infinite has both epistemic and ontological priority over the finite.

We have already seen this reflected in Descartes' argument that all finite perceptions are preconditioned by an intuition of the infinite.[158] In response to claims that the infinite is a negative concept, Descartes argued that it is, in fact, the *indefinite* rather than the infinite that is a negative concept. The indefinite is that which arises from the mere negation of the finite. Consider Descartes: "I never use the word 'infinite' to mean only what has no end, something which is negative and to which I have applied the word 'indefinite,' but to mean something real, which is incomparably bigger than whatever has an end."[159] Schleiermacher expressed similar sentiments when he argued that all that is finite exists, as it were, as if it were "carved out" from the infinite. It is precisely such a claim that the infinite enjoys ontological priority over the finite that Pannenberg deploys with regard to the concept of the infinite in his doctrine of God.

I need mention Spinoza only briefly as an example of what happens when the priority of the infinite is taken to an extreme. In Spinoza's thought, it is the infinite that is. God is identified with the infinite in such a way that it is only the infinite God who truly exists. What, then, according to Spinoza, are the bodies that we experience in the physical world? They are merely determinate modes of the divine, infinite existence. Some have characterized Spinoza's position as pantheistic, while others, including Pannenberg, argue that acosmism (the claim that nothing but God exists) is a better description. In either case, this makes evident one of the problems that arises with some frequency when the concept of the infinite is applied to God: The all-encompassing nature of the infinite may tend toward pan-

---

158. See above, p. 40.
159. Descartes, cited in Moore, *Infinite*, 77.

theism or one of its related positions. Given Pannenberg's own position on the metaphysical sense of infinity, our analysis will need to consider whether Pannenberg himself successfully avoids pantheism.

Kant

Since Immanuel Kant attempted to provide a bridge between the empiricists and the rationalists, a brief stop to consider his contributions to the discussion concerning the concept of infinity is warranted. Kant's proposed solution to the debate between the empiricists and the rationalists was to argue that humans possess innate categories of understanding that make experience possible. All human experience, then, is grasped as the mind imposes these innate categories of understanding upon given raw percepts. Without the categories, there would be no way to unify the percepts into a given experience; without experiences, the mind would have nothing upon which to impose the categories of understanding. Kant captured the point in his well-known dictum: "Concepts without percepts are empty. Percepts without concepts are blind." The compromise between the empiricists and the rationalists that Kant proposed was, in essence, to say that both were right in some sense, that both innate categories and perceptual experience are necessary.

In his philosophy, Kant made perhaps the strongest distinction between appearance and reality since Plato, and it was just this distinction that opened the possibility for Kant to show the relation between the metaphysical and the mathematical infinites. On the one hand, it is the "real" world, the unknowable world that Kant called the "noumenal realm," that is metaphysically infinite. On the other hand, the everyday world of appearances, which Kant called the "phenomenal realm," is the place where the metaphysical infinite is expressed by means of the mathematical infinite. In other words, the metaphysical infinite is given piece by piece to be received by receptive reason. However, as Aristotle had pointed out, an infinite totality given in this way can never be fully experienced and, therefore, can never be actual. This led Kant to argue that, while he affirmed the metaphysical infinitude of space and time, there could be no such thing as the physical world as a whole. Why? Since everything physical is appearance and must be such that it can be given to experience, and since the totality of the physical world corresponds to the unexperienceable mathematical infinite, there can be no such thing as the physical world as a whole because it cannot be experienced as a whole. If one examines Kant's resolutions to the antimonies of reason, one will find that each is closely connected to this line of argument. So far, Kant's position, sympathetic as it is to the priority of the infinite, seems consistent with the objectives Pannenberg has in deployment of the concept of the infinite in the doctrine of God. However, as Pannenberg points out, there are irremediable tensions within Kant's position.

The position described above is the position that Kant detailed in the section of *Critique of Pure Reason* entitled "Transcendental Aesthetic." There Kant embraces the notion of infinite space as a positive concept, meaning that the whole has priority over the parts. This is the upshot of the arguments outlined above. However, in "Transcendental Analytic" Kant argues that all intuitions are dependent upon space and time and that they are, in fact, extensive magnitudes so that "the representation of the parts makes possible . . . the representation of the whole."[160] In other words, as Pannenberg says, "while according to the 'Transcendental Aesthetic' the intuition of the infinite whole of space (and also, analogously, of time) first makes possible the comprehension of the individual therein, according to the 'Transcendental Analytic' the representation of the parts *precedes* that of the whole."[161] Consequently, while Kant's analysis of the infinite is generally recognized as making a significant contribution, Pannenberg is leery of placing too much weight on Kant's arguments. It seems that Hegel provided a more thorough analysis. Because of the significance of Hegel's thought to Pannenberg's project, I will undertake a more detailed examination of Hegel's work.

Hegel

There is a sense in which Hegel plays Aristotle to Kant's Plato. Hegel/Aristotle strongly rejected the appearance/reality distinction that played such a major part in Kantian/Platonic philosophy. According to Hegel, the infinite manifests itself precisely in appearance so that, ultimately, appearance and reality are one. In a sense, then, appearance mediates the infinite to us. While Hegel agreed with Kant that reality is a self-contained, absolute whole, they differed in that, for Hegel, this self-contained, absolute whole was the world in which we live, not something separate and distinct from it. Comparing Hegel with Aristotle, Moore writes that "whereas Aristotle thought that what was required was a new conception of the infinite, as something that could be understood in spatio-temporal terms, Hegel thought that what was required was a new conception of the spatio-temporal, as something that could be understood in terms of what was now recognizable as the truly infinite."[162] Moore suggests the extent to which the infinite takes priority in

---

160. I. Kant, *Critique of Pure Reason* (trans. N. K. Smith; New York: St. Martin's Press, 1965), 198. See Pannenberg's citation in *Metaphysics and the Idea of God* (trans. P. Clayton; Grand Rapids: Eerdmans, 1990), 32.

161. Pannenberg, *Metaphysics and the Idea of God*, 32.

162. Moore, *Infinite*, 97.

Hegel's thought: One does not change the concept of the infinite to correspond to perceptions of the physical world; rather, one's understanding of those perceptions must be modified in order to be brought into line with the concept of the infinite.

Given the epistemic and ontological priority of the infinite generally affirmed by the rationalist tradition, it comes as no surprise to find a similar line of thought in Hegel. As Lauer writes, "Hegel not only intends that the concept of 'infinity' be thoroughly intelligible . . . but also sees its intelligibility as the necessary condition for the intelligibility of whatever else the human mind is to understand."[163] More specifically, Moore observes that Hegel held that "knowledge of infinite being is prior to knowledge of finite beings—the former a logical precondition, so to speak, for the latter."[164]

Hegel affirmed the priority of the infinite in very strong terms. Consider his claim from *Science of Logic*: "It is not the finite which is real, but the infinite."[165] And again, "The proposition that the finite is ideal [ideell] constitutes idealism. The idealism of philosophy consists in nothing else than in recognizing that the *finite has no veritable being*" (emphasis added).[166] For Hegel, the infinite is fundamentally affirmative being, while the finite, which is *primarily the negation* of the infinite, is fundamentally nonbeing. Hegel used such terms as "self-sufficient," "absolute," and "unconditioned" to describe the infinite, while he used the corresponding negative terms, such as "conditioned" and "limited," to describe the finite. It is true that Hegel sometimes referred to the infinite as the negation of the finite, but to grasp fully what he had in mind, one must make a couple of observations. First, Hegel spoke of the infinite in two senses: (1) the true infinite and (2) the spurious infinite (*die schlechte Unendlichkeit*). I shall have more to say about this momentarily, but for now we only need recognize that within the idea of the infinite, Hegel saw one concept as an inadequate (spurious) expression of the infinite. Second, we must remember that for Hegel the finite is already a negative concept; therefore, to say that the *true* infinite is a negation of the finite is merely to say that it is a negation of the negation. Again, the true infinite is a positive concept.

Recall from the discussion of early Greek conceptions of the infinite that the infinite was often seen as negative because it was associated with indeterminacy, indefiniteness, and formlessness. Hegel turned these ideas upside down by arguing that it is the finite that is indeterminate and there-

---

163. Q. Lauer, *Hegel's Concept of God* (Albany, NY: SUNY Press, 1982), 162.

164. Moore, *Infinite*, 168.

165. G. W. F. Hegel, *Science of Logic* (trans. A. V. Miller; Atlantic Highlands, NJ: Humanities Press International, 1995), 149.

166. Ibid., 154.

fore negative, and it is the infinite that is supremely determinate and therefore supremely positive. It is true that Hegel also spoke of the finite as determinate, but only as it is determined by another. Hence, the finite does not contain its determinations within itself and is, then, ultimately and of itself, indeterminate. On the other hand, the infinite contains all of its determinations within itself so that it is not definitively determined by any other.[167] One of its determinations is to be in opposition to the finite (in the sense noted above), but another determination of the true infinite is to overcome that opposition so as not merely to be "other" to the finite. At first blush, of course, it sounds contradictory to be opposed to the finite but also to overcome the opposition. However, it is Hegel's position that these contradictions are transcended and overcome (*aufgehoben*) in the true infinite so that a higher unity is achieved. This is reminiscent of the position of Nicholas of Cusa, who argued that finite categories fail at the level of the infinite so that contradictions are overcome. Because the infinite contains all possible determinations within itself and because the finite is devoid of determination in itself, Hegel argued for the supremacy of the infinite and for its ultimate determinateness.

An important point for grasping Pannenberg's theology is his deployment of Hegel's distinction between the true infinite and the spurious infinite. According to Hegel, if we think of the infinite merely as the other of the finite, then we make the infinite itself finite. In his analysis, Hegel points out that the finite is characterized by limitation, boundedness, and the like. However, if we think of the infinite merely as that which is opposed to the finite, then the boundary between the infinite and the finite becomes a boundary for the infinite, thus finitizing it. This, Hegel argued, cannot be the true nature of the infinite. To capture the deficiency of such a conception of the infinite, he used the adjective *schlecht*, which literally means "bad" and which is often translated in this context as "spurious" to describe any conception of the infinite that never truly rises above finitude. To overcome this, that which is truly infinite cannot merely be defined by the determination that defines it as that which is opposed to the finite. Instead, the true infinite, while it must be conceived as that which is opposed to the finite, must also be conceived as *that which overcomes that opposition*. As we shall see in more detail subsequently, it is precisely this claim concerning the nature of the true infinite that Pannenberg most uses in his theology. For example, if God is to be conceived as infinite, then the doctrine of God must allow for the unity of God to be understood as a differentiated unity so as to allow for both the divine transcendence (its difference from the finite world of creatures) and the divine immanence (its

---

167. See, for example, Hegel, *Science of Logic*, 148ff.

presence with that world). In short, if God is to be conceived as the metaphysical infinite, he must be conceived as the true infinite (opposed, yet overcoming the opposition) and never as the spurious infinite (merely opposed to the finite). Pannenberg writes that in light of Hegel's analysis, "from now on, the only understanding of God that can be called monotheistic in the strict sense will be that which is able to conceive the one God not merely as transcending the world; at the same time, this 'God beyond' must be understood as immanent in the world."[168]

Elsewhere Pannenberg observes that the philosophical requirements imposed by a proper understanding of the infinite are so pressing that whatever stands in opposition to it cannot be part of an acceptable doctrine of God. In fact, Pannenberg believes this understanding of the true infinite has important implications for the Christian doctrine of the triune God.

Since I have observed the distinction between the metaphysical and the mathematical infinite, it is appropriate to consider how Hegel characterized each. In the first place, it seems obvious that the conception of the infinite that Hegel most affirmed is the metaphysical infinite. In fact, Lauer argues that Hegel held the mathematical infinite to be the most insignificant form of the infinite. And in places, Hegel characterized the mathematical infinite as the spurious infinite, as mentioned earlier. According to Hegel, the problem with the mathematical infinite is that though it strives to become infinite, it never is able to extend itself beyond its own finitude. Specifically, Hegel recognized that any finite quantity can always be increased by one more. In the act of increase, the finite, argued Hegel, reaches out to become infinite, striving to extend beyond its finitude to become infinite quantity. However, all that is realized is a larger finite quantity. This process can continue on ad infinitum, and yet the finite never becomes the infinite. Moore captures the point nicely:

> The mathematically infinite was what Hegel described as a spurious, or bad, infinity—a mere succession of finite elements, each bounded by the next, but never complete and never properly held together in unity. It seemed at turns nightmarish, then bizarre, then simply tedious, but always a pale reflection of the truly infinite. Moreover, it was a kind of infinity that *could* be set in contradistinction to the finite.[169]

This line of reasoning is reminiscent in some ways of the distinction between the actual and the potential infinite articulated by Aristotle. However, Hegel and Aristotle, though with similar concerns, came to different conclusions:

---

168. Pannenberg, *Metaphysics and the Idea of God*, 36.
169. Moore, *Infinite*, 99.

The upshot of all of this, we now see, was one of the great ironies in the history of thought about infinity. By dint of similar metaphysical recoil, Aristotle and Hegel arrived at positions that were the exact mirror-image of each other. Aristotle had explicitly repudiated a metaphysical conception of the infinite in favor of a mathematical one. Hegel explicitly repudiated a mathematical conception of the infinite in favor of a metaphysical one. They represent polar opposites in this dialectical history.[170]

While there is more to consider in Pannenberg's deployment of these concepts, this discussion has placed Hegel within the historical development of the concept of the infinite and outlined the primary points Pannenberg appropriates from Hegel's work.

Georg Cantor

While Pannenberg does not depend upon Cantor in any overt way, it is important to consider Cantor's work to see if it raises serious objections to the insights, primarily Cartesian and Hegelian, that Pannenberg adopts. First, as Moore points out, though Bertrand Russell was generally sympathetic to Cantor's work, he "petulantly dismissed the idea that the mathematically infinite was a 'false' infinite, a vain attempt to reach 'true' infinity."[171] As we have seen, the essence of Hegel's argument was that the mathematical infinite could only be potential, never actual. It was Cantor's work in set theory that provided resources to argue against Hegel's conclusion. Consider, for example, the set of all positive integers, those whole numbers greater than zero. Cantor's point is simply this: Even if we cannot name every member of this set (which would be designated {1, 2, 3, . . .}), we certainly know what it would take to be a member of the set, and we can certainly say what would disqualify a given number from being a member of the set. Further, this is a set that clearly has an infinite number of members and is, therefore, *an actually infinite set.* In fact, there are many such sets: the set of all real numbers, the set of all rational numbers, the set of all even numbers, and so on. In this way, Cantor believed he had shown the error in thinking of the mathematical infinite as the spurious infinite along the lines of Hegel.

In what has come to be known as transfinite mathematics, Cantor showed not only that there exist sets that are actually infinite but also that various infinities, contrary to intuitions, differ in size. In fact, he was able, in some sense, to scale the relationships between various infinite sets, thereby

---

170. Ibid.
171. Ibid., 117.

showing that these infinities had far more determinancy than heretofore had been thought. Does this apparent rehabilitation of the concept of the mathematical infinite call into question any of the Hegelian insights that Pannenberg appropriates? There are several reasons to hold that the answer is no.

In the first place, certain apparent paradoxes of transfinite mathematics led Cantor to argue that there were infinities so large that not even their relative sizes could be determined. In some places, Cantor himself referred to these infinities as "absolute infinities." In language strangely reminiscent of Hegel, Cantor wrote that "the Absolute can only be acknowledged, never known, not even approximately."[172] Consequently, while Cantor may have shown that Hegel's characterization of the mathematical infinite was nowhere near adequately nuanced, there is justification for the distinction between the infinite and the absolutely infinite, which seems closely related to Hegel's distinction between the "spurious" and the "true" infinite. Second, it is important to note that Cantor was a very devout man, who spent the later part of his life in religious studies and theology. According to Moore, he believed that

> he had a God-given gift to effect a mathematical study of the infinite and thereby, in a way, to vindicate certain cherished views about the divine against the charge of incoherence. . . . And this Absolute that had revealed itself in his own formal work, in a way that was so reminiscent of more traditional views of the infinite, was embraced by Cantor as a vital part of his conception of God.[173]

It is of some significance that Cantor himself believed that there were theological implications to his work on the infinite, and it seems we can conclude that Cantor's work does not obviate the points that Pannenberg appropriates from the history of thought on the infinite.

Pannenberg's Deployment of the Concept of the Infinite

I have already broached the subject of Pannenberg's deployment of the concept of the infinite, and I will cover the implications of the concept for specific aspects of Pannenberg's doctrine of God in subsequent chapters. Now, however, given the divergence of thought we have seen so far, we need to assess the persuasiveness of Pannenberg's appropriation and deployment of a specific concept of the infinite. My first step will be to summarize those points already identified as important to Pannenberg's work. Then I will

---

172. Cantor, cited in ibid., 128.
173. Ibid.

expand my examination, especially of Hegel's work, in certain areas not yet considered.

At the outset, I noted that there are two of what W. T. Jones called a "fundamental parting of the ways" in the history of thought concerning the infinite: (1) the question of whether the infinite should be taken primarily in a mathematical or a metaphysical sense, and (2) the question of whether the infinite is potential or actual. It has become evident in the course of our examination that those who are a part of what can be roughly characterized as the empiricist/analytic tradition tend to take the former option in each case. More specifically, these philosophers and theologians tend to see the infinite as (1) essentially a mathematical concept and (2) nowhere actualized and, therefore, better understood as potential. Those in what can be roughly characterized as the rationalist/idealist tradition, however, tend to take the latter option. More specifically, the rationalist/idealist tradition tends to see the infinite as (1) primarily a metaphysical concept and (2) actualized in some way. Given Pannenberg's positioning within the rationalist/idealist tradition, it is no surprise that he finds the metaphysical notions of the infinite to be of far more importance than mathematical notions. In fact, he seems sympathetic to Hegel's judgment that mathematical conceptions of the infinite are of least significance. Further, since he argues that God is the reality who corresponds to the "true infinite," it is clear that he sees the infinite as actualized. Consequently, Pannenberg understands the important notion of the infinite to be metaphysical in nature, and he intends to show how the Trinitarian God of the Christian tradition is the reality who corresponds to the metaphysical (or "true") infinite. This is the first point of significance in Pannenberg's appropriation of the concept of the infinite.

The second is the manner in which Pannenberg understands the infinite to be structured (specifically, as both to stand opposed to the finite and to overcome that opposition). Pannenberg accepts Hegel's distinction between the "true" and the "spurious" infinite, with Pannenberg's attention focused upon the nature of the true infinite. In many places throughout Pannenberg's three-volume *Systematic Theology*, he utilizes the structural implications that follow from the true infinite to make a variety of points about the divine nature. Pannenberg believes that conceiving the divine nature in accord with the structure of the true infinite—which is both other than the finite and yet, in some sense, to be identified with the finite—encourages us to maintain a proper balance between the divine transcendence and the divine immanence. Both Hegel and Pannenberg refer to conceptions that fail to maintain this balance as "one-sided" and therefore inadequate.

Third, Pannenberg concurs with the assessments of both Descartes and Schleiermacher concerning the priority of the infinite over the finite. Further, it is clear that Pannenberg affirms both the epistemic and the ontological priority of the infinite. As to epistemic priority, Pannenberg writes that Descartes "regarded the infinite as such, and not being, as the first intuition of the intellect *on which all knowledge of other things depends.*"[174] In various places throughout Pannenberg's writings, he describes this "first intuition" as "pre-thematic," "non-thematic," "confused," and as a "preconception." By using these terms, Pannenberg does not mean to downplay the significance of the epistemic priority of the infinite, which he clearly sees as the precondition for all perceptions/knowledge of finite things. Instead, he is merely highlighting the fact that, for most, the epistemic priority of the infinite never becomes an item of explicit reflection. Consequently, many never recognize the epistemic priority of the infinite. However, when one comes to explicit reflection, Pannenberg believes that the argument from Descartes' third meditation establishes the point.

As for ontological priority, one might cite Descartes' argument that the idea of infinity, which we all have, must have a source that is ontologically adequate.[175] In essence, Descartes argues that there must be as much ontological reality in the source of an idea as in the idea itself. Consequently, an idea of the infinite must have the infinite as its source. One might also cite Schleiermacher's claim that "all that is finite exists only through the determination of its limits, which must, as it were, be 'cut out' from the Infinite."[176] One might also appropriate the arguments underlying Hegel's claims that it is the infinite that is real or that the finite has no veritable being. In each case, the point is to establish the ontological priority of the infinite over all finite realities.

There are two additional steps in Hegel's articulation of the nature of the true infinite that Pannenberg is willing to take. First, regarding Descartes' connection of the infinite with the concept of God, we have seen that Pannenberg criticizes Descartes for making that connection in too facile a fashion.[177] There Pannenberg argues that the idea of God is far too conceptually rich to be expressed adequately by the philosophical concept of the infinite. He believes that Hegel's treatment of the infinite in his *Science of Logic* "suggests that Hegel judged the category of the Infinite to have a rather limited assertorical force."[178] This would indicate that Hegel

---

174. W. Pannenberg, *Systematic Theology* (vol. 1; trans. G. W. Bromiley; Grand Rapids: Eerdmans, 1991), 350 (emphasis added).

175. R. Descartes, *Meditations on First Philosophy* (3rd ed.; trans. D. A. Cress; Indianapolis: Hackett, 1993), 78.

176. F. D. E. Schleiermacher, *On Religion: Speeches to Its Cultured Despisers* (trans. R. Crouter; Cambridge: Cambridge University Press, 1988), 103; quoted in Pannenberg, *Metaphysics and the Idea of God*, 25.

177. See above, p. 41.

178. Pannenberg, *Metaphysics and the Idea of God*, 36.

likely would have agreed with Pannenberg's criticism of Descartes and, hence, would have realized the need for additional argument.

Second, in assessment of the work of Gregory of Nyssa and Duns Scotus, Pannenberg argues that "the Infinite is one because it has no other outside itself; and since it also cannot be conceived as divided, the Infinite is identical with the One."[179] Here we are reminded of Plotinus's identification of the infinite with the One. Hegel, in light of his identification of the infinite with the metaphysical rather than the mathematical infinite, prepared the way for the further identification of the infinite with the Absolute, "which does not need any other for its Being. All-sufficiency . . . is therefore shown to be the true content of the concept of the Infinite."[180] This analysis suggests many of the positive predicates of the infinite that we noted earlier, such as wholeness, completeness, and self-sufficiency. These predicates are, of course, consonant with identification of the metaphysical infinite with the concept of God. The extent to which Pannenberg believes the notion of the infinite bears upon the doctrine of God is clear when he writes that "whatever stands in contradiction to the notion of the infinity of God cannot be a component of a rationally demonstrable notion of the one God."[181] We may conclude, then, that Pannenberg sees the concept of infinity as playing something of a regulative role in the doctrine of God.

God as the Metaphysical Infinite

At the beginning of this chapter, I identified the primary question as whether the concept of infinity could reasonably be applied to God. At this point, we turn our attention to two distinct sets of arguments aimed at answering this question—one set from the philosophical/theological tradition and one from the scriptural tradition. Of course, the Scriptures were not written in such a way as to overtly deploy metaphysical categories. Consequently, our task will be primarily to examine certain scriptural evidence to determine if it is consistent with conceiving God as the infinite. As usual, I will present the various arguments first and subsequently engage in their critical assessment.

Philosophical/Theological Arguments

Pannenberg considered Gregory of Nyssa's use of the concept of the infinite as central to the doctrine of God an "epochal contribution." Let us begin, then, by considering Gregory's primary argument for the infinity of God. In

---

179. Ibid., 34.
180. Ibid., 35.
181. Ibid., 34.

The Life of Moses, Gregory considers Moses' own growth from infancy to death as a metaphor for the ascent of the soul to God. There is a sense, then, in which this work of Gregory is an examination of the life of increasing virtue. In the prologue, Gregory addresses the question of a stopping point in the life of virtue. His answer is straightforward: "In the case of virtue we have learned from the Apostle that its one limit of perfection is that it has not limit."[182] Why does Gregory argue that the limit of the perfection of virtue is that it has no limit? Because Gregory argues that "no Good has a limit in its own nature but is limited by the presence of its opposite," for example, "as life is limited by death and light by darkness."[183] Consequently, since virtue is a good, it could be limited only by the presence of its opposite. However, perfect goodness would be only goodness and would, therefore, have no opposite. With no opposite, nothing would limit such goodness; consequently, according to Gregory, it would be unlimited.

Gregory then takes the next step: "The Divine One is himself the Good (in the primary and proper sense of the word)."[184] Further, if God is himself the Good, then the divine perfection would require that he be the perfect Good. However, as we have just seen, the Good can be limited only by the presence of its opposite, and, of course, owing to the divine perfection, there can be no opposite to the Good in the divine nature. Consequently, the Good that is itself God must be unlimited, and, as Gregory writes in *Contra Eunomius*, "the unlimited is the same as the infinite."[185] At the end of Gregory's line of argument is the conclusion that God is the infinite. Further, given the nature of the arguments that Gregory employs, it is clear that he intends to equate God with the metaphysical infinite. Thus, Gregory provides us one reason to believe it is appropriate to identify God with the infinite.

In addition, if one considers the sorts of positive predicates that must be affirmed of God, there will be an interesting correlation between those predicates and the predicates attributed to the divine, for example, by Plotinus. Since God is the source of all that exists yet has no source outside himself for his own being, God is the Unconditioned One. Another way of capturing this is to speak of God as the Self-Sufficient One, which is a predicate we have already seen applied to the infinite. Again utilizing the notion of God as the source of all there is, we could speak of God as the One who unifies all else that exists. Since God has no lack in himself, he is the One who is whole, and again we have seen predicates such as wholeness applied

---

182. Gregory of Nyssa, *The Life of Moses* (trans. A. J. Malherbe and E. Fergusen; New York: Paulist Press, 1978), 30.

183. Ibid.

184. Ibid., 31.

185. Gregory of Nyssa, *Contra Eunomius*, 107.

to the metaphysical infinite. We could expand the list, but we would find only more of what we have already seen: Those terms that are generally predicated of God are very much the same as those that various thinkers have applied to the metaphysical infinite.

Finally, while it is certainly not a formal argument for the application of the concept of the infinite to the doctrine of God, the bulk of the Christian tradition has affirmed that the omni-attributes are, in fact, expressions of the divine infinity.[186] I observed earlier Origen's denial of the infinity of God in certain senses; nevertheless, he is one in a remarkably small minority. At the same time, however, among those who propose that God is to be conceived as the infinite, those who propose to make the concept of infinity *primary* are a small minority. So even if we accept the tradition's majority position of applying the concept of infinity to God, we are still left with an important pair of questions: (1) Should the concept be made primary as Pannenberg proposes? (2) Is the concept to be understood in the way Pannenberg takes it? Before addressing these additional issues that have arisen in the course of our inquiry, let us turn our attention now to the Scriptures to see what grounds we might find for conceiving God as the infinite.

Scriptural Bases for God as the Infinite

Pannenberg readily admits that "infinity is not a biblical term for God."[187] However, in a particularly important passage concerning his view of the relation between the concept of infinity and the doctrine of God, he writes:

> [The concept of Infinity] is implied, however, in many biblical descriptions
> of God, and especially clearly in the attributes of eternity, omnipotence, and
> omnipresence that are ascribed to him. The confession of God's holiness is
> also closely related to the thought of his infinity, so closely, indeed, that the
> thought of infinity as *God's* infinity needs the statement of his holiness for
> its elucidation, while eternity, omnipotence, and omnipresence may be
> viewed as concrete manifestations of his infinity from the standpoints of
> time, power, and space.[188]

I shall say more about certain of these issues in chapter 7, which deals with the divine attributes. However, as Pannenberg suggests, our consideration

---

186. The omni-attributes are those attributes of God that correspond to relationship between the divine infinity and certain aspects of the cosmos. For example, the infinity of God's presence is the divine omnipresence, and God's infinity as related to time is the divine eternity.

187. Pannenberg, *Systematic Theology*, 1:397.

188. Ibid.

of whether the Scriptures justify incorporating the concept of infinity within the Christian doctrine of God will proceed by examining the manner in which the Scriptures speak of the divine relation to other concepts and whether that relation involves the concept of infinity.

Time

There are frequent references within the Scriptures to the fact that God is without beginning or end. For example, Deut 33:27 refers to God as "the eternal God"[189]; in Exod 15:18 the writer affirms that "the LORD will reign for ever and ever"; in Ps 90:2 the psalmist writes: "Before the mountains were brought forth, or ever thou hadst formed the earth and the world, from everlasting to everlasting thou art God." Finally, in Rev 10:6, God is referred to as "him who lives for ever and ever." Such passages seem to support the claim that God is infinite temporally. However, intuitions are deeply divided on this issue. Can we speak of God's eternity as infinite in the sense Pannenberg intends, with all of the trappings indicated previously? Or ought eternity to be considered as never ending, somewhat in the sense of Aristotle's potential infinite? While these passages seem clearly to indicate a relationship between God and time that is suggestive of infinity, it is not clear *what* sense of the infinite is intended. In fact, in speaking of the Old Testament passages regarding the divine eternity, Pannenberg comments that "Hebrew has no other term for eternity than unlimited duration, whether past or future."[190] So does Scripture warrant a connection between the concept of infinity and God as regards the divine experience of time? Yes, but the question as to the sense of infinity suggested will have to await the more detailed analysis of the next chapter.

Space

In my assessment of the manner in which the Scriptures speak of God's relation to space, my findings are similar. Consider Jer 23:24, which affirms that the Lord's presence fills the heavens and the earth, or Ps 139, which indicates that no matter where one might go, even if one goes down to Sheol, one never escapes the presence of God. Also, 1 Kgs 8:27 indicates that not even the totality of "heaven and the highest heaven" can contain the divine presence. So again we find passages that suggest that the divine presence is "everywhere," transcending his creatures whose spatial pres-

---

189. All references to Scripture are from the Revised Standard Version.
190. Pannenberg, *Systematic Theology*, 1:401.

ence is of a much more limited kind. It is not yet clear whether these notions can reasonably be connected with the concept of the true infinite, which Pannenberg takes as definitive for the divine infinity; again, it seems that adequate warrant exists for conceiving God's relation to space as characterized by the concept of infinity.

Power

This brings us to the question of God's power. Consider Job 42:2: "I know that thou canst do all things, and that no purpose of thine can be thwarted." In Rom 1:20, Paul affirms that the "eternal power" of God is made manifest in his creative works. And Jeremiah affirms that nothing is too hard for God (32:17). Further, through the biblical conception of God's sovereignty, it is clear that God is seen as having complete authority over his creation. Interestingly, upon close examination of these notions, there seems to be reason to think of the divine omnipotence as structured in accord with the true infinite as laid out in this chapter. First, the passages cited above suggest, at least, that God's power is unlimited, and the divine sovereignty suggests that even the power the creatures have is not beyond God's authority. Further, the very concept of creature (having been created, particularly in the Christian sense of having been created from nothing) suggests that even the power that the creatures have is not ultimately their own. So may one argue that the divine omnipotence reflects the true infinite in that God has power *over* all creatures while at the same time God's power appears as the gift of limited power *to* creatures? While one might justifiably argue that such biblical assertions are not intended to carry such metaphysical weight, it is not unreasonable to argue that they are suggestive of such a conception of the divine essence and, therefore, provide *prima facie* justification for such a connection.

Critical Assessment

In the course of the critical assessment that follows, we must keep two considerations in mind. On the one hand, I will assess various elements of the proposals for their plausibility: Does the conclusion of the examined argument coherently give support to the proposal? Plausibility is not a decisive standard, as there is generally more than one plausible conclusion that can be drawn from a set of data. On the other hand, I will attempt to evaluate the overall persuasiveness of a given argument. The objective of any argument, of course, is to persuade individuals to accept certain conclusions; the more persuasive an argument is, the more likely are individuals to accept its conclusions.

Gregory's Arguments for the Divine Infinity

While the argument from Gregory for conceiving God as the infinite is historically interesting, it is not clear that, as presented, it accomplishes what he intends. In the first place, one might reasonably argue that the Good, which is reminiscent of Plato's form of the Good, is merely an abstraction. Or rather than denying that the Good is actual, one might simply take a more skeptical route by asking what exactly is meant by "the Good" and asking what reasons we have for thinking that it exists as anything more than a conceptual construct. An idealist response might proceed along the lines that ideas have the highest degree of reality. However, of course, this idealist thesis is highly debatable and would be generally unpersuasive to, say, analytic philosophers. Consequently, it seems that even the plausibility of Gregory's argument is highly dependent upon the fundamental metaphysical commitments an individual brings to the argument. Therefore, it is hard to see Gregory's argument as making much headway in justifying connection of the doctrine of God with the concept of the infinite to those not inclined to intuit such a connection.

Recall that Pannenberg states that Gregory's argument proceeds from the idea of the divine perfection, thereby implying that the divine perfection leads one to conclude that God is the infinite. Is this, however, necessarily the case? More specifically, does perfection imply infinity? If so, precisely what is the nature of the implication? Further, in various contexts, what does it mean to affirm perfection of something? Consider a manufactured steel ball. Further imagine that technology was adequate to produce it such that its surface was perfectly smooth. Does this mean that such a "perfect" ball would be "infinite," or would you ever call it "perfect" in any generalized sense? The response would no doubt be that this example misses the point. In the case of the divine perfection, we are talking about such attributes as perfect in goodness, perfect in wisdom, perfect in being. But the question remains: What precisely does this mean? Does perfect in wisdom, for example, mean infinite in wisdom, or merely wisdom without error? While I am sympathetic to the connection that Pannenberg intends to make here, it is hard to see how such an argument would be very persuasive unless one were antecedently inclined to understand the divine nature in this way.

Philosophical Considerations

The more persuasive argument seems to come from consideration of the predicates one might apply to God and that seem very closely connected to the idea of the infinite. Let us consider what it means for two objects to have the same or similar predicates. First, we must distinguish between essence predicates, those that an object must have in order to be that type of object, and nonessence predicates, those that may describe a particular instantiation of a certain type of object but are not necessary to that type of object's essence. For example, an essence predicate of a ball is "round." While a given ball may be red, balls are not necessarily red; thus "red" would be a nonessence predicate. Now consider some pair of objects x and y that have some set of essence predicates, $P_E(x)$ and $P_E(y)$, and some nonessence set of predicates, $P_{NE}(x)$ and $P_{NE}(y)$. If x and y have the same set of essence predicates, then they are the same *type* of object. If, however, they have the same set of essence and nonessence predicates, then the two objects are identical. Intuitions on these matters are fairly straightforward. Since Pannenberg argues that the idea of God is far more conceptually rich than that of the idea of the infinite, it is clear that he does not see the infinite as identical with God.

So the question becomes whether the idea of God implies the essence predicates of the concept of the infinite so that God may be conceived as the metaphysical infinite. (Remember that the reverse need not be true since I am not arguing for identity.) Recall the sorts of predicates applied to the metaphysical infinite: self-sufficiency, unconditionedness, wholeness, completeness, and unity or oneness. These are precisely the sorts of predicates that have been either directly or indirectly predicated of God within Christian history. While the Christian tradition has not generally affirmed the emanationist understanding of the creation of the world as Plotinus held, it has nevertheless affirmed the oneness of God (even if Christian monotheism has an internal Trinitarian structure) and that everything that exists apart from God has God as its source. Hence, one can conceive of God as "the One" without implying the position of Plotinus. Further, the other predicates listed above are related to perfections of one sort or another, and, of course, the tradition has consistently affirmed that God has all perfections to the maximal degree. Therefore, given what we have considered so far, it seems reasonable to affirm that the essence predicates of the infinite are realized in God.

There are additional essence predicates that Pannenberg argues belong to the concept of the infinite. These are the predicates that arise from our consideration of the infinite as the "true" infinite—those related to the fact that the true infinite can be conceived not merely as opposed to the finite, but also as overcoming that opposition. In the Christian doctrine of God, these predicates encourage the proper balancing of the notions of God's transcendence and his immanence. Within the Christian tradition, there have been those who have emphasized one side or the other of this pair. Nevertheless, the tradition as a whole has generally recognized that one must not lose sight of either. Hence, Pannenberg's assertion that the predicates of the true infinite must also be applied to God seems correct, thereby making plausible the utilization of the concept of the infinite within the Christian doctrine of God.

Scriptural Considerations

Finally, as for the arguments from Scripture, it is reasonably clear that, at a minimum, something like the concept of infinity is suggested by a number of passages. Of course, the question of the precise concept of the infinite is not entirely resolved by appealing to Scripture. For example, it will require further examination to determine whether the divine eternity should be taken as unlimited duration, which seems to correspond to the mathematical infinite, or in some other sense. My brief examination of the divine omnipotence suggested that the structure of the true infinite could be applied to at least some of the omni-attributes. Applying the concept of the infinite to God is indeed plausible. Finally, such a conclusion is further warranted by the fact that so many within the Christian tradition have affirmed that God is the infinite One.

Epistemic Considerations

In our consideration of whether the concept of the infinite can be plausibly incorporated into the Christian doctrine of God, we have essentially taken it for granted that the concept of the infinite that Pannenberg uses is a coherent idea. Ultimately, however, this ought not be taken for granted, and so we must turn to this and related questions. We begin with the claim that the infinite has epistemic priority over all finite perception, as when Pannenberg claims that the infinite is the precondition of the possibility of all finite perceptions. But what exactly does that mean? The force of the claim is that awareness of any finite object requires a prior conception of the infinite. In chapter 2, we examined arguments to the effect that any finite object is recognized only as it is delimited from the others around it. In other words, to become cognizant of some finite object requires recognizing the boundaries of that object, and those boundaries become evident only as they are contrasted with something else. Broadly speaking, there are only two possibilities for these others: (1) another finite object or (2) the other of the finite as such, namely, the infinite. Hence, at least by implication, every finite perception carries with it a prior conception of the infinite.

However, one might question whether an awareness of the infinite (even if vague and nonreflective) is really a precondition of every finite perception. For example, must I have an awareness of the infinite to recognize the boundaries around the computer at which I type? It seems I need only be aware of the other finite objects that serve as the background against which the boundaries of the computer may be distinguished. We have already seen that the other that serves as the background for distinguishing an object may be another finite object. So it seems there are finite perceptions that are not preconditioned by an awareness of the infinite, at least not directly. However, Pannenberg does not indicate that all finite perceptions must be *directly preconditioned* by the infinite. For example, he writes that this awareness is often "by connotation, certainly not always explicit."[191] The frequently implicit nature of this awareness of the infinite is evident when Pannenberg writes that finite perceptions *suggest* the infinite, so that "both [the Infinite and the finite] are suggested by the border that is contained within the very notion of the finite: the finite in its specificity suggests the other finite from which it is distinguished; and the finite as finite per se, in its generality, suggests the Infinite."[192]

Hegel has argued, rightly it seems, that one cannot think of any bounded or finite object without already thinking what lies on the far side of the boundary. However, one can always think of a larger bounded object and so on and so on. If one follows this line of thought, would one not be justified in arguing that the concept of the infinite that arises is really the potential infinite of Aristotle? Hegel and Pannenberg would argue that, conceptually, the ultimate other implied by finitude would be characterized by totality, wholeness, and so forth—in other words, the metaphysical infinite. At the end of the day, it seems at least plausible to claim that the metaphysical infinite precedes all finite perceptions.[193]

Ontological Considerations

We can consider the ontological priority of the infinite briefly. To argue for the ontological priority of the infinite, one must engage the question of whether the metaphysical infinite actually exists. If it does not, how could it have ontological priority over the finite? And, of course, if it does exist, how could it not? The divide in intuitions on the question likely will fall along the empiricist/idealist lines I have previously pointed out. However, once again, to the extent that conceiving God as the metaphysical infinite is plausible, the position Pannenberg lays out to defend the ontological priority of the infinite would be plausible.

---

191. Pannenberg, *Metaphysics and the Idea of God*, 25.
192. Ibid.
193. In conversation with Pannenberg, he was adamant on this point. The attempt to conceive ever-larger finite objects is representative of the mathematical infinite, which is the spurious infinite in his view and, therefore, not adequate. The metaphysical infinite must be the ground from which spring all finite perceptions.

The Metaphysical Sense of the Infinite

To what extent ought we to go with Pannenberg and others in the tradition who emphasize infinity in its metaphysical sense over against the mathematical sense? Reflection upon some of the essential characteristics of the concept of infinity leads us quickly to see why these philosophers and theologians judge mathematical infinities to be spurious. First of all, we must note that limit "is precisely what characterizes things that are finite."[194] So if the essence of infinity is primarily to be understood as the other of the finite, then infinity must be characterized as unlimited or unbounded. Yet many mathematical infinities are bounded. Consider, for example, that there are an infinite number of points between any two points on the number line. Here we have a set (all the points between two given points) that has an infinite number of set members, yet should one really say that this is an *infinite* set? Of course, an infinite set in mathematics is generally defined as one that has an infinite number of members. But does this definition do justice to logical analysis of the concept of infinity?

Hegel's solution was to recognize the importance of the notions of both boundedness and unboundedness, affirming both of the true infinite, that is, the metaphysical infinite. So, as Pannenberg writes:

> Any infinity that we conceive as only abstractly transcendent, as standing in opposition to the finite, is itself finite. In order to truly be conceived as infinite, the Infinite must not only be set in opposition to the finite but must at the same time overcome this opposition. It must be conceived both as *transcendent* in relation to the finite, and as *immanent* to it.[195]

Hence, mathematical infinities, such as the set of all points between two given points, are infinite in that no matter how many points are located, one more may yet be identified. However, this bounded infinity can never be truly infinite in the sense of the all-encompassing totality that both includes and transcends all boundaries. Only such an all-encompassing conception of the infinite could satisfy the logical requirements of the very idea of infinity. In fact, it is just such a "true infinite" (to use Hegel's and Pannenberg's phrase) that would be the logical ground, not only of all finite reality, but of these bounded infinities as well. One can see that only the infinite in its metaphysical sense could ever be adequate to the term "infinite." Consequently, I believe Pannenberg is correct in arguing that should any existing being correspond to the metaphysical infinite, then it

---

194. Pannenberg, *Metaphysics and the Idea of God*, 36.
195. Ibid.

should be expected to exhibit the characteristics of the "true infinity" in all their robustness.[196]

The Infinite as Fundamental for the Christian Doctrine of God

The last question concerns whether Pannenberg is justified in asserting the primacy of the infinite in the Christian doctrine of God. The response to the question of why Pannenberg proposes this move can be reasonably brief. In addition to the implications of the conceptual analysis in the preceding, Pannenberg believes the concept of infinity to be far more conceptually rich than the idea of God as the first cause of the universe, which the tradition generally seems to embrace as the primary category in the doctrine of God. We can get at his point by considering the implications of what follows from each concept. If God is to be conceived primarily as First Cause, what seems to follow is that he is Creator of the universe. It follows, for example, that he is very wise and powerful. It does not follow, however, that he is omniscient or omnipotent. If God is conceived primarily as corresponding to the metaphysical infinite, what seems to follow, first, are all of the omni-attributes, such as omniscience, omnipotence, and eternity. Next, given the fundamental description of the metaphysical infinite, God would be conceived as self-sufficient, complete, and without lack of any kind. Finally, given the description of the true infinite, God would be conceived as both transcendent and immanent. Consequently, if the connection between the metaphysical infinite and the doctrine of God is ultimately justified, one can see why Pannenberg believes it should be elevated to primacy. Of course, by elevating it to primacy, he does not intend to exclude other concepts; for example, the notion of infinity does not imply personality, but as we shall see, Pannenberg believes that God must be conceived as having personality.

Conclusions

At this point, we are ready to pull together the threads of the various arguments of this chapter in order to draw some final conclusions concerning Pannenberg's proposal. In the first place, while we have found some of the arguments examined more widely accepted than others, we have generally found that Pannenberg's construal of the metaphysical infinite and his attempts to incorporate it in the Christian doctrine of God are quite plausi-

---

196. It is worth noting that Pannenberg readily admits that "none of these concepts yet entails the idea of an *existing being* [*Wesen*] that possesses infinity, absolute perfection, and necessary existence" (Pannenberg, *Metaphysics and the Idea of God*, 37).

ble and persuasive. Will the arguments outlined herein persuade all to accept Pannenberg's construal of the infinite and its deployment within the doctrine of God? I rather doubt it, but such a standard would surely be too high, would it not? At the very core of Pannenberg's understanding of the relationship between the concept of infinity and the concept of God is a strict analysis of the concepts themselves. Quite apart from, yet suggested by the question of whether either objectively exists in the world, what exactly is implied by the concepts themselves?

Upon such analysis of the concept of infinity, Pannenberg concludes that mathematical senses of the infinite do not adequately express the unbounded and limitless character of the true infinite. The infinite in its metaphysical sense does; hence, this must be infinity in its truest form. What is implied by the concept of God? A good many things, but metaphysically the concept of God implies the underlying ground that is the source and unity of all else that exists. The concept of God is the expansive, all-encompassing totality upon which all finite being is contingent. From this perspective, Pannenberg observes, the concepts of God and of the infinite in its metaphysical sense are mutually implicative. The question of the existence of God is not settled with this conceptual analysis, but this analysis persuasively connects the two concepts such that if God exists, God would exemplify the characteristics noted of what we have called "the true infinite."

With our initial examination of the concept of the infinite and assessment of Pannenberg's methodology behind, I now turn my attention to the specific details of Pannenberg's doctrine of God. In the next chapter, I consider a number of provocative proposals that are captured by the phrase so frequently deployed by Pannenberg: God is the power of the future that determines everything that exists. Given the central place that Pannenberg assigns to the concept of the infinite as articulated in this chapter, we should expect to find it deployed in some fashion in each of the following chapters. This will, in fact, be the case and will provide us the opportunity to assess the viability and utility of the concept in more detail before we draw our final conclusions.

CHAPTER 4

God, the Future, and Human Freedom

As we extend our examination into the details of Pannenberg's doctrine of God, we will have the opportunity to explore a number of innovative proposals that are part of his attempt to move the theological enterprise in the direction of a "rather radical revision"[197] to the classical doctrine[198] of God. In this chapter, I examine one of the proposals that has consistently engendered a great deal of critical response, specifically, his emphasis upon the futurity of God. Pannenberg expresses this in a variety of ways. For example, in several places he refers to God as the power of the future (*die Macht der Zukunft*). In others, he expands the notion somewhat to call God the power of the future that determines everything that exists.[199] Pannenberg's close connection between the idea of God and the future has a significant role to play in the manner in which his overall theological enterprise is understood. Some have gone so far as to argue that futurity is the fundamental category of his work, while others have used his orientation toward the future as the basis for grouping his work as part of the "theology of hope" movement.[200] However one characterizes Pannen-

197. W. Pannenberg, *An Introduction to Systematic Theology* (Grand Rapids: Eerdmans, 1991), 23.

198. Again, I use this phrase for convenience, not because there is such a thing as *the* classical doctrine of God.

199. For a detailed discussion of these connections, see W. Pannenberg, "The God of Hope," in *Basic Questions in Theology* (vol. 2; trans. G. H. Kehm; Philadelphia: Westminster, 1971), 234–49.

200. See, for example, S. J. Grenz and R. E. Olson, *20th Century Theology* (Downers Grove, IL: InterVarsity Press, 1992), 170 n. 99.

berg's work, there can be no doubt that the idea of the future plays a vital role in its articulation.

The pregnant phrase "God is the power of the future that determines everything that exists" raises at least three important constellations of issues. First, to speak of the future raises the question of God's relation to time. Hence, the doctrine of the divine eternity must be addressed in this chapter. While the doctrine of eternity may also be properly addressed within a treatment of the divine attributes, its importance to this set of issues requires our treating the subject here rather than in a subsequent chapter. Second, conceiving God as the power of the future has led Pannenberg to assign *ontological priority* to the future. Once again, this is a provocative proposal that has engendered much controversy; we will have to examine it to determine first its meaning and then comment upon the appropriateness of deploying it within the Christian doctrine of God. Third, Pannenberg believes that his proposal for conceiving God as the power of the future opens up resources for dealing with the issue of human freedom. However, some have questioned whether speaking of God as "a power that determines" everything that exists does not directly or indirectly imply a deterministic theology. Pannenberg rejects this charge; hence, we will have to consider the extent to which conceiving God in this way either alleviates or exacerbates the problem of human freedom.

The Eternity of God

In the Christian tradition, contrary to what seems to be common opinion,[201] there have been three ways of conceiving the divine eternity. First, there is the strand of the tradition that holds that God transcends temporality by virtue of his infinite duration. Those who hold such a position might cite such biblical passages as Ps 90:2:

> Before the mountains were brought forth,
> or ever thou hadst formed the earth and the world,
> from everlasting to everlasting thou art God.

According to this position, God takes up a temporal position just as we creatures do; in other words, the divine essence exists at a particular point in time along with the rest of the created world. "Now" for God is the same as

---

201. Consider, for example, A. Padgett, *God, Eternity, and the Nature of Time* (New York: St. Martin's Press, 1992). In this work, Padgett has a tendency to collapse the views of Augustine and Plotinus, a rather common error. Consider D. Braine's similar observations: "Here we are lighting upon the first of Padgett's key philosophical oversights, the fact that there are not just two views of the status time . . ." (D. Braine, "God, Time, and Eternity: An Essay in Review of Alan G. Padgett, *God, Eternity, and the Nature of Time,*" *Evangelical Quarterly* 66, no. 4 (1994): 340.

"now" for us. Let us say that those who hold this view conceive God as "everlasting," and hence, the divine eternity is understood as everlastingness.

The other two positions might cite John 8:58 as support: "Jesus said to them, 'Truly, truly, I say to you, before Abraham was, I am.'" Notice that Jesus does not say, "Before Abraham was, I *was*," but rather "Before Abraham was, I *am*." Of course, this passage can be taken many ways, and some believe that it suggests a divine transcendence of time that is radically different from that noted above, which simply affirms God as everlasting. Let us expand our discussion in order to consider both positions that might use such an argument.[202]

On the one hand, there are those who conceive God's eternity, following Augustine, such that God stands completely outside of time. God, according to this construal, "sees" time—all that is past, present, or future according to human perspective—all at once, though he is not in any way "in" time. This position has been called Augustinian timelessness, and I will adopt this term for this discussion. On the other hand, there are those who argue that the entire course of human history stands before God all "at once" in undivided wholeness, but God is "in" rather than "out" of time. According to this strand of the tradition, rather than conceiving God as atemporal, one might argue that God's relation to time is such that his experience of time is superlatively temporal in that all times are actually present to him in undivided wholeness.[203] I will use the term "eternalist" to describe this view of the divine eternity.

In light of the incorruptibility of God, it may seem obvious that he must be conceived as everlasting, but what about either Augustinian timelessness or the eternalist conception of God's eternity?[204] Within modern philosophy and theology, one finds several different opinions. Elenore Stump and Norman Kretzmann have pointed out that both positions have had a firm place within the Christian tradition since at least the time of Augustine. Stump and Kretzmann believe the tradition has affirmed these positions because "no life that is imperfect in its being possessed with the radical incompleteness entailed by temporal existence could be the mode of existence of an absolutely perfect being."[205] Then again, scholars such as David

---

202. I have set aside the complex set of questions relating to the appropriateness of using this particular passage in this way. Rather, I refer readers desiring further consideration of the biblical data to W. Pannenberg, *Systematic Theology* (vol. 1; trans. G. W. Bromiley; Grand Rapids: Eerdmans, 1991), 401ff.

203. Terminology for the third position is notoriously difficult and can be quite confusing. For example, to say that God experiences all of human history "simultaneously" seems to reintroduce the notion of temporality. Consequently, I will generally use the phrase "undivided wholeness" to capture the fact that this position affirms that God experiences all that we experience sequentially as the course of human history without any aspect of that history dropping from his actual presence.

204. Note that one may affirm that God is everlasting without holding that the divine eternity is constituted wholly by everlastingness.

205. E. Stump and N. Kretzmann, "Eternity, Awareness, and Action," *Faith and Philosophy* 9, no. 4 (October 1992): 463.

Braine believe that passages like the one cited from the Gospel of John demonstrate that such views of the divine eternity are supported by Scripture and, therefore, must be taken seriously.[206] Of course, some who adhere to the eternalist position or Augustinian timelessness do so for both philosophical and biblical reasons. There are those, however, such as Richard Swinburne[207] and Nelson Pike[208] who believe that both positions are inadequate philosophically and/or theologically. Consequently, Swinburne and Pike both conclude that these positions ought to be rejected in favor of a conception of eternity as merely everlasting. One might proceed at this point by providing critical assessment of each position. However, since our objective is to examine Pannenberg's doctrine of God, our primary focus will be upon the position that Pannenberg embraces. In what follows, I will begin with some brief comments concerning inadequacies that lead Pannenberg to reject two of the positions but that will be secondary to analysis of Pannenberg's proposal. As we shall see, the position Pannenberg embraces is, to a large extent, that advanced by Plotinus in the *Enneads*, which is the position I have termed the "eternalist position."

Pannenberg's Rejection of Eternity as Merely Everlasting Duration or Timelessness

Early in Pannenberg's treatment of the eternity of God, he addresses the concept's development within the biblical tradition: "Hebrew has no other term for eternity than unlimited duration, whether past or future."[209] However, in the very next paragraph, he goes on to claim, "This does not mean that we are to think of eternity in the O.T. only as a process, as unlimited time."[210] He goes on to draw attention to Old Testament passages in which the intent seems to be to communicate more than just unlimited duration. In particular, he cites Ps 90:4, wherein it is written, "A thousand years in thy sight are but as yesterday when it is past." Pannenberg believes that the significance of the phrase "when it is past" is intended to signify completeness in that yesterday is the time that, for humans, stands completed. He goes on to argue that, of course, the significance of "one thousand years" is not to identify literally that span of time, but rather to indicate that time stands before God as if past, that is, in completeness. Consequently, Pannenberg goes on to argue that "all time is

---

206. See, for example, Braine, "God, Time, and Eternity."

207. See R. Swinburne, *The Coherence of Theism* (Oxford: Clarendon, 1993), particularly the section "Timelessness" on pp. 223–29.

208. See N. Pike, *God and Timelessness* (New York: Shocken, 1970).

209. Pannenberg, *Systematic Theology*, 1:401.

210. Ibid. One might recognize already in Pannenberg's language a rejection of a mathematical conception of infinity, ever adding more years but never reaching infinity.

before the eyes of God as a whole."[211] It is not entirely clear that this passage can carry as much metaphysical weight as Pannenberg intends, but for now let us grant the interpretation for the sake of argument.[212] The interpretation given above would support either the eternalist position or Augustinian timelessness. We must carry our analysis further to discover why Pannenberg rejects the latter.

Who can say for sure how much the early Christian theologians and philosophers adopted Platonic categories for deployment within their theological constructions? Nevertheless, it seems clear that conceptualizing with regard to the relation of time and eternity was one area where this occurred. Pannenberg suggests that one of the strongest reasons for favoring Platonism had to do with Christian teaching about the eternal God and "Platonic teaching about the eternity of the ideas and the deity."[213] Pannenberg is not entirely happy, however, with the tradition's appropriation of Plato relating to the eternity of God because time and eternity were understood to be antithetically related in Platonism. Time was defined primarily in terms of change; in fact, Plato's discussion of time derived the concept from the notion of celestial change and movement. As opposed to this, eternity was defined primarily in terms of constancy and freedom from change and movement. As Pannenberg points out, "This agreed with the one aspect of the biblical witness to God's eternity (Ps. 102:25ff) but not with the thought that God as always the same embraces all time and has all temporal things present to him."[214] Thus, in Christian theology articulated in Platonic categories, change and mutability came to be associated with the notions of time and temporality, while constancy and immutability came to be associated with the notion of eternity. This had corresponding implications for certain divine attributes such as the divine immutability.

Pannenberg argues that Augustine, incorporating certain of these notions in his own doctrine of God, maintained the opposition of time and eternity.[215] He saw time as a creation of God that stood in distinction from eternity. So since time did not exist prior to its creation, there could be no time in God's eternity; rather, it was seen as separated from all time. God's eternity, then, was understood in terms of timelessness. Augustine incorporated the biblical insight that all time stands before God at once and articu-

---

211. Ibid.

212. Of course, there is John 8:58 cited above, and Pannenberg himself identifies other Old and New Testament passages that suggest the undivided wholeness of the divine experience of time. And, of course, this interpretation of the divine eternity is by no means rare within the tradition. Consequently, my granting of the interpretation "for the sake of argument" is not that much of a stretch.

213. Pannenberg, *Systematic Theology*, 1:403.

214. Ibid.

215. Ibid., 1:409. See also Augustine, *Confessions* 11.26.33 (Library of Christian Classics; trans. A. C. Outler; Philadelphia: Westminster, 1955), 263–64.

lated this by conceiving God as occupying a timeless realm that transcends the temporal world and from which all times (what is past, present, and future to us) are "visible" to God simultaneously. Subsequently, the position known mostly as "classical Augustinian timelessness" came to be perhaps the most widely accepted conceptualization of God's eternity in the West. During the modern period, as Pannenberg points out, there has been a growing awareness that positions that maintain the opposition of time and eternity are in need of revision. For example, he writes that "there is widespread agreement that eternity does not mean timelessness or the endlessness of time."[216]

The primary problem, according to Pannenberg, is precisely the fact that Augustinian timelessness leaves time and eternity in opposition to each other. By this, Pannenberg means primarily that time and eternity are seen as the negation of each other so that their relation is a negative one. This follows directly from the definitions that relate temporality to mutability and change, for example, and eternity to immutability and changelessness. At this point, Pannenberg's understanding of the true infinite as detailed in the last chapter makes an important contribution. Pannenberg believes that Augustinian timelessness puts a one-sided stress upon the transcendence of God by making God's eternity utterly different from human temporality. This corresponds to the "spurious" infinite, which does not overcome the opposition between itself and the finite. Pannenberg believes that the Augustinian position leaves no adequate means of affirming God's immanence with his creation, and Pike in *God and Timelessness* comes to very similar conclusions.[217] Pike concludes that by placing God in a timeless realm outside of time, one is left with no adequate means for conceiving God's actions in time.[218] Consequently, Pike argues for conceiving God as imperishable and immortal but as occupying a temporal position along with his creatures. Since the precise natures of the concerns are not identical (Pannenberg is concerned to conceive time and eternity as positively related, while Pike is concerned with the coherence of divine action in a timeless construal of God's eternity), it is not surprising that they come to different solutions. While there is more to say about this, for now I will merely note Pannenberg's reason for rejecting Augustinian timelessness.

Since the concept of the divine eternity as everlasting duration is fairly self-evident, we need not bother describing it. Essentially, Pannenberg has two objections to this position. First, the concept of the true infinite mili-

---

216. Pannenberg, *Systematic Theology*, 1:407. Of course, conceptions of time remain in a good deal of flux.

217. Those who argue against Pike's conclusions, such as Stump and Kretzmann, tend to be eternalists, which suggests that Pike's concerns relate more specifically to Augustinian timelessness.

218. Pannenberg agrees; see *Systematic Theology*, 1:408ff.

tates against the concept of eternity as everlasting duration. Just as the concept of timelessness provided a one-sidedly transcendent understanding of God's relation to time, eternity-as-everlasting-duration, according to Pannenberg, provides a one-sidedly immanent view. Further, eternity-as-everlasting-duration would correspond to the mathematical infinite, which is always potential but never actually infinite. Hence, Pannenberg argues that Pike's position finitizes God: "This idea makes God into a finite being if it implies that like ourselves God at every moment of his life looks ahead to a future that is distinct from the present and sees the past fading away from him. . . . If God is, then his whole life and all things created by him must be present to him at one and the same time."[219] Along the lines of my conclusion in chapter 3, it seems that Pannenberg's argument is sound. Of course, Pannenberg's objections are the subject of some debate, but for now we will simply recognize that he rejects these two positions for these reasons.

Pannenberg's Embrace of the Eternalist Position

Pannenberg embraces the eternalist view of God's eternity, as this position is able to meet the requirements imposed by the concept of the true infinite. He believes that a proper understanding of the divine eternity must adequately provide for both the divine transcendence and the divine immanence, must not lead to finitization of God, and must be reflective of wholeness and completeness. Given Pannenberg's appropriation of certain aspects of Plotinus's concept of eternity, I will briefly outline Pannenberg's position and its relation to that of Plotinus.

First, Pannenberg believes that just as there is a positive relation between the finite and the true infinite (the latter being the precondition of the former) there must be a positive relation between time and eternity. Second, Pannenberg argues, for both scriptural and philosophical reasons, that all times stand before God in undivided wholeness. This means that even the most remote past and the most distant future (to us) are all present in God's eternity. Third, Pannenberg's position is not to be understood as Augustinian timelessness, but rather is what I have called the eternalist position. A fair characterization of this position, drawing a rough analogy to spatial omnipresence, might be "temporal omnipresence." God has all times present to him, not successively, but in undivided wholeness, just as he has all spaces present to him at once. So rather than referring to the divine experience of temporality as "nontemporal," I suggest that a better way to describe God's temporality in Pan-

---

219. Ibid., 1:405.

nenberg's construal of the divine eternity is to say that God's experience of time is *superlatively* temporal. It is not that God has no experience of time, as the term "nontemporal" would suggest, but rather that God's experience of time is an undivided wholeness that may well transcend our ability to grasp fully. With this barest outline of Pannenberg's position, let us turn our attention now to Plotinus.

Time and Eternity in Plotinus's *Enneads*

Our examination will focus upon what Mackenna has called "the only extended discussion in ancient philosophy of the theory of time apart from that of Aristotle in *Physics*."[220] This discussion appears in Ennead 3, tractate 7 of Plotinus's *Enneads*, and it contains his most important passages on the subject. There are, however, passages from other tractates that will be brought to bear as appropriate. Plotinus begins his discussion of time and eternity by making two points: (1) While "Eternity and Time [are] two entirely separate things" (3.7.1), (2) time is image to Eternity the original.[221] In other words, there is a radical difference between eternal and temporal existence, yet there exists a positive relationship between the two modes of existence; one is image, one is original. Plato had called time a moving copy of eternity, and yet his definitions retained the opposition between the two, thus retaining a negative relationship. At the end of Ennead 3.7.1, Plotinus says that he will proceed first to investigate eternity and then to articulate the manner in which time can be said to be its copy.

In Ennead 3.7.2, Plotinus writes that whatever eternity is, it must possess some sort of perpetuity, though not the kind "of perpetuity in the time-order." Ennead 3.7.3, which undoubtedly has one of Plotinus's most important statements about the nature of eternity, reads:

> We know it [eternity] as a Life changelessly motionless and ever holding the Universal content [time, space, and phenomena] in actual presence; not this now and now that other, but always all; not existing now in one mode and now in another, but a consummation without part or interval. All its content is in immediate concentration as at one point; nothing in it ever knows development; all remains identical within itself, knowing nothing of change, for ever in a Now since nothing of it has passed away or will come into being, but what it is now, that it is ever.

---

220. S. Mackenna, Summary to the Seventh Tractate, "Time and Eternity," in Plotinus, *The Enneads* (trans. S. Mackenna; New York: Penguin, 1991), 213. My quotations from Plotinus are from *The Six Enneads* (trans. S. Mackenna and B. S. Page; Great Books of the Western World; Chicago: Encyclopedia Britannica, 1952).

221. Ibid.

Here is perhaps the fundamental claim made by Plotinus regarding the nature of eternity: The universal content of the totality of life stands in actual presence in eternity. Applying this to God, the entire course of temporal existence stands before God in undivided wholeness, not just in memory of the past or foreknowledge of the future, *but in actual presence.* Plotinus elucidates his position: The eternal mode of existence is changelessly devoid of becoming, it has no part or interval, nothing ever passes from or enters into that eternal now, and it constitutes a life that is entire and complete in any and every way imaginable. He continues:

> What future, in fact, could bring to that Being anything which it now does not possess; and could it come to be anything which it is not once for all?
>
> There exists no source or ground from which anything could make its way into that standing present; any imagined entrant will prove to be not alien but already integral. And as it can never come to be anything at present outside it, so, necessarily, it cannot include any past; what can there be that once was in it and now is gone? Futurity, similarly, is banned; nothing could be yet to come to it. Thus no ground is left for its existence but that it be what it is.
>
> That which neither has been nor will be, but simply possesses being; that which enjoys stable existence as neither in process of change nor having ever changed—this is Eternity. Thus we come to the definition: the Life—instantaneously entire, complete, at no point broken into period or part—which belongs to the Authentic Existent by its very existence, this is the thing we were probing for—this is Eternity.

It is particularly important to note that the emphasis in this attempt to describe the eternal mode of existence is not upon the *simultaneity* of God's experience, but rather upon the *wholeness* or *completeness* of that experience. The point is that nothing escapes the actual living presence of God. No event that has ever occurred is lost to God, and no future can ever enter eternity but that which was already present. This is the same point intended by Stump and Kretzmann in the quotation cited above.[222] Humans live in an utterly durationless[223] present that moves inexorably from moment to moment, leaving those moments experienced in the untouchable past and looking forward with anticipation and expectation to those not yet present. In the Plotinian view of eternity, it is as if that durationless present some-

---

222. See above, p. 93.

223. Perhaps "utterly durationless" sounds too strong. However, consider the "infinitely" small quantities used in physics; for example, current equations calculate the state of the physical universe back to within roughly 10^{43} seconds of the big bang. What is the smallest measurable quantity of time? Perhaps calling our present "utterly durationless" is too strong, but not much.

how expands to embrace all aspects of lived experience, whether past, current, or future to us.

Of course, this mode of life is radically different from anything we finite, merely temporal creatures experience. In fact, it is so radically different from everyday experience that one issue we shall have to address is whether this conception of eternity is coherent. However, clarity of meaning is the first issue, and for now we need to consider other passages from Plotinus in an effort to make clear his claims. First, consider the contrast Plotinus sees between the divine eternity and normal, temporal existence as recorded in Ennead 5.1.4:

> Soul deals with thing after thing—now Socrates; now a horse: always some one entity from among beings—but the Intellectual-Principle is all and therefore its entire content is simultaneously present in that identity: this is pure being in eternal actuality: nowhere is there any future, for every then is a now: nor is there any past, for nothing there has ever ceased to be: everything has taken its stand for ever, an identity well pleased, we might say, to be as it is.

We need not delineate Plotinus's hierarchy of being to understand his point here. The temporal experience of what Plotinus calls "Soul" is the same as the experience of time that humans have, and that experience is, as we know, of one thing after another, or as Plotinus writes, "now Socrates; now a horse." This is radically different from God's experience of time, which is characterized in the terms already noted, and now Plotinus adds "pure being in eternal actuality." Here he seems to suggest what we have called the undivided wholeness of such experiencing.

Plotinus recognizes the difficulty in articulating his understanding of the divine eternity. In particular, he recognizes that temporally tinged terms are virtually unavoidable; hence Ennead 3.7.6: "Observe that such words as 'always,' 'never,' 'sometimes' must be taken as mere conveniences of exposition: thus always—used in the sense not of time but of incorruptibility and endlessly complete scope—might set up the false notion of stage and interval." While we may, in fact, be forced to use terms that suggest temporality, this is a consequence of the limitation of our language. We use such terms because they are available, a convenience, as Plotinus says, not because they accurately reflect the facts of the matter. Plotinus argues that such terms as "always" and "never" are to be taken in the sense of indicating perfection of a whole and actual existence. These terms, applied to the divine existence, are not to be taken as suggesting finitude, as Plotinus sees it, of a one-thing-after-another temporality. There is one more point we need to draw from Plotinus's writings before we begin to assess his position.

Remember that one objection Pannenberg raised vis-à-vis the positions of Plato and Augustine was that their conception of the divine eternity maintained the opposition between time and eternity. One of the strengths of Plotinus's position, according to Pannenberg, is that it has the potential of changing the manner in which time and eternity are understood to be related. In Ennead 3.7.11, Plotinus writes:

> Time at first—in reality before that first was produced by desire of succession—Time lay, self-concentrated, at rest within the Authentic Existence: it was not yet Time, was merged in the Authentic and motionless with it. But there was an active principle there, one set on governing itself and realizing itself (=the All-Soul), and it chose to aim at something more than its present: it stirred from its rest, and Time stirred with it. And we, stirring to a ceaseless succession, to a next, to the discrimination of identity and the establishment of ever new difference, traversed a portion of the outgoing path and produced an image of Eternity, produced Time.

While this passage suggests something of the rationale that Plotinus sees in the separation of time from eternity, the primary point is the claim that time once existed potentially within the "Authentic Existence," potentially since Plotinus writes that time existed within, but *not yet as time*. Time comes to be, then, as a fall from eternity, or as Pannenberg writes, "Time is now seen as the dissolution of the unity of life into a sequence of separate moments, and yet it is constituted a sequence by the reference to the eternal totality."[224] Rather than seeing time and eternity in opposition as with Plato, who identified time with change and eternity with immutability, Plotinus argues that time is what comes to be when the unity of eternity is dissolved into succession. Pannenberg, then, argues that eternity becomes the precondition of temporal succession so that eternity is constitutive for time. There, a positive relation between time and eternity is set forth.

Summary of Plotinus's Position

We can summarize now the three primary points taken from this brief examination of Plotinus's concept of eternity. First, Plotinus understands eternity to be such that it holds the totality of life present in actual, undivided wholeness. There is no past, present, or future in the divine eternity, since they are all taken up into one divine experience of all times. It could be argued that this is a fundamentally nontemporal way of experiencing; however, I have suggested that it would be better to term this sort of experi-

---

224. Pannenberg, *Systematic Theology*, 1:404.

encing "superlatively temporal." Second, Plotinus seems primarily to argue for this conception of the divine eternity rather than the normal human experience of time because the latter is fragmentary and radically incomplete, and such a mode of experiencing life would be unworthy of God. He argues that the conception of eternity he pursues provides the sort of wholeness that must be an essential element of the divine life. Finally, by seeing time as a dissolution of eternity into a succession of temporal moments, Plotinus suggests that eternity is the basis for the unity of all times. This establishes a positive relation between time and eternity, thereby overcoming the weakness of those positions that see time and eternity in opposition.

Assessment of Plotinus's Position

Since the only mode of existence we have ever known is one wherein time passes and events come one after another, it is difficult for us to imagine what this eternal mode of existence would be like. However, we must recognize that even if we conclude that one simply cannot imagine what this superlatively temporal mode of experiencing would be like, this recognition alone would not be adequate to dismiss Plotinus's proposal.[225] With these cautions in mind, let us assess Plotinus's view of the divine eternity. One difficulty is evident from the following question: How can one make sense of the claim, for example, that Plato's birth and death are both actually present to God? To make the concern more explicit, consider whether the following propositions must both be true in the divine eternity:

1. Plato is alive now.
2. Plato is dead now.

Certainly these two propositions stand in stark contrast to each other, and one is justified in asking how they might both be true in the divine eternity. How might Plotinus respond? In the first place, he might note that there is a very misleading ambiguity in applying these two propositions in the same fashion to both the sequentially structured human experience of time and the superlatively temporal experiencing of the divine eternity. In the sequentially structured experiencing of time, the two "nows" mean entirely different times, say 427 BC and 347 BC. By contrast, in the nonsequentially

---

225. In an interesting article dealing with divine knowledge of the future, Alvin Plantinga argues that simply being unable to say *how* God may know the future is inadequate to deny such knowledge. In fact, Plantinga goes on to point out that since God has no body or sense organs, it is just as problematic to say how God has any knowledge, but we do not deny divine knowledge on this account. See A. Plantinga, "Divine Knowledge," in *Christian Perspectives on Religious Knowledge* (ed. C. S. Evans and M. Westphal: Grand Rapids: Eerdmans, 1993). So the mere fact that the divine mode of experiencing is beyond our grasp is by no means a decisive argument against it.

structured experiencing of time, according to Plotinus, all times are present to God in undivided wholeness in what might be called an eternal "now." Consequently, Plotinus would likely say that both propositions are, in fact, true in the divine eternity "now," since "now," in the undivided wholeness of the divine eternity, does not indicate temporal distinction. Plotinus cautioned about this when he warned that temporally defined terms are merely conveniences of language and not to be taken literally when used in relation to the divine eternity.

It surely does not follow, however, that because the divine eternity has all times present in undivided wholeness, God therefore has no means of distinguishing between events that are experienced sequentially by humans. It would seem that the divine omniscience would take care of this. Consider the following three propositions:

3. In sequentially ordered time, July 1, 2005, comes before July 2, 2005.
4. In sequentially ordered time, event *a* occurred on July 1, 2005, and event *b* occurred on July 2, 2005.
5. Therefore, in sequentially ordered time, event *a* occurred before event *b*.

With the appropriately selected *a* and *b*, certainly these propositions are all true. Further, if one takes God's omniscience to mean that God knows all true propositions, then God knows these propositions. Consequently, even if Plotinus's construal of the divine eternity is correct, there is no reason to conclude that the undivided wholeness of God's experiencing precludes his knowing the temporal structuring of events that are sequential for humans. Of course, when we use propositions such as 3, 4, and 5, the introductory phrase "in sequentially ordered time" is utterly taken for granted because this is the only sort of experiencing that humans know. However, since we are contrasting the divine eternity with the human experiencing of time, the introductory phrase is necessary for the level of precision required for our analysis. If we were to apply this lesson to propositions 1 and 2, we would see that "now" would be replaced with the appropriate temporal indicators. Let us turn our attention now to some proposals intended to help clarify the claim that God holds all times in actual presence in undivided wholeness.

Augustine attempted to provide "an analogy between the human experience of time and the simultaneous present of eternity"[226] with the phenomenon of the time-bridging present that is evident in the human experience of music. Even though a given melody actually occurs as a

---

226. This description is from Pannenberg, *Systematic Theology*, 1:409.

sequence of notes, Augustine pointed out that we are able to cause our attention to expand so as to embrace, by recollection, what is past and, by anticipation, what is yet future in the melody so that we enjoy the melody as a whole rather than merely as a sequence of notes. Similar things happen in language. Even though at any instant during the course of uttering a sentence only a particular syllable is spoken, we can unite those syllables that have been spoken and often anticipate those that have yet to be spoken so that we can participate not just in syllable uttering but in the communication of information, often very complex and detailed information. If we were not able to extend attention in this way, we could neither communicate nor enjoy a melody. The human ability to integrate experience is, in this matter, very limited, and Augustine's analogy is merely intended to give a degree of clarification. If humans can integrate small pieces of sequential experience into a greater whole to yield a form of experiencing greater than merely experiencing individual instants, why think that the superlatively temporal experiencing of the divine life does not integrate all time?

Closely related to the Augustinian notion of the time-bridging present is the idea of the "specious present" used by William James in *The Principles of Psychology*. In a chapter entitled "The Perception of Time," he writes:

> We do not first feel one end and then feel the other after it, and from the perception of the succession infer an interval of time between, but we seem to feel the interval of time as a whole, with its two ends embedded in it. . . . To sensible perception its elements are inseparable, although attention looking back may easily decompose the experience, and distinguish its beginning from its end.[227]

The specious present is, humanly speaking, that duration of time that the mind integrates in its living of some particular experience. Note that James is not speaking of integrating an experience from memory after it is experienced. He is, instead, talking about the way we actually experience life. We do not experience life in discrete instants (can we even say what that would look like?), but rather in events that integrate an appropriate set of instants. William Alston suggests that such a concept could make intelligible the claim that God experiences life in undivided wholeness: "The psychological concept of the specious present provides an intelligible model for a nontemporal knowledge of a temporal world. . . . A being with an infinite specious present would not, so far as his awareness is concerned, be subject to temporal succession at all. *Everything* would be

---

227. W. James, *The Principles of Psychology* (vol. 1, chap. 15; Mineola, NY: Dover Publications, 1950); quoted in Stump and Kretzmann, "Eternity, Awareness, and Action," 481, n. 21.

grasped in one temporally unextended awareness."[228] I have opted for the phrase "superlatively temporal" to describe the experiencing of life in eternity as understood by Plotinus, rather than the term "nontemporal" as used by Alston. This is because in the Plotinian proposal what is experienced sequentially by humans is experienced in undivided wholeness by God. Consequently, God does experience what occurs in time, which nontemporal experiencing may seem to deny; it is just that he does not experience it piecemeal as do humans. It seems to me the phrase "superlatively temporal" captures this much more accurately than the frequently used "nontemporal." In any case, James and Alston, with the concept of the specious present, offer a conceptualization of what the undivided wholeness of the divine life might be like.

Before moving on, let us examine another way to give content to this construal of eternity. First, recall that contemporary physics teaches that the speed of light in space is finite. Consequently, for example, as a result of the distance to the star Sirius, the light that impinges upon human retinas on earth from Sirius left Sirius about eight years ago. Therefore, when we look up at Sirius, we do not see Sirius as it is today; we see it as it was about eight years ago. If one could travel into space exactly one light-year's distance from earth and look back with a very powerful telescope, one would see the events that occurred upon earth exactly one year prior to looking through the telescope. In fact, we can generalize the claim:

6. If one occupies a position x light-years from earth and looks through a very powerful telescope, one sees z from x years ago, where z is defined as the complex image that would impinge upon a human retina if a human retina were so located.

Further, for every x there is a corresponding z such that a true proposition can be constructed. Therefore, given the divine omniscience, every one of these true propositions, as well as the corresponding x's and z's needed to make the proposition true, exists already in the divine mind.

Let me attempt to clarify this claim by way of an example. Let us say that three hours ago I was working out in the gym. My claim is that there exists in the divine mind a proposition in the form of 6, where x is three light hours and z is an image of a portion of my workout routine. In this moment, three hours after my workout, the image of my workout, as a consequence of the divine omniscience, is still before the mind of God. Since a proposition of the form of 6 can be constructed for any z that has existed in the past, by choosing the correct x, there is a very large (perhaps

---

228. W. P. Alston, "Hartshorne and Aquinas: *A Via Media*," in W. P. Alston, *Divine Nature and Human Language* (Ithaca, NY: Cornell University Press, 1989), 136; quoted in Stump and Kretzmann, "Eternity, Awareness, and Action," 481 n. 22.

infinite) number of images in the divine mind, exactly one of which corresponds to every lived experience upon the earth. Consequently, it seems clear that not just descriptive propositions but the actual images of the totality of lived experience are before the mind of God simultaneously.

At this point, it is appropriate to add some clarifying comments and cautions to our assessment. First, I do not claim that this proposal is an actual representation of the divine eternity. Instead, I merely seek to respond to those who claim that the idea of the undivided wholeness of Plotinus's doctrine of eternity is unintelligible by showing that, at least as regards past events, something similar to this undivided wholeness is a direct result of the limiting speed of light and God's omniscience. Second, I have chosen to use the idea of "images formed upon the human retina" because this represents the most data-rich form of human experiencing. Modern computer science has demonstrated that complex visual images can be reduced to collections of digital data so that computer programs can perform tasks based upon those data. Of course, humans do not know the precise nature of divine experiencing. Since God has no body and since the five human senses require a body, God's method of experiencing anything must be radically different from our own. Consequently, the use of the notion of visual images is only intended to show the plausibility of the undivided wholeness of Plotinus's (and, ultimately, Pannenberg's) conception of eternity. Finally, I have already shown that the presence, for lack of a better word, of temporal locators in these propositions does not in any way affect the proposed undivided wholeness of the divine experiencing in Plotinus's proposal.

At this point, the objector may say that this is all well and good but that the real problem, the real incoherence, is in claiming that God knows the future. The charge of incoherence, then, hinges upon the claim that propositions of the following form are incoherent:

7. Z is what one would see if one viewed the earth from near its surface on y, where z is the complex image that would impinge upon a human retina if a human retina were so located and y is some future date.

Here x, which was essentially a past temporal locator, has been replaced by y, which is a future temporal locator. To make proposition 7 more clear, consider an example. Let us assume that Henry Smith is elected president of the United States on November 3, 2008. Proposition 7 says that some of the many images in the divine mind are ones that correspond to events that occur on November 3, 2008. Of those images, a subset will be those that correspond to Smith's being elected president. Of course, the images may be as detailed as you like. One could take the image that shows the final total of the voting, or one could take every individual image of persons voting. Again, one may consider as many as one pleases, for as a consequence of the divine omniscience, they all exist in the divine mind.

The charge is often advanced that propositions of the form of 7 are incoherent, but why think that? They seem clear enough in meaning. As Alvin Plantinga has pointed out, they seem to have a truth value, and they do not seem to entail contradictions.[229] Of course, it is possible that no such true propositions (and in our case, images that make them true) exist about events that are future to us, but it is not clear that they do not, and it is certainly true that an important and large strand within the Christian tradition has affirmed that God does have knowledge of the future and, therefore, that such propositions exist. Some have argued that propositions such as 7 are unknowable, but again Plantinga has reminded us that we cannot draw that conclusion merely on the grounds that we cannot say *how* God would know them. Interestingly, Plotinus lets the question stand by merely affirming that God knows them by a means "transcending the process of cogitation."[230]

In summary, this is what I believe our analysis has shown so far:

1. Since the limiting speed of light and God's omnipresence and omniscience lead directly to the affirmation that all of past history is "seen" by God, the usual objections about this being an incoherent means of experiencing are mistaken. I make no claim, however, that the divine eternity is actually like this.
2. Since all of the past history "seen" by God in undivided wholeness has what I have called "temporal locators," the fact that they are present all at once in undivided wholeness does not mean that God is unaware of the way in which humans experience them.
3. The claim that the eternalist position is incoherent is often a function of the fact that we cannot say how God knows events that are future to us. But, of course, this alone does not justify rejection of the Plotinian position.

Consequently, we have yet to find adequate reason to believe that the position of Plotinus, the position I have called the eternalist position, is to be rejected as false or incoherent.

Because the eternalist view of the divine eternity is so difficult to conceptualize and because charges of incoherence and unintelligibility run rampant, it is worthwhile to consider one more manner of conceptualizing the eternalist view. According to well-accepted scientific theory, as objects

---

229. See Plantinga, "Divine Knowledge."
230. Plotinus, *Six Enneads* 4.4.12, p. 164.

approach the speed of light, their experience of time slows down. Here one recalls the example of two identical twins, one of whom leaves the earth and spends twenty years in a spaceship traveling at near the speed of light, while the other remains on earth. Upon the first brother's return, the second brother will have aged twenty years, while the first will have aged only a very small amount of time. In other words, the passage of time for the first brother slowed down as a function of his speed. If one were to travel at the speed of light, the passage of time for the traveler's frame of reference would come to a halt. If God were zipping around the universe in a ship traveling at the speed of light, no time would pass in his frame of reference, while billions of years might pass in ours. In fact, the entire history of the universe could pass in this frame of reference, while none would pass in the divine frame of reference. However, by virtue of the divine omniscience, God still would know all that happened in our frame of reference, even if it all stood in undivided wholeness, "at once," before him. Of course, I do not propose this to be the actual character of the divine life; I do not believe God is traveling around the universe in a superlatively fast spaceship. However, this scenario gives additional intelligibility to the eternalist's position and helps one to grasp the plausibility of the proposal.

Let us turn our attention now to the second issue: Plotinus's concern for the wholeness of the divine eternity. The first matter concerns the meaning of the term "wholeness" in the context used by Plotinus. Interestingly, the earlier quotation from Stump and Kretzmann expresses the belief that the sequential temporal existence that humans experience would be radically incomplete and, thus, inadequate to characterize the perfect existence of God. Stump and Kretzmann share Plotinus's view that the human experience of time is fragmentary in that, of all the times experienced in our lives, only the instantaneous "now" is in actual presence. The perfection of the divine life, so the eternalist says, could not be so fragmentary as to be bound in that instantaneous now, separated from all the other moments of the divine life. For this fragmentariness to be overcome, so the argument goes, the divine life must be such that it integrates all the moments of life into a complete totality that is ever held in actual presence. In addition, Plotinus expresses concern that the divine life must be such that nothing could ever enter it from outside. In other words, nothing could ever exist in the divine life that was not there all along. Likewise, he argues that nothing that ever existed in the divine life could ever fade away. Consequently, Plotinus develops his understanding of the divine eternity as the totality of life present in undivided wholeness. Such a mode of existence transcends the problem of missing wholeness implied by the human experience of time. To clarify this, let us consider an analogy that might show the weight the term "wholeness" is intended to carry. The explanation that Plotinus gives is more suggestive than precise, so my attempt to flesh out his meaning will require a bit of speculation.

A number of examples help clarify Plotinus's point. First, consider a parent's experience of seeing his or her child grow up. While parents are constantly excited and amazed at the marvelous experiences they enjoy as their children mature, surely every parent has, from time to time, lamented that the teenager is no longer an infant who can be held and nurtured in the way only an infant can be. Or once the child is an adult, parents miss the day-to-day interaction of having the child at home. A children's story entitled *Love You Forever*[231] tells of a mother who, as her son grows to manhood, sneaks into his bedroom from time to time to rock him just as she had done when he was an infant. I suspect virtually all parents would love the chance to "go back" from time to time to relive other moments in the lives of their children. But, of course, this is impossible in the human experience of time, for once a time is past, it can never be present again. There is a sense in which one could term the human experience of time (the experience of one moment at a time) as radically incomplete as compared to one who has all of the moments of life present in undivided wholeness. If Plotinus is correct, there is no point at which past events become "lost" to God's living presence so as to exist only in the divine memory (as the child eventually becomes "lost" to the parent); rather, the divine eternity holds the totality of life in actual presence. There can be no question that the kind of superlatively temporal experiencing that Plotinus has in mind could be characterized by the term "wholeness."

Finally, two points that we discussed in chapter 3 are relevant for the current analysis. The first is Pannenberg's understanding of the relation between the philosophical categories of part and whole. Recall that he argues that the category "whole" has priority over that of "part." It is precisely this ordering that guides his understanding of eternity as constitutive for time. In other words, the whole (eternity) makes the parts (discrete times) what they are, since, according to Pannenberg, the interrelation of all the parts, which is evident only in the whole, is constitutive for the essence of each of the parts. Second, Pannenberg believes that conceiving the relationship of time and eternity in this way is consistent with the structure of the true infinite in contrast to timelessness, which corresponds to the spurious infinite:

> The thought of eternity that is not simply opposed to time but positively related to it, embracing it in its totality, offers a paradigmatic illustration and actualization of the structure of the true Infinite, which is not just opposed to the finite but also embraces the antithesis. On the other hand the

---

231. R. Munsch and S. McGraw, *Love You Forever* (Willowsdale, Ont.: Firefly Books, 1991).

idea of a timeless eternity that is merely opposed to time corresponds to the improper infinite which in its opposition to the finite is defined by it and thereby shows itself to be finite.[232]

By "positively" versus "negatively" related, Pannenberg means to draw attention to the matter of whether time is merely the opposite of eternity (negatively related) or whether eternity is also seen as the total integration of all times (positively related). Here, in connecting the eternalist position with the "true infinite," Pannenberg recognizes that there is a sense in which time and eternity are opposed (in the way that part and whole are opposed) but that the opposition is overcome once we see that eternity is all-encompassing of time and serves to unify it into a totality. That totality, then, is never separated from the divine life.

Summary

It is appropriate at this point to draw some interim conclusions concerning the doctrine of eternity that Pannenberg deploys. First, the primary question is the plausibility and coherence of the eternalist position, that is, of conceiving the experience of time as a totality in undivided wholeness. In this construal of eternity, God would experience in undivided wholeness what we humans experience sequentially. The radically different nature of this from normal human experience has led to the claim that the very notion itself is unintelligible. However, while I have granted that a thorough understanding of the divine eternity might be beyond human capacity, my analysis has reasonably shown that the eternalist position is intelligible. Consequently, it cannot be rejected on these grounds. Second, my analysis has also shown that objections often reduce to our inability to say *how* God is able to experience time this way. This, however, is not a decisive objection. Third, I have found plausible biblical and philosophical grounds for the eternalist position. My interim conclusion, then, is that Pannenberg's proposal for the doctrine of the divine eternity is plausible. Consequently, we are ready to proceed to examine (1) the relationship between conceptions of the divine eternity and the claim that God is the power of the future, and (2) the relationship between these notions and human freedom.

God's Power and Being

In *An Introduction to Systematic Theology*, Pannenberg writes, "The word 'God' refers to a power. A God without power is no God at all."[233]

---

232. Pannenberg, *Systematic Theology*, 1:408.
233. Pannenberg, *Introduction to Systematic Theology*, 8.

In fact, the pervasive nature of the power of God is evident as Pannenberg continues: "The word 'God' implies as its semantic minimum the idea of power on which all finite reality depends."[234] Pannenberg goes on to recognize that the simple concept of divine power does not necessarily imply a coercive power or a violent power. In this Pannenberg is attempting to establish the importance of the concept of power within the doctrine of God while avoiding an interpretation of God's power as one-sided or tyrannical.[235] Pannenberg later expands these ideas in order to make a very close connection between the power/rule of God and his being/ essence. In fact, he argues that God's power/rule *is* his being/essence.

While Pannenberg generally seems to take this connection as virtually self-evident, one can construct the argument that he likely would use. In the first place, Pannenberg argues that while it is not necessary to God's being that he create a world, it is hardly consistent with the idea of God to think that a world could exist that he did not rule.[236] This indicates a very close connection between the idea of God's rule and the biblical concept of the kingdom of God, since the kingdom of God is precisely where he rules. And, of course, it is by God's power that he rules his kingdom, and thus we see how the notions of rule, power, and kingdom become very closely associated. In light of the scriptural claim that God is Lord of his kingdom, Pannenberg writes, "From the biblical standpoint the being of God and that of the kingdom are identical, since the being of God is his lordship."[237] Pannenberg's argument reduces to this: (1) If a world exists, to say that God did not exercise lordship over it would contradict the very idea of God; (2) since the world exists, God must exercise lordship over it; and (3) since the divine lordship is essential to God's being God, God's being is his lordship.

When is it that God exercises lordship over the world? The short answer is only when God's existence is definitively revealed and his lordship is no longer a subject of debate. Undoubtedly, God exercises lordship over the world, in some sense, even today, but the very fact that the debatability of God's existence is still a reality in the world of human experience

---

234. Ibid.

235. Two points are worth mentioning here. First, Pannenberg and other modern theologians (Moltmann, for example) express concerns with conceptions of divine sovereignty and omnipotence that leave no room for significant human action; thus, his comments here. Second, this should make clear that his emphasis upon the concept of power is not intended to deemphasize other divine characteristics. For example, as we shall see subsequently, he argues that the divine nature is to be characterized as love, so the emphasis upon power must be taken as the power of love.

236. Or as Pannenberg observes, "the world as the object of [God's] lordship might not be necessary to his deity, since its existence owes its origin to his creative freedom, but the existence of a world is not compatible with his deity apart from his lordship over it." Pannenberg, *Systematic Theology*, 313.

237. W. Pannenberg, *Basic Questions in Theology* (vol. 2; trans. G. H. Kehm; Philadelphia: Westminster, 1971), 240.

means that the definitive revelation of God has not yet occurred.[238] In fact, recall that we have already witnessed Pannenberg's claim that only with the final appearing of the kingdom of God is the debatability of God's existence put to rest forever. This means, and in this there is no surprise, that there is an eschatological element to the kingdom of God. More specifically, the kingdom does not definitively arrive until the eschaton appears.

Now comes the frequently debated thesis that connects these thoughts about God's being/rule/power with the idea of futurity. If the kingdom of God is not actualized until the eschaton, and if the kingdom/rule of God is his being, then it follows that there is some sense in which God's being is not yet actualized. Since God's being is not yet actualized but will be someday, the actualization of the rule is a future event. Therefore, the actualization of God's being is also in the future. This is primarily what Pannenberg means when he says that the future has ontological priority for the being of God; the time when God's being will be actual is in the future. Or as Pannenberg writes, "To this extent, the God to whom the hope of the kingdom refers is characterized in a radical and exclusive sense by 'futurity as a quality of being.'"[239] A number of issues need to be sorted out in these claims, but there is a very important paragraph in which Pannenberg captures several of these matters very succinctly:

> The idea of the future as a mode of God's being is still undeveloped in theology despite the intimate connection between God and the coming reign of God in the eschatological message of Jesus. What is the meaning of this intimate connection? For instance, is the future of his lordship, the kingdom of God, inessential to his deity, something merely appended to it? Is not God God only in the accomplishment of his lordship over the world? This is why his deity will be revealed only when the kingdom does come, since only then will his lordship be visible. But are God's revelation of his deity and his deity itself separable from each other? The God of the Bible is God only in that he proves himself as God. He would not be the God of the world if he did not prove himself to be its Lord. But just this proof is still a matter of the future, according to the expectations of Israel and the New Testament. Does this not mean that God is not yet, but is yet to be? In any case, he exists only in

---

238. Obviously, there is a very close relationship between epistemic and ontological concerns here, since Pannenberg's argument implies that universal awareness is essential. In short, his claim seems to be that God cannot be the ruler unless he is known as such. However, it seems that one could reasonably argue that God could be ruling in a hidden way. Nevertheless, as we see in the next quotation, the biblical revelation promises the definitive arrival of the kingdom of God so that no doubt about the deity of God remains. Since this has not yet occurred, it leaves the claim "God rules" hypothetical. However, when the deity of God is definitively revealed, Pannenberg argues, that eschatological revelation will have eternal consequences in that we will then see that God has, in fact, ruled all along.

239. Pannenberg, *Basic Questions in Theology*, 2:240. The last phrase is a quotation from Ernst Bloch's *Das Prinzip Hoffnung*.

the way in which the future is powerful over the present, because the future decides what will emerge out of what exists in the present. As the power of the future, God is no thing, no object presently at hand, which man could detach himself from and pass over. He appears neither as one being among others, nor as the quiescent background of all beings, the timeless being underlying all objects. Yet, is being itself perhaps to be understood as in truth the power of the future? As the power of the future, the God of the Bible always remains ahead of all speech about him, and has already outdistanced every concept of God. Above all, the power of the future does not rob man of his freedom to transcend every present state of affairs. A being presently at hand, and equipped with omnipotence, would destroy such freedom by virtue of his overpowering might. But the power of the future is distinguished by the fact that it frees man from his ties to what presently exists in order to liberate him for *his* future, to give him his freedom.[240]

There is a sense in which all of the major themes of this chapter appear in this quotation. As we soon shall see, it is precisely Pannenberg's understanding of the divine eternity that allows him to propose that the future has ontological priority without, as I have suggested, losing the existence of God in the present. Here also he begins to work out what it means to say that God is the power of the *future*. Finally, toward the end of the passage, Pannenberg begins to address the relationship between the concepts of eternity, the divine power, and God's futurity on the one hand, and human freedom on the other.

Development and Assessment

With this initial introduction to what Pannenberg means when he says that God is the power of the future, we now turn our attention to five questions that will guide us in finishing the task. First, Pannenberg clearly argues that his understanding of the futurity of God is an expression of the eschatology of both the Old Testament and the proclamation of Jesus. Thus, we must consider how the futurity of God follows from biblical eschatology. Second, Pannenberg makes quite a claim when he states that the decisive revelation of the deity of God is an essential part of what it means to be the God of Abraham, Isaac, and Jacob. Is this correct? For example, would it be possible (not in the broadly logical sense, but in the narrower sense of a real, live option) for God to exercise his deity definitively while remaining totally hidden? Third, if futurity is the primary mode of the divine existence, then one must ask, in what sense and to what extent does God exist

---

240. Pannenberg, *Basic Questions in Theology*, 2:242–43.

in the present? Fourth, what does Pannenberg intend when he assigns priority to the future? Finally, Pannenberg claims that the future exerts power over the present. To many this surely will seem an odd claim, so we must ask, in what sense does Pannenberg mean to say that the future exerts power over the present?

Futurity in Biblical Eschatology

In *The Dawn of Apocalyptic*, Hanson argues that the rise of apocalyptic in Israelite literature resulted when the hope for the definitive appearing of the kingdom of God within space-time history began to collapse as events seemingly called into question God's rule over the world of Israel's experience.[241] In apocalyptic, the hope for definitive appearance of God's reign was pushed off into the distant future, and extraordinary (sometimes mythical) language is used to describe the battle that ensues between God and those who oppose him. The hope for the definitive demonstration of God's rule over the cosmos is not given up, but it becomes an eschatological hope rather than one to be realized in the current space-time setting. Whether or not one attaches significance to the fact, there is little debate that this hope is evident in the apocalyptic writings of both the Old and New Testaments, as well as in the proclamation of Jesus.[242]

Of course, Pannenberg recognizes that the message of Jesus regarding the coming reign of God contains elements of both the present in-breaking of that reign and the promise of its future, full realization. There is the nowness that relates to the present rule of God in the hearts of believers, which Jesus modeled through his life of obedience and self-subjection to the Father. Further, we have an anticipation of the final arrival of the kingdom evident in the resurrection of Jesus. Nevertheless, it is only in the eschaton that the glory of God will be fully visible and, thus, that the kingdom will make its decisive appearance. Thus, in commenting upon the writings of Isaiah, Pannenberg asserts that "the deity of Yahweh as the God of Israel depends upon the future action which he declares and which will show all peoples that he is the one true God."[243] Only as God brings to reality what he promises is he shown truly to be God. Surely, eschatology is primary for the proclamation of either the hope of Israel or the message of Jesus, but the pressing question for our examination is whether the eschatological expectations of the Scriptures can bear the metaphysical weight Pannen-

---

241. P. D. Hanson, *The Dawn of Apocalyptic* (Philadelphia: Fortress, 1975).

242. As is often the case, of course, many of these claims are contested. However, an important strand within the Christian tradition has consistently affirmed such an eschatological hope for the arrival of God's kingdom.

243. Pannenberg, *Systematic Theology*, 1:193.

berg intends concerning the nature of the divine life. Much of the answer to this question hinges upon our analysis of the issue of the relation between the deity of God and the revelation of that deity.

God's Deity and Its Revelation

In the long quotation from Pannenberg above, he asks whether the deity of God can be separated from the revelation of that deity.[244] The immediate context indicates that Pannenberg believes that the answer to this question is no. In taking this position, Pannenberg draws an extremely close identification between issues of epistemology and those of ontology. In fact, if Pannenberg intends to argue, as it seems he does, that the deity of God is inseparable from the revelation of that deity, then the being of God (expressed in his deity) cannot be fully realized without the universal awareness (expressed in the universal knowledge) of his deity. One of the first implications of this is that, since the debatability of God's existence presently precludes universal awareness of his deity, this proposed relation between ontology and epistemology leads Pannenberg to write, *"It is necessary to say that, in a restricted but important sense, God does not yet exist."*[245] To the ears of most theologians and Christian philosophers, this is no doubt a peculiar claim. But before we can consider this in detail, we must ask whether there are adequate reasons to believe the underlying claim that the deity of God and the revelation of that deity are inseparable.

We must pull together the strands of the preceding arguments to analyze Pannenberg's thesis. First, let us grant for the sake of argument the series of claims that express identity between God's power/rule/kingdom and his deity. Let us also agree that when we use the phrase "deity of God," we are attempting to express the deepest sense of what it means to be God. The question then becomes, can we speak of the kingdom as God's kingdom if God himself remains unrevealed? Or can we speak of God ruling the cosmos if the cosmos is not aware that God rules it? We have used the term "lordship" to express the rule of God over his kingdom, and intimately involved in the idea of lordship is the idea of a lord exercising authority over his subjects. We may then rephrase our questions: Can one be lord over another if that lordship is not recognized? If this line of argument is correct, it seems that Pannenberg's claim that the deity of God and the revelation of that deity are inseparable is, at a minimum, plausible in light of the manner in which the Christian tradition has

---

244. See pp. 112–13.
245. W. Pannenberg, *Theology and the Kingdom of God* (ed. R. J. Neuhaus; Philadelphia: Fortress, 1977), 56.

generally conceived God. Those parts of the biblical witness that promise the definitive appearance of God's kingdom are particularly relevant here. The existence of the God of Abraham, Isaac, and Jacob remains a hypothetical assertion, as does the claim that he exercises lordship over the cosmos. For God to be fully God, it seems plausible to claim he must be recognized as such, though when he is so recognized, it will have eternal consequences such that it will be seen that God has ruled all along.[246] Perhaps the underlying significance of the scriptural claim that at the final judgment every knee will bow and every tongue will confess that Jesus is Lord to the glory of God the Father also relates to the necessity of God's open demonstration of his rule. In other words, when the lordship/deity of God is actualized, it will necessarily involve the decisive revelation of that deity. We must ask what it means for Pannenberg to write that in some sense God does not yet exist.

Another way of getting at the same point is to ask, given Pannenberg's proposals, in what sense God may be said to exist now. Of course, the Christian tradition has overwhelmingly conceived God as active in the world and in the present, and it is hard to see how a God who does not yet exist could be conceived as actively involved in the world today. It is at this point that we must bring together various strands from our analysis and combine them with Pannenberg's doctrine of the divine eternity. This, in turn, will clarify a number of issues, not the least of which will be to expand our understanding of the claim that the future has ontological priority for the existence of God.

God's Present Existence

In chapter 2, I discussed the influence of a German philosopher of history, Wilhelm Dilthey, upon the thought of Pannenberg. Dilthey argued that the essence of our life is bound up with its meaning, but the meaning of life can be understood only against some horizon of meaning. Since circumstances change, horizons of meaning change, and therefore, our own essences are, in a sense, in a state of flux. Dilthey's solution to the problem of the ambiguity of life's meaning was to argue that only from the horizon of meaning formed by the context of one's death, that point at which all of the events of life could be seen in their totality and interrelation with other events, would one be able to say definitively what the meaning of one's life was.[247] Dilthey went on to say that to determine the meaning/essence of the totality of human history, one would need a vantage point beyond all possible

---

246. See, for example, Pannenberg, *Systematic Theology*, 1:330ff.
247. See p. 31.

changes to the horizon of meaning. For Pannenberg, the eschatological revelation of the kingdom of God constitutes such a vantage point. Consequently, the eschatological future has priority in that it plays a definitive role in determining the meaning and significance of every single event and experience in the course of human history.[248]

Additionally, Pannenberg argues for the ontological priority of the future on the basis of the identity between God's being and his rule coupled with the fact that the definitive revelation of the rule of God will occur only with the decisive arrival of the kingdom in the eschatological future. So for Pannenberg, the eschatological future plays a decisive role in determining the meaning of all human history. Further, if his argument identifying essences and meanings is correct, then this argument also turns out to be an argument for the ontological priority of the future.[249] Now let us combine these points with the earlier discussion about the nature of the divine eternity as Pannenberg sees it. In God's superlatively temporal mode of experiencing, all times, which are experienced as sequentially structured by humans, are present in undivided wholeness. However, from what we have just seen, Pannenberg argues that in that eternal divine life, what is future, from our perspective, has priority over all other times. The two important questions are these: (1) What exactly does this mean? (2) Is it plausible?

Since humans do not experience life in the same way as God, human language does not readily have the terms we need. So we shall have to improvise. When speaking of the human, sequential experience of time, I will use the terms "past," "present," and "future" in their common senses. However, since I have already argued that there is no reason to think that the superlatively temporal way of experiencing life leaves God confused about the order in which events are experienced by us, I will add the word "logical" to "past," "present," and "future" to indicate God's ability to recognize that sequential ordering of experiences, even though he does not experience them in that way. So in human experience, we can talk about, for example, the primordial past, the present, and the eschatological future. Though, according to Pannenberg, God has all of these present in undivided wholeness, we still can speak of their logical relations.

With these terminological distinctions in place, let us consider what it means to say that the eschatological future has priority for the existence of God. First, does Pannenberg's assertion of an ontological priority of the future rob the present of God's active and living presence? I believe the

---

248. Pannenberg readily admits, however, that many things will turn out to be just as we expected all along.

249. Even if Pannenberg's attempt to draw together epistemology and ontology is not successful, it seems clear that this latter argument establishes something of the epistemological priority of the future in that the final meaning of human history becomes evident only in the light of the eschatological kingdom of God.

answer to this question is no. Earlier in this chapter, I suggested that the eternalist position, rather than being confused with Augustinian timelessness, ought to be conceived in terms of temporal omnipresence. In other words, since in God's eternity all times are ever present to the divine life, we can think of this as roughly analogous to the claim that all of space is present to God in undivided wholeness. If all times are present to God in this way, then it is equally true that God is present to all times. From our perspective and using the tensed language that applies to sequential temporal experiencing, then, God was present to all past times, is present now, and will be present to all future times up to and including the eschatological future. Of course, from the perspective of the divine eternity, these tensed terms carry logical weight only as outlined above.

The Priority of the Future

At this point, one may be inclined to ask, if this is the case, why then does Pannenberg insist that the future has priority for the divine life? There are at least four identifiable reasons, each of which requires brief assessment. First, along the lines of the preceding discussions concerning the coming of the kingdom and the manifestation of the deity of God, Pannenberg believes that the future has priority as regards the being of God. Second, consistent with Pannenberg's deployment of the Diltheyian historical hermeneutic, he believes that the future has decisive significance for the meaning of the totality of the world's history. Third, Pannenberg argues that the future is the source of contingency, and as it turns out, this connects with his understanding of human freedom. Finally, Pannenberg argues, again with implications for human freedom, that the future is the locus of the wholeness of the divine knowledge. Let us examine these four issues in this order, recognizing that with the third and fourth issues we transition to our last major topic for analysis: the issue of human freedom.

In light of the previous discussions, I can be quite brief concerning the first two points. As regards the first, if one finds plausible Pannenberg's arguments for making an intimate connection between God's being and his rule, then, as I have already pointed out, since God's rule is only decisively present at the eschaton, then the eschatological future has ontological priority for God's being. However, we must not lose sight of the implications of connecting this assertion with Pannenberg's understanding of the divine eternity. Since the life of God is present to all times in undivided wholeness, the one and same being of God must be present to all those times. This means that while we who experience time sequentially will not experience the full deity of God prior to the eschaton, once the eschaton dawns, we will see that God is who he has always been. This is why Pannenberg often uses a locution that asserts that what is revealed as true in the eschaton will be seen as having always been true. The priority of the future, from the perspective of the all-at-onceness of the divine life, is purely logical (in the sense outlined above) rather than temporal. If one were able, as it were, to snatch God out of his eternity so that he had to live his life sequentially as we do, then one would have to affirm becoming of the divine essence. This is why, in the earlier quotation from *Theology and the Kingdom of God*, Pannenberg states only that there "is a sense" in which it must be said that God does not yet exist. The "sense" in which God can be said not to exist yet is a direct implication of the ontological priority of the future. Yet by virtue of the divine eternity as described here, there is also a sense in which it must be said that God has always existed. It is the undivided nature of the divine life that takes all these changes up into itself.

For Pannenberg, the all-embracing horizon of meaning presented by the arrival of the eschaton has decisive implications for the meaning of all the world's history. Recall that according to Dilthey, the essence of events (which he takes to be identical with their meaning) is contingent upon the nexus within which an event is situated. Since that nexus changes with changing horizons of meaning (which occur as new events shed light on past ones), the essence of a given event is not finally determinative prior to the arrival of the eschatological future. Hence, the future (as eschaton) has priority in determining the meaning of all things.

The third issue relates to Pannenberg's assertion that the future is the source of contingency. As usual, our first issue is to clarify what he means by this. In the first place, Pannenberg seems to hold that if there were no God, there would be no contingent events. All that could possibly occur would be the unfolding of the causal influences inherent in what exists at any given time. Hence, the universe would be fundamentally mechanistic in nature: What would come to be would be mainly that which was already present such that it could not help but come to be. Likewise, what is not already present could never come to be. If this mechanistic unfolding of the world were to be overcome, it could not be overcome from the past, since the past is the source of what already is. Neither could it be overcome by the present alone, since the present is merely where what was potentially present becomes actually present. However, the future is the realm of the possible, and according to Pannenberg, as such it is the source of the possibility of transcending the causal influences of the past. Consequently, it is God, as the power of the future, who comes to individuals and presents them with possibilities that enable them to become more than the mere outworking of the causal influences of the past. Human freedom has its source, says Pannenberg, in the futurity of God.

One might reasonably challenge this line of reasoning by saying, for example, that one need not conceive the future as the source of freedom. Rather, one might conceive God's creative power in such a way that the world has contingency "built in," perhaps through the mystery of human freedom. Of course, this is a real possibility. However, it seems to miss the point that perhaps what we have from Pannenberg is a proposal about the very nature of that mystery. One way of conceiving human freedom is to trace back antecedent causes of a given event until one arrives at the point where a choice made by an agent may be identified. At the point where choice is identified, we have reached a point at which the action cannot be further reduced. However, I suggest that what we have in Pannenberg is an attempt to establish human freedom on a rather different basis. According to his alternative theory, freedom would not necessarily be conceived as a "faculty" or "power" inherent in human nature. Rather, freedom would always be conceived as a gift from God, who comes to individuals and empowers them to transcend their own pasts by presenting them with possibilities for actualization that extend beyond what would be possible without God's interaction. Since God comes presenting possibilities that have not yet been actualized, Pannenberg argues that this power, which God is and which gives humans their freedom as a gift, comes from the realm of the undecided, that is, the future. Pannenberg captures this with a suggestive question: "Is freedom possible as something constituted by the subject as such, or can it only be thought of as a freedom given to him, or even only as the experience of liberation at some particular time?"[250] All of this, of course, raises the question of how the future can be a causal influence in the present.

Future as Causally Impacting the Present

In Pannenberg's thought, there exist at least three distinct notions of how the future might impact the present. The first of these I will refer to as the power of "inspiration" or the power of "deliverance." The second has been described as "anticipation," and we have already seen its central role in Pannenberg's theological enterprise. The third has often been referred to as "reverse causality." Let us consider each; however, before proceeding, we must pause to consider what might be expected from attempts to describe a causal power that acts from the future. Obviously, such a power would need to be conceived in a radically different sense than our normal conceptions of causality. For example, the very definition of causality indicates a

---

250. W. Pannenberg, *The Idea of God and Human Freedom* (trans. R. D. Wilson; Philadelphia: Westminster, 1971), 92.

temporal ordering such that the cause comes before the effect. So defined, there could be no causal efficacy of the future. In the cases of inspiration/ deliverance and anticipation, a more accurate description might involve talking in terms of causal influences.

Perhaps the two best examples of what I am calling deliverance or inspiration arise in consideration of the drug addict and the artist. The drug addict, by virtue of his past choices, has given up his freedom so that those past choices have become decisive for present and future choices. While the addict may not be able to transcend the past on his own, God, as the power of the future, may come to the addict and empower him to realize possibilities that do not follow from his past. In this case, it is empowerment to turn from his addiction. The artist, when inspired, is raised beyond herself, and in that experience she finds herself presented with new possibilities for creative expression. God, as the power of the future, encounters the artist with the opportunity to transcend her own past. While in both of these cases the actual presentation of the possibility and the choosing by the subject occur in the present, there is a sense in which these examples can be viewed as a sort of "future causality," for it is the presentation of future possibility (and the power to actualize it) that results in the coming to be of something new.

Moving on to "anticipation," this occurs anytime an individual expects an occurrence in the future and then chooses specific acts in the present based upon that anticipation. For example, if one anticipated that a particular airline flight would meet with disaster on a certain date, that anticipation would influence one's decision about flying. For Pannenberg, God has given humanity an insight into the end that he intends for his creation by causing the eschaton to make a proleptic appearance in Christ. As Pannenberg writes, in Christ "the end of history is already here" so that "in the person of Jesus the end of history is already anticipated."[251] This anticipation calls individuals to decision and opens the possibility to orient their lives based upon what has been revealed about the future. Pannenberg summarizes by saying that "it is characteristic of Jesus' message about the nearness of the reign of God that the eschatological future of this reign does not remain a distant beyond, but rather becomes a power determining the present without thereby losing its futurity."[252] In this way, God's future, by virtue of his having revealed it in Christ, becomes an effective cause in the present. Of course, it does not overpower the freedom of individuals but nonetheless presents opportunities to realize possibilities that would not be otherwise available. As in the previous case and for the same reasons, here we can speak of future causality only *in some sense*.

---

251. W. Pannenberg, *Basic Questions in Theology* (vol. 1; trans. G. H. Kehm; Philadelphia: Westminster, 1971), 36.
252. Ibid., 1:178.

The third form of future causality is much more problematic than the first two. It has been referred to by many as "reverse causality"[253] and can best be understood as the power of the future drawing the present to itself but, according to Pannenberg, doing so contingently. It is extremely difficult to know what to make of this sort of future determination of the present. In the first place, "determine" is being used in a radically different sense than we normally recognize, for as Pannenberg observes, "determinism is a clear idea only on the basis of a scheme where past events determine the future outcome of the process."[254] In the same passage, Pannenberg uses quotation marks around the word "determine" and subsequently writes, "'Determination' of the present by the future is not the same sort of determination as in the case of past events that determine the future outcome."[255] By these comments, does Pannenberg mean to collapse this form of future causality into the other two we have analyzed? That the talk of future causality can be reduced to the first two forms is suggested when Pannenberg writes, "Eternity, of course, is not only future, but also (as future) prior to the other modes of time."[256] Here the term "prior" is used in the logical sense noted earlier. Even with these sorts of comments, however, ambiguity remains. If Pannenberg means to assert a future causality of a different form, then we must ask that he spell out in more detail precisely what is meant so that we are able to assess the claim.

Human Freedom and the Future

These comments have already launched us into the discussion of human freedom, and we must now turn our attention to the intended force of the term "determines" in the phrase "God is the power of the future that determines everything that exists." There are at least three senses in which the word "determines" could be intended.[257] First, "determines" could be intended in the sense of grounds and establishes parameters for all that exists. Second, it could be intended in the sense Polk refers to as "epistemological,"[258] wherein the meanings (for Pannenberg, the "essences") of events are retroactively determined in light of the future of God. Third, it could be

253. Consider, for example, D. P. Polk, "The All-Determining God and the Peril of Determinism," in *The Theology of Wolfhart Pannenberg* (ed. C. E. Braaten and P. Clayton; Minneapolis: Augsburg, 1988), 152–68.

254. W. Pannenberg, "A Response to My American Friends," in *The Theology of Wolfhart Pannenberg* (ed. C. E. Braaten and P. Clayton; Minneapolis: Augsburg, 1988), 322.

255. Ibid.

256. Ibid.

257. See Polk, "All-Determining God and the Peril of Determinism," for a discussion of the difficulty in translating the German word that underlies "determines."

258. Ibid., 160.

intended in the sense that God actively participates in determining the course of human history.

The first sense, which means that God determines that there be a creation rather than nothing at all separate from himself and that he determines the parameters of creaturely existence, is one that the overwhelming majority of the Christian tradition has affirmed. Similarly, it presents no threat to human freedom, since this position seems to follow directly from the notions of *creatio ex nihilo* and divine freedom. If God creates of no necessity or lack in himself, then it follows that he freely determines whether anything else will exist. If he creates freely from nothing, then he determines the forms that will exist as well as those that will not. Examples of such "determination" might include determining the range of intellectual capacities for humans, determining the sort of world that would be made available to them, and determining the boundaries within which their freedom might be exercised. In short, it would mean that no aspect of creaturely existence would extend beyond the range intended by God. We have seen that this position does not threaten human freedom, but we can go further, following Polk: "Even the strongest doctrine of *creatio ex nihilo* must want to affirm that God creates his creatures as they are, which means in the case of the human creatures, that human freedom itself is to be conceived as God's creation."[259] So God has determined that the actions of humans not be predetermined by God, which means that human freedom and autonomy are not abstract things outside of God's involvement.

"Determines" might also be taken in the sense Polk refers to as epistemic:

> Pannenberg may intend to assert only that, since it is the ultimate future which finally decides the essence of what becoming occurrences in history actually *mean*, therefore the future possesses the power of *ascertainment* of the true character of all reality. Not existence per se but the *essence* of what comes to exist is fully a consequence of God's all determining power.[260]

From our previous discussion of Pannenberg's incorporation of the work of Dilthey, it seems there can be no question but that Pannenberg sees God's future as having a determinative effect upon the meaning of individual events.[261] Only from the eschatological future, when the final contextual

---

259. Pannenberg, "A Response to My American Friends," 322–23.

260. Polk, "All-Determining God and the Peril of Determinism," 160.

261. However, I am concerned that Polk's language may imply more than Pannenberg intends. One gets the impression from Polk that humans can do whatever they want only to have God trump their intentions, thereby finally deciding everything. In personal conversation with Pannenberg in January of 1994, he indicated that while he affirms the future as constitutive for the meaning of events, he allows that many (most?) events will turn out to have the meaning we intended all along. In the main discussion, I will affirm Pannenberg's view. However, I would encourage caution, and it is my opinion that he would reject a construal that led to seeing God as arbitrarily overruling the intentions of his creatures.

horizon of meaning is reached, can one be sure that no further transcendence of meaning is possible. This is why God's future can have a determinative effect upon present events. It seems clear that Pannenberg intends "determines," at least in some places, in this sense.

Polk holds that such a construal of God's determinative power indicates that humans are not truly free, since God's future and not human intention is the final determiner of meaning. I cannot agree with this assessment. While it might be true that free agent A's act—intended to have meaning M(1)—will turn out to have meaning M(2) in light of the future, it is not at all clear how this will affect A's ability to bring about the intended physical state of affairs or how it will prevent God from judging the agent's act accordingly. First, Polk seems to imply that unless an agent has explicit awareness of the meaning an action will have in light of God's future, the action in question is not free. With such a definition, it is hard to see how any acts are free. Second, consider a counterexample. Free agent A, who happens to be a vandal, slashes the tires on B's car parked in front of A's house. As a result, B is unable to leave for work. Coincidentally, on the same morning, an electrical fire starts in B's garage. Since B is home, he is able to discover the fire and prevent serious damage to his house. If he had been at work, his house would have burned. In light of the end, A's vandalism has the result of saving B's house. However, one would not expect this happy coincidence to have much weight with the police or with God, who judges the intents of free agents. While all this might mean that humans are not free to have the final word, so to speak, whether all the consequences of their intentions are actualized, we must conclude that determination of essences by God's future does not preclude human freedom or God's ability to judge human intentions.

The third sense in which "determines" may be taken actually allows for a subset of interpretations. In order to highlight them, consider the following analogy.[262] Imagine that God's future power, which is actively drawing the creation to himself, is a gravitational field centered upon some point in space. Imagine that creation is like a vessel being drawn through space toward the center of that gravitational field. There are a number of possible relations between the gravitational field and the path the vessel will follow. If the field is infinite in power, the energy expended

---

262. I discussed the following analogy with Pannenberg in December 1993. He termed it "perhaps helpful" but cautioned against a possible misunderstanding. First, he noted that the example had a "deterministic bias" because it failed to have "future" as one of the indices. Second, he also expressed concern that one might conclude that creatures and Creator were on "the same level," which is not correct. He went on to say that we must be careful not to think of creaturely freedom as something exempted from God, for we must recognize that whatever degree of freedom creatures enjoy is precisely so because God has created it as such. So, for Pannenberg, the central point is that we must conceive of human freedom as created by God, not something "in addition to what God is doing."

by the ship will not make a difference in the path it follows to the center. The path will be a straight line.

If we imagine the gravitational field as very strong but less than infinite in power, then the vessel, by expending its own energy, may be able to traverse a less direct path to the center, though the vessel still would be drawn to the center. In applying this analogy back to the question of God's futuristic determinative power, we would say that the destiny of the creation as such (the vessel) is to arrive at the kingdom of God (the center of the field), but there is a fair amount of freedom in the course by which it arrives at the kingdom. In order to include the possibility of individuals being lost to God, one could imagine the vessel's path such that it could allow some to escape from the vessel and thereby escape the destiny God offers to humanity. Even in this case, however, we must be careful not to claim that the individuals really escape from God—the psalmist has noted that even if one should make his bed in hell, he does not escape God's presence.

One could also imagine a third scenario: The gravitational field is not strong enough to determine that the vessel will ever arrive at the center. Perhaps it will expend its energy to arrive at another destination altogether. However, this analogy cannot be a real possibility for expounding Pannenberg's view since in this case God would be only one of the realities of human existence that may be transcended. This is where our analogy breaks down, for it is at least logically possible (Pannenberg concurs) that no humans would be saved. However, when Pannenberg speaks of the coming of the kingdom, he intends the definitive coming of the kingdom to correspond to the definitive revelation of the deity of God. In this way, the coming of the kingdom is not dependent upon the actions of humans. While this last scenario is not consistent with Pannenberg's position, the other two are. Consequently, we may conclude that, minus scenario three, Pannenberg's position has the conceptual richness to satisfy the alternative interpretations of the term "determines." Further, none of these interpretations is problematic for human freedom. However, before concluding this discussion on the issue of human freedom, we must consider the implications of Pannenberg's doctrine of the divine eternity for human freedom.

Eternity, Foreknowledge, and Freedom

It has been argued that if the divine omniscience means that God knows the future, then humans are not free. One of the arguments aimed at making this point is that if God knows the future and if God cannot be wrong about anything he knows, then humans cannot act in any way inconsistent with God's knowledge about the future. Since I can do tomorrow only what God already knows I will do, I cannot be free; therefore, my very actions are predetermined. This problem is generally referred to as the "foreknowledge" problem. Does the nature of the divine eternity as understood by Pannenberg carry deterministic implications, or does it actually help resolve this problem? As one might expect, Pannenberg believes his position provides the resources both to affirm that God's knowledge includes all true propositions—whether they are past, present, or future from our perspective—and to affirm human freedom, while at the same time agreeing that foreknowledge implies predeterminism. We will now see how.

In an essay entitled "Speaking about God in the Face of Atheistic Criticism," Pannenberg's agreement that foreknowledge implies predeterminism is evident:

> If the eternity of God is thought of as the unlimited continuance of a being which has existed from the first, then the omnipotence and omniscient providence of this God must have established the course of everything that takes place in the universe in all its details from the very first. In this case there is no room for genuine freedom on the part of any creature.[263]

Similar sentiments are expressed in numerous places throughout Pannenberg's writings. Just because Pannenberg believes that foreknowledge implies determinism does not make it so. In what follows, however, my focus is first upon understanding Pannenberg's position. Subsequently, I will comment further upon his criticism of alternative positions.

In addition to this quotation, which shows Pannenberg's concurrence with the claim that foreknowledge precludes human freedom, consider his rejection of alternative solutions to the foreknowledge problem that have been advanced within the tradition.

> Neither the solution that God foresees free actions as such, nor the consideration that the eternity of God is simultaneous at any point in time and therefore does not predetermine temporal events, could be convincing as long as the being of God was thought of as already perfect and complete in itself at every point in past time and therefore at the beginning of all temporal processes.[264]

Again, these alternate positions cannot be decisively refuted merely by *claiming* they are false, but we begin to see why Pannenberg finds certain positions inadequate. The reader may be surprised to find that Pannenberg

---

263. W. Pannenberg, "Speaking about God in the Face of Atheistic Criticism," in *The Idea of God and Human Freedom* (trans. R. A. Wilson; Philadelphia: Westminster, 1973), 108.

264. Ibid.

believes that "the consideration that the eternity of God is simultaneous at any point in time" does not alleviate the problem. At first this sounds like Pannenberg's own eternalist position, but this is another place where Pannenberg believes that deployment of the priority of the future resolves the difficulty. The real problem, he thinks, is conceiving God "as already perfect and complete in itself" at the beginning.

In order to get at the meaning of Pannenberg's point, let us focus our attention upon the nature of the divine omniscience and its relation to the divine eternity. Pannenberg argues that in the superlatively temporal mode of the divine life, God is actually present to all times in undivided wholeness. Consequently, every free decision that any free agent makes is present to God (though as I have argued, there is no reason to believe that God is unable to see "logical" relations between events, and thus he would be aware of the sequential ordering of events as we experience them). Therefore, God has "always" (in our logical sense) known what every free agent would do in every set of circumstances. However, and this is how he believes he avoids the foreknowledge problem, Pannenberg claims that the eschatological future has priority with regard to the divine omniscience. Think of it this way: In the sequentially ordered, temporal experience of life that is human existence, we come to know what free agents freely choose after they have chosen. But in the "logically structured," superlatively temporal experience of life that is God's, all of those free choices are present in undivided wholeness. Since these free choices are present to God in this way, one can say that there are the logical distinctions that allow God to distinguish between what is "before" and "after" for us. Consequently, in this logical sense, we may say that God knows the results of free choices "after" they occur. The point of correspondence—the "place" where the knowledge that arises from the temporally structured experiencing of humans and the knowledge that arises from the "logically" structured experiencing of the divine life are identical—is the eschatological future.

Let us suppose that it is possible, during the course of the world's history, to record every one of the free choices made by free agents. At the eschaton, this hypothetical knowledge base would be complete. In the "all-at-onceness" of the divine life, the eschaton is just as present as all other times. However, what Pannenberg is claiming is that, as regards the divine knowledge base, it is complete at the same point as this hypothetical knowledge base, that is, at the eschaton. This is the force of the claim that the future has priority as it regards the divine omniscience. God does know what is future to us *as future*, but only because he experiences all times "at once" in undivided wholeness. If it were possible to somehow remove God from the divine eternity so that he took up a temporal position alongside humans, then according to this construal, he would not know the future.[265] In other words, God's omniscience is a direct consequence of the divine eternity.

If, on the other hand, the primordial past were given priority with regard to the divine omniscience, the divine omniscience would constitute foreknowledge and, Pannenberg believes, the loss of human freedom would be a consequence. This is where Pannenberg utilizes the notion that once the eschaton arrives, we will find that what is true in light of the eschaton will turn out to have been true all along.[266] In other words, all true propositions about all states of affairs will turn out to have always been true in God's eternity. This is because God's eternity embraces all times and thus all temporal processes and decisions. Perhaps an example will be helpful. Consider the following true proposition:

8. Martha Dandridge married George Washington.

This proposition, so goes Pannenberg's claim, has always (in the logical sense) been true in God's eternity precisely because in the divine eternity, the wedding date is present to God with all other times in undivided wholeness. However, Martha could have married someone else; had she done so, the *corresponding true proposition* always would have been true in God's eternity.[267] Whatever turns out to be true at the eschaton will be so precisely because that is what the individual chose (even if from our perspective those times are yet future). In this way, Pannenberg believes that his understanding of the divine eternity coupled with his argument for the ontological priority of the future resolves the foreknowledge problem without surrendering any of the traditional divine attributes. With the presentation and assessment of Pannenberg's claim that "God is the power of the future that determines everything that exists" complete, we may now draw final conclusions from this examination.

Summary and Conclusions

While the issues addressed in this chapter are essential to an examination of Pannenberg's doctrine of God, there is a sense in which they could justify a monograph of their own. Consequently, my examination and assessment have been selective, focusing more upon the positive aspects of Pannenberg's proposal than his criticisms of other positions. Nevertheless, we must first point out the degree to which the set of proposals we have examined in this chapter are mutually supportive. The doctrine of eternity

---

265. Pannenberg agreed with this assessment in private discussion in October 1999.

266. See, for example, Pannenberg, *Systematic Theology*, 1:330, where this notion is expressed, even if it does not contain this precise locution.

267. In private conversation, Pannenberg has concurred with this analysis.

that Pannenberg deploys leads to his understanding of the ontological and epistemological priority of the future, which, of course, leads to his reference to God as the power of the future. These things together lead to the manner in which he understands human freedom and God's interaction with it.

The various discussions of this chapter have shown that Pannenberg's doctrine of the divine eternity is plausible. While one must grant that it conceives God's experience of time in a radically different way from that of human experiencing, Pannenberg's position has adequate resources to rebut the charges of unintelligibility and incoherence. The various analogies and examples I have used, while I do not claim that they directly correspond to the nature of the divine life, at least enable one to grasp what it would mean to enjoy such a mode of existence. It also seems that Pannenberg's proposal is superior to both the conception of God as everlasting and the notion of timelessness as in the Augustinian tradition. God never suffers the lack of wholeness that I have argued follows from the sequential experience of time, while he is yet intimately involved in the times of his creatures rather than merely transcendent to them as in Augustinian timelessness. As with many things in philosophy and theology, intuitions will be divided on this issue; however, I believe Pannenberg has given us adequate reasons to accept the broad contours of his proposal.

The extent to which one finds the thesis of ontological and epistemological priority of the future persuasive will be at least somewhat dependent upon the extent to which one finds persuasive Pannenberg's appropriation of Dilthey's work. This, in turn, may be related to the extent to which one accepts the ordering of the concepts of whole and part that gives priority to the former. At a minimum, I have argued that these claims are plausible. In our discussion of the manner in which the future "determines" the present, we discovered a number of ways in which the future may be said to act upon the present. However, it seems unlikely that the future can truly be conceived as having causal efficacy in the present. In Pannenberg's attempt to refute the claim that his position is deterministic, he argues that determinism must be understood as predeterminism. In other words, to be deterministic, causes must precede effects. However, to be determined means to be caused, so if Pannenberg's position cannot be taken as deterministic because "causes" come after effects, then the future cannot determine the present in the sense of having causal efficacy. Pannenberg's position suffers from some ambiguity here, and he will have to provide additional details if we are to be able to clearly assess this position.

Given this outline of Pannenberg's position, his view of human freedom follows. However, Pannenberg raises what seems to me to be a very valid caution when he points out that we must not simply think of human freedom in some abstract sense but rather remember that even the freedom that humans have is within the determination of God. We must not elevate freedom to the point that it is conceived as a means of escaping the divine presence. Even in our God-given autonomy, we are still creatures. Pannenberg's proposal gives a plausible account of human freedom that brings together in an interesting way both human freedom and divine providence. Whether it will be accepted by the tradition remains to be seen, of course, but Pannenberg's proposal seems to provide the resources to resolve some issues that, from a historical perspective, have been quite bothersome.

Is Pannenberg's overall position as laid out in this chapter persuasive? I believe the answer to this question is yes. This set of issues is highly contested, and the final judgment on it may, in fact, turn out to depend upon the persuasiveness of the totality of Pannenberg's doctrine of God. For now, I will proceed by recognizing the plausibility and inner coherence of those proposals we have examined in this chapter. In the next chapter, I take up Pannenberg's treatment of the doctrine of the Trinity. Pannenberg believes, in light of what he calls the regulative role of the concept of the true infinite, that the only plausible doctrine of God is one that conceives God as a differentiated unity. I want now to turn to the manner in which Pannenberg understands and deploys the doctrine of the Trinity within his overall doctrine of God.

CHAPTER 5

Father, Son, and Holy Spirit:
The One God

WE LIVE DURING A TIME of resurging interest in the doctrine of the Trinity. What is perhaps more remarkable is the fact that recovery of Trinitarian doctrine has been necessary from time to time. Of course, the most significant objection to the Trinitarian conception of God, which has been raised by those inside as well as outside the Christian faith, is the challenge to the very coherence of the idea. How can one coherently affirm monotheism while at the same time affirming that this *one* God is constituted by *three* persons? To many, this has sounded like polytheism.

The Cappadocian fathers (Gregory of Nyssa, Gregory Nazianzus, and Basil the Great) are generally credited with working out the technical language of the Trinitarian doctrine: The Godhead is composed of three hypostases and one common substance. Yet the development of this language did not stave off all objections. From within the tradition, Erasmus once argued that while among the common people it could not be admitted that Christians worship three gods, it could be so admitted among the learned.[268] Additionally, the Socinians, in the sixteenth century, went so far

---

268. Erasmus wrote, "According to the dialectical logic it is possible to say there are three gods. But to announce this to the untutored would give offense." Quoted in R. Bainton, *Hunted Heretic: The Life and Death of Michael Servetus, 1511–1553* (Boston: Beacon, 1953), 30–31. In fact, Bainton cites others as well. In this work on the burning at the stake of Michael Servetus, he identifies certain anti-Trinitarian tendencies within the tradition. First, he cites Pierre D'Ailly, who said that "it is a special gift of God to believe correctly [in the Trinitarian doctrine]." John Major went a bit further, arguing that "on account of the infidels the saints did not admit a plurality of gods. Yet the case may be so understood among the experts."

as to reject the doctrine of the Trinity. From outside the tradition, both Jews and Muslims have consistently denied that Christians can rationally call themselves monotheists. Is it possible that the doctrine of the Trinity has lost emphasis from time to time because the charges of irrationality are too difficult to refute?

While the precise reasons that the Trinitarian doctrine has seemed to wax and wane from time to time are the subject of a good deal of debate, Pannenberg believes that the doctrine tends to be lost when it is not understood to be essential to the doctrine of God. It is as if Christian theologians undertake seriously the challenge to refute objections to the doctrine of the Trinity only when a threat to it can be construed as a threat to the very concept of God itself! Consider Pannenberg's comments:

> I think that the trinitarian conception of God has a good claim to be considered the specifically Christian idea of God. It is not a doctrine of only secondary importance in addition to some other basic concept of the one God: If the issue is considered in terms like that, the case for trinitarian theology is lost. *It can be defended only on the condition that there is no other appropriate conception of the God of Christian faith than the Trinity.*[269]

At this point, it is not necessary to assess whether Pannenberg is correct in his assertion; the point is rather to show the extent to which Pannenberg takes seriously the doctrine of the Trinity. He is not alone. In the second half of the twentieth century, the resurgence of attention to the doctrine was evident in the work of a broad range of theologians. These include Karl Rahner, a representative of the Catholic tradition; Eberhard Jüngel and Jürgen Moltmann, two of Pannenberg's fellow Germans; and Robert Jenson, an American Lutheran. All of these theologians have sought to reestablish the essential role the doctrine of the Trinity plays in Christian doctrine.

Consider, for example, the similarity between the preceding quote from Pannenberg and the following from Jenson: "Christians do not have 'a God,' about whose ideas Jesus then perhaps contributes some information. They have the particular God of whom the man Jesus is one identity, and who therefore is *triune in the first rather than the second place.*"[270] Again, we need not debate the accuracy of Jenson's substantive claim, as

---

269. W. Pannenberg, "The Christian Vision of God: The New Discussion on the Trinitarian Doctrine," *Asbury Theological Journal* 46 (1991): 28 (emphasis added). Pannenberg delivered these comments as part of a lecture series at Asbury Theological Seminary.

270. Quoted in R. Olson, "Wolfhart Pannenberg's Doctrine of the Trinity," *Scottish Journal of Theology* 43 (1990): 176 (emphasis added).

the point here is merely to show that Pannenberg fits within a broader group of theologians who agree with his concern that the doctrine of the Trinity tends to be ignored when it does not occupy the central position in Christian doctrine.

Pannenberg emphasizes the concern by noting that as soon as "it appears that the one God can be better understood" without it, Trinitarian doctrine seems to be treated as "a superfluous addition to the concept of the one God even though it is reverently treated as a mystery of revelation."[271] Shortly after this statement, Pannenberg indicates what he believes hangs in the balance: "The doctrine of the deity of Christ could not itself endure apart from the doctrine of the Trinity. Jesus would simply be viewed as a divinely inspired man and the church as a human fellowship of faith which arose under the impress of his personality, as in Schleiermacher's *Christian Faith.*"[272] The fact that Jesus spoke of God as Father and distinguished himself from the Father leads directly to Pannenberg's assertion here: If Jesus is to be understood as divine and yet speaks of another as God, then there must be distinction of some sort within God himself. The doctrine of the Trinity, of course, provides just such a distinction. Our overarching task in this chapter is to determine whether Pannenberg is successful in demonstrating that only with the doctrine of the Trinity can a coherent doctrine of the Christian God be constructed. Beyond that, we will consider the implications that Pannenberg believes follow from a robust embrace of the Trinitarian doctrine.

The significance of the doctrine of the Trinity for Pannenberg is evident. However, given that Pannenberg has argued for the need to modify the doctrine of the Trinity as traditionally understood, we must consider the precise nature of the Trinitarian doctrine that he intends. There are, he claims, five specific areas where modification is necessary:

1. "The Trinity cannot be deduced from a general concept of God as spirit or love," but rather must be derived from the revelation in Christ.
2. To understand the nature of the relations between the members of the Trinity, it is necessary to recognize the mutuality of those relations rather than seeing them simply as one-way relations of origin.
3. The concept of the self-distinction of the Son from the Father is central to a proper understanding of the Trinitarian relations.
4. The monarchy of the Father alone does not adequately account for a mutuality of relations between the Trinitarian persons.

---

271. W. Pannenberg, *Systematic Theology* (vol. 1; trans. G. W. Bromiley; Grand Rapids: Eerdmans, 1991), 291.

272. Ibid., 1:292.

5. A proper understanding of the contribution of the Son and Spirit to
   the kingdom of the Father is essential to understanding the unity of
   the divine essence.[273]

During the course of our examination, I will touch upon each of these
proposals. In so doing, I will proceed as follows. First, I will consider Pannenberg's analysis of the problems with the manner in which the tradition
has generally sought to develop the Trinitarian doctrine. Once I complete
my review of Pannenberg's critical analysis, I will turn my attention to
Pannenberg's proposal for how the doctrine ought to be derived. Third, I
will examine Pannenberg's proposal concerning the mutuality of the
inner-Trinitarian relations. Next I will undertake Pannenberg's argument
for the unity of the divine essence; thus, we will consider the implications
of the concept of infinity for the doctrine of the Trinity. Finally, I will
summarize my critical analysis of Pannenberg's proposals and assess its
overall persuasiveness.

History of Attempts to Derive the Trinitarian Doctrine

Given the commitment of Judaism to a monotheistic conception of God
and Christianity's origin within that tradition, one might first ask, why did
a Trinitarian conception of God arise within Christianity in the first place?
At the beginning of a section entitled "The God of Jesus and the Beginnings
of the Doctrine of the Trinity," Pannenberg writes: "At the heart of the
message of Jesus was the announcing of the nearness of the divine reign.
But Jesus called this God whose reign was near, and even dawning with his
own coming, the (heavenly) Father. God shows himself to be Father by car-
ing for his creatures."[274] Again and again throughout the preaching of
Jesus, he speaks of God as Father. However, to conceive God as Father is
not without precedent in the Old Testament, and if Jesus' proclamation
could have been conceived as merely a continuation of this Old Testament
theme, it might have been an easy matter to connect the God to whom
Jesus referred as Father with the one God of Jewish monotheism and be
done with it. However, Jesus claimed an authority for his message such that
"God is to be understood only as the heavenly Father whom he declared
him to be,"[275] thus implying a unique relation between himself and God.
Even in light of these claims by Jesus, Pannenberg believes it was the resurrection of Jesus from the dead that "was seen as a divine confirmation
of the claim implied in his earthly ministry, Jesus in light of Easter had

---

273. For more detail on these points, see Pannenberg, "Christian Vision of God," 31–35.
274. Pannenberg, *Systematic Theology*, 1:259.
275. Ibid., 1:264.

to appear as the Son of the Father whom he proclaimed."[276] Pannenberg cites Rom 1:3–4 as the passage most clearly connecting the resurrection with the sonship of Christ and, consequently, with his deity.[277] In other words, if Jesus proclaimed, even if by implication, that God was the Father of Jesus as Son, and if the resurrection is seen as the divine confirmation of the proclamation of Jesus and of his deity, then Jesus had to be seen as having the unique relationship with the Father implied by Jesus' own preaching. In this way, the early church was faced with the quandary of trying to explain how it could take Jesus' proclamation seriously without deserting monotheism. Of course, the difficulties did not end there.

Throughout the period of the Arian controversy,[278] the primary focus of debate was upon the ontological status of Jesus Christ. Was he divine? Was he a creature? Was he more than human but less than God? At the same time, an examination of the various creeds produced during this period reveals that the question of the status or rank of the Holy Spirit was also becoming an important issue. Was the Holy Spirit a creature or something more? Once it became evident that Jesus was to be identified with the Eternal Son, which led to affirmation of the divinity of Christ, the tradition was faced with the fact that differentiation within the Godhead had been admitted. While the early church fathers were by no means anxious to expand membership within the Godhead, this development opened the way to take seriously the arguments that were advanced in favor of the divinity of the Holy Spirit. In fact, Basil the Great provided a set of arguments aimed at showing that the Holy Spirit was to be ranked with the Father and the Son.[279] Not the least persuasive of these was the fact that the three—Father, Son, and Holy Spirit—are frequently ranked together in the Scriptures. That the triple invocation at baptism was commanded by Jesus was particularly significant, and Basil argued that it would not be appropriate for deity and creature to be grouped together in this way. Thus, all three must be members of the Godhead. In the overwhelming majority of the arguments advanced for the divinity of both the Son and the Spirit, the appeal was to the biblical record of the revelation in Christ.

---

276. Ibid.

277. At this point we must recognize a distinction between two separate issues that Pannenberg identifies with regard to his treatment of the Scriptures. As we have seen in chapter 2, Pannenberg argues that one cannot take the truthfulness of the Scriptures for granted but rather must demonstrate their truthfulness. Yet in this chapter, in particular, he frequently cites the Scriptures as warrant for the positions he takes. This seems to stand somewhat in tension with what was observed earlier. However, as regards the contents of the Christian faith, Pannenberg holds that the Scriptures are normative in that they define what constitutes the faith. Consequently, he can cite passages in the context of presenting the content of the faith. The second question becomes, then, given that the Christian faith is thus-and-so, how do we know that thus-and-so is true?

278. For excellent detail concerning the issues and characters involved in the controversy, see R. P. C. Hanson, *The Search for the Christian Doctrine of God* (Edinburgh: T&T Clark, 1988).

279. See Basil, *On The Holy Spirit* (Crestwood, NY: St. Vladimir's Seminary Press, 1980).

As we have seen, it was the resurrection of Jesus that served as the divine confirmation of the message of the pre-Easter Jesus and of his divinity. In assessing the evidence for the divinity of the Spirit, Pannenberg comments that within the Scriptures "the Spirit of God is either presupposed or expressly named as the medium of the communion of Jesus with the Father and the mediator of the participation of believers in Christ."[280] The latter point in particular is also raised by Basil: To affirm that the Holy Spirit mediates divinity implies the divinity of the Holy Spirit. Pannenberg summarizes the point by saying that "all sonship, then, rests on the working of the Spirit."[281] Later Pannenberg argues that in the act of raising the Son, the Spirit plays the primary role.[282] Pannenberg draws the implications for the Trinitarian doctrine: "The involvement of the Spirit in God's presence in the work of Jesus and in the fellowship of the Son with the Father is the basis of the fact that the Christian understanding of God found its developed and definitive form in the doctrine of the Trinity and not in a biunity of the Father and the Son."[283] By the time the divinity of the Holy Spirit was affirmed, the difficulty was not simply in showing how the biblical witness of two distinctions within the Godhead was to be reconciled with the affirmation of the one God of monotheism; rather, it now had to deal with the question of how these three distinct "somethings" could be one God. Adding to the difficulty, while one might argue that the deity of Father, Son, and Holy Spirit is a reasonable inference from Scripture, there is no clearly expressed statement of the relations between the three or how the three are to be conceived as one God. Already we see the sorts of problems one is likely to face in articulating a doctrine of God that affirms God's triune nature. On the one hand, those who emphasize real distinctions between the three members of the Trinity will have to show how they have avoided lapsing into polytheism. On the other hand, those who emphasize the "oneness" of the triune God will have to show how they have avoided collapsing the three, thus denying concrete distinctions within the one God.

Excursus: Personhood

The term "person" came to be the standard means of identifying the bearers of the distinctions within the divine life. At this point we must make a brief excursus to develop an understanding of the manner in which Pannenberg intends and deploys the term. First, Pannenberg understands personhood to be a relational concept; it requires interaction with another.

---

280. Pannenberg, *Systematic Theology*, 1:266.
281. Ibid.
282. Ibid., 1:315.
283. Ibid., 1:268.

This means that the doctrine of the Trinity is what makes it possible to understand God as personal without the creation of the world, since the relationality essential to personhood is present in the interrelations of the three Trinitarian persons. If the unity of God, Pannenberg argues, could not be conceived as differentiated in some sense, then either God would be impersonal or the world would be necessary for God's becoming personal.

In the modern period, however, the concept of person came to be understood primarily in terms of autonomy and individuality.[284] One can trace the so-called classical definition of personhood back to the sixth-century work of Boethius, who understood "self-consciousness as the constitutive element of personhood" rather than relationality. This conception Pannenberg refers to as the "absolute" concept of personhood, and he makes the distinction between it and the relational conception as follows: "the 'absolute' concept of person, which is limited to the individual that exists for itself, and the 'relational' concept, which looks rather to the conditioning of the ego by the Thou and by society."[285] While Pannenberg holds relationality to be of critical importance, he does not reject this "absolute" concept but rather attempts to overcome the apparent opposition between the two.

Important for our discussion is the distinction made between the "I" and the "self" in psychoanalytic theory. As Wood writes, "The 'self' represents the substance of what a person is, its true potentiality to be what it can be. The 'I' represents the agency of the self; it is the mere subject who acts." These two elements, when properly integrated, constitute the two primary ingredients of one's self-consciousness. In this, we see Pannenberg's affirmation of the "absolute" concept of person. However, these elements arise only in the course of interaction with the community of others with whom one shares society, and, of course, this represents the relational element of self-identity/personhood. At this point, it is more my intent to identify Pannenberg's conception of personhood rather than critically examine it in great detail. We have recognized the importance of the concepts of both relationality and self-consciousness in Pannenberg's conception of personhood, and with this briefest of outlines behind us, we return to Pannenberg's unfolding argument concerning the manner in which the Trinitarian doctrine has been derived within the tradition.

The early church's unfolding understanding of the triune nature of God arose predominantly as a consequence of the manner in which God seemed revealed in the life of Christ. The first question, then, that had to be

---

284. In what follows, unless noted otherwise, I am indebted to an unpublished paper by Laurence Wood entitled "Pannenberg's Concept of 'Person.'"

285. W. Pannenberg, *Anthropology in Theological Perspective* (trans. M. J. O'Connell; Edinburgh: T&T Clark, 1985), 236.

answered was how the *unity* of this "three-personed" God was to be understood. Pannenberg observes that the early church's affirmation of the "biblical confession of the unity of God accompanied the development of Christian statements about the deity of the Son and the Spirit."[286] In other words, as the early theologians dealt with the claim that both the Son and Spirit shared the divine essence, they attempted to preserve the oneness of God (thus maintaining consistency with Christianity's monotheistic roots) without dissolving the distinctions of the persons. Pannenberg observes that these attempts generally developed in one of two ways. On the one hand, the deity of the Son and Spirit was seen as derived from the Father, who was conceived as the source or "fount" of deity.[287] On the other hand, the Son and Spirit were viewed as different expressions of the self-consciousness of the Father.[288] Pannenberg's analysis aims to determine whether either provides an adequate defense of both the unity and the differentiation implied in the doctrine of the Trinity.

Son and Spirit Derived from the Father as Fount

Pannenberg analyzes certain aspects of the theology of the Cappadocian fathers to demonstrate the problems he sees with deriving the deity of the Son and Spirit from the Father as the fount of deity. They claimed that the inner-Trinitarian relations were definitive for the distinctions between Father, Son, and Holy Spirit. However, their concept of relations focused upon *relations of origin*, so that the Father was seen as "the source and principle of deity" from which the Son and Spirit derivatively receive their deity.[289] Relations of origin, however, run only one way. The Son and Spirit are God only derivatively, and the Father, since he is conceived as the fount of the deity of Son and Spirit, is inevitably "God in the fullest sense," since he needs nothing outside of himself for his deity.[290] One must ask, however, whether this can establish a true equality of deity among the three persons. Are not causes always ontologically superior to their effects? Pannenberg points out that the Arians had used this very argument in their attempt to deny the divinity of the Son and Spirit. The Son and Spirit could not be fully God since they were generated by the Father, who was the one not generated, or ingenerate.[291] Consequently, we see how the one-way relations of origin immediately suggest the ontological subordination of the

---

286. Pannenberg, *Systematic Theology*, 1:274.

287. As, for example, in the theologies of the Cappodocian fathers.

288. See Olson, "Wolfhart Pannenberg's Doctrine of the Trinity," 180ff., for more details. This line of thinking is generally traced back to the psychological analogies of Augustine, which I shall address in due course.

289. Pannenberg, *Systematic Theology*, 1:279.

290. Ibid., 1:289.

291. See, for example, Hanson, *Search for the Christian Doctrine of God*, 202–7.

Son and Spirit to the Father. Even if one could argue that the distinctiveness of the persons could be maintained in this fashion, it seems clear that the equal divinity of the three is, at best, compromised.

Pannenberg does not object to using the concept of the inner-Trinitarian relations to define the distinctions between Father, Son, and Spirit. Rather, the problem is concerning the relations as one-way. In fact, one infers from Pannenberg's presentation that he thinks the Cappadocians would have done better to retain Athanasius's insight concerning "the logic of the relation that is posited when we call God 'Father.'"[292] This would have encouraged a move in the direction of a mutual relation. According to Athanasius, the Father could not be Father without the Son. Consequently, the Father would be dependent upon the Son for his deity in that being Father is essential to the Father's deity. Pannenberg believes that a proper understanding of the distinctiveness of the persons, an understanding that maintains their ontological equality, must be based upon reciprocal relations, a concept that is essential to Pannenberg's Trinitarian doctrine.

Continuing his analysis of Cappadocian theology, Pannenberg moves from examination of relations of origin aimed at establishing the distinctions within the Trinity to his consideration of the manner in which the Cappadocian fathers attempted to articulate the unity of the persons. In *On Not Three Gods*, Gregory of Nyssa argued that the unity of the Godhead refers to the unity of their operations. In fact, he argued that the term "Godhead" "is not significant of nature but of operation."[293] While it is true that distinction is made between humans who engage in the same operation (for example, we speak of three philosophers or three lawyers), there is a unity of operation, according to Gregory, among the persons of the Trinity that is very different from that among humans. This, he believed, opened space for affirming the unity of the three persons. Gregory, using the inner-Trinitarian relations for establishing distinctions, did not need to be overly concerned with the fact that prior to the fourth century the identification of the differing spheres of operation had been used to establish those inner-Trinitarian distinctions. He was, of course, now reversing this by attempting to ground the unity of God in their unity of operations. However, as Pannenberg observes, "the idea of a collective cooperation of ontologically independent beings is not, then, ruled out, so that the charge of tritheism cannot be dismissed in this manner."[294] Pannenberg concludes that attempts to derive the three persons from relations of origin or to derive the unity of the essence from the Trinitarian operations inevitably lead to these sorts of problems.

---

292. Ibid., 278.

293. Gregory of Nyssa, *On Not Three Gods* (Nicene and Post-Nicene Fathers, series 2, vol. 5; ed. Philip Schaff; Albany, NY: AGES Software, 1996–1997), 334.

294. Pannenberg, *Systematic Theology*, 1:278–79.

Son and Spirit Derived from
the Father's Self-Consciousness

The second approach for deriving the Trinitarian distinctions does so by deriving the three persons from the self-consciousness of the Father. Pannenberg traces this approach back to the "psychological analogies" expressed by Augustine in *The Trinity*, though as we shall see, it made a later appearance in the work of Hegel. It is interesting that Augustine did not intend the psychological analogies for deriving the Trinitarian distinctions; rather, he intended them more as aids for understanding how the disparate notions of plurality and unity might be related. Perhaps the main issue for Augustine was to show the reasonableness of the Christian faith— here, particularly, the doctrine of the Trinity. By showing that there are cases in which we readily think of something as three in one sense while thinking of it as one in another, and by showing that these sorts of "trinities" exist in our everyday experience of life, Augustine hoped to show that grasp of the doctrine of the Trinity is not as foreign to us as it might initially seem. However, Pannenberg explains that these analogies "also figure in the development of what later became the normative structure of the doctrine of God to the extent that the doctrine of the unity precedes the treatment of the Trinity."[295] This captures Pannenberg's primary concern: Can one adequately develop the doctrine of the Trinity if one begins with the unity of the divine essence?

Augustine intended to treat the triune nature of God as a pure, impenetrable mystery of faith. Interestingly, he found support for this in the Cappadocian idea that the unity of the Trinity was to be found in the unity of the divine actions.[296] If the actions of the triune God are such that they appear to be the act of a single subject, then all attempts to get at the distinctions on the basis of the actions are ruled out from the beginning. I have already remarked that tritheism cannot be ruled out on the grounds of positing the unity of action on the part of the Trinitarian persons. Now an additional problem arises: If no distinctions are evident in their works, so that the acts appear to be those of a single subject, could they not be the acts of a single divine subject who simply appears in different modes? As a consequence, efforts at deriving the real existence of the Trinitarian persons from the unity of the essence seem to invite modalism. The reality of this problem, specifically with regard to Augustine's analogies, was not a late discovery, for as Pannenberg observes, as early as the twelfth century, Gilbert de la Porree "rejected as Sabellianism the attempt to derive the

---

295. Ibid., 1:282.
296. Ibid., 1:283.

Trinity from the unity with the help of Augustine's psychological analogies."[297] Gilbert's objection did not apply directly to Augustine's work, since he intended them merely as ways "to illustrate the Trinity in whom one already believes,"[298] but rather to the misapplication of the analogies.

Aside from the psychological analogies, there were other attempts to derive the Trinitarian persons from the unity of the one God. One, toward which Pannenberg is somewhat sympathetic, appeals to the concept of love. For example, Richard of St. Victor argued along the lines that "love defined as *caritas* has to be love of another. . . . Hence it demands a plurality of persons."[299] Further, Richard argued that the only worthy "other" to whom the love of God may be directed must also be divine. In this way, Richard believed that he had demonstrated the need for a plurality of divine persons within the one Godhead that is characterized by *caritas*. One of the advantages of such a derivation, says Pannenberg, is that the notion of love "truly leads to the idea of personal encounter."[300] Another advantage of deriving a plurality of persons from the concept of love is that the expression of unselfish love requires three. Why? Because where only two are involved, the lover may hold selfishly and exclusively to the one loved, both in the sense of orienting all of one's love toward the beloved and in the sense of insisting the beloved give his or her love to no one else. When three are involved in mutual love, such selfishness is precluded. However, Pannenberg also has concerns with Richard's proposal. Are the persons constituted by love, or must they be presupposed? Are the second and third persons generated by the love of the first? If so, then we are back to a single divine subject who gives rise to the second and third; consequently, we return to an implicitly modalist position. The important thing for Pannenberg is that if the divine essence is to be conceived as love, it must be conceived as an aspect of the divine reality that is shared by all three persons and is not just the possession of the first person.[301]

Similar problems plagued Hegel's attempt to renew the doctrine of the Trinity. As a matter of fact, Pannenberg refers to Hegel's adoption and expansion of Lessing's attempt to ground the Trinity "in the concept of Spirit as an expression of the self-understanding of God in self-awareness" as the "classical form" of the "doctrine of the Trinity in terms of self-conscious Spirit."[302] Interestingly, Pannenberg takes the fact that the doctrine of the Trinity needed speculative revival as evidence that "the decay of

---

297. Ibid., 1:282 and 287.
298. Ibid., 1:287.
299. Ibid., 1:286.
300. Ibid.
301. Olson, "Wolfhart Pannenberg's Doctrine of the Trinity," 183.
302. Pannenberg, *Systematic Theology*, 1:292.

the doctrine of the Trinity in Protestant theology was an expression and consequence of inadequate linkage with the concept of the divine unity."[303] Of course, even Hegel's efforts failed to make the appropriate linkage, for, according to Pannenberg, Hegel's proposal involves a single divine subject whose self-expression takes on three forms. Later, says Pannenberg, Barth's attempt to reground the doctrine of the Trinity in the revelation of Christ fell short of its goal when he used the "formal concept of revelation as self-revelation" wherein Barth posited an object, a subject, and a revelation itself.[304] Once again, Pannenberg finds underlying Barth's proposal a single divine subject that precludes any real space for a plurality of persons.[305]

According to Pannenberg, all these attempts at explicating the Trinity, both those focusing upon relations of origin and those attempting to derive the Trinitarian persons from the concept of self-consciousness, fell short in a very fundamental way: They failed to forge adequately an "inner linkage"[306] between the Trinitarian statements about the three persons on the one hand and the unity of God on the other.[307] Pannenberg argues that in the sixteenth century, this led to a number of attacks from various quarters that challenged the supporting biblical exegesis and questioned the very reasonableness of the notion of a three-personed God.[308] Likewise, in the seventeenth and eighteenth centuries, many theologians focused their attention upon discovering the doctrine in revelation.[309] Olson comments that this gave the impression that the unity was rationally demonstrable while the Trinity was a matter of special revelation. He goes on to say, "From there it was a small step to the atrophy of the doctrine in Enlightenment religion and liberal Protestant theology."[310] Concluding his assessment of various attempts to derive the doctrine of the Trinity, interestingly in a section entitled "The Place of the Doctrine of the Trinity in the Dogmatic Structure and the Problem of Finding a Basis for Trinitarian Statements," Pannenberg writes: "Any derivation of the plurality of Trinitarian persons from the essence of the one God, whether it be viewed as spirit or love, leads into the problems of either modalism on the one hand or subordina-

---

303. Ibid.

304. Ibid., 1:296.

305. Of course, Barthian scholars might well object to Pannenberg's construal of Barth's Trinitarian theology. My point here, however, is to understand Pannenberg's arguments underlying his proposal for the appropriate grounding of the Trinitarian conception of God.

306. By using the phrase "inner linkage," I believe that Pannenberg is expressing his concern that the connection between the trinity and the unity of God must not appear as accidental, coincidental, or superfluous. An "inner linkage" would show the necessity of the relation between the Trinitarian persons and the unity of the one God.

307. Pannenberg points this out once on each of three consecutive pages of *Systematic Theology*, vol. 1: 290, 291, and 292.

308. See *Systematic Theology*, 1:290ff., for the details of Pannenberg's arguments.

309. Ibid., 1:291ff.

310. Olson, "Wolfhart Pannenberg's Doctrine of the Trinity," 183.

tionism on the other. Neither, then, can be true to the intentions of the trinitarian dogma."[311] If the Trinity cannot be derived from the presupposed unity of God, then how can it be derived? Pannenberg argues that we must begin with the revelation of Father, Son, and Holy Spirit in salvation history.

Pannenberg's Proposed Derivation of the Trinitarian Doctrine

Pannenberg writes that in order "to find a basis for the doctrine of the Trinity, we must begin with the way in which Father, Son, and Spirit come on the scene and relate to one another in the event of revelation,"[312] specifically, the revelation of God in Jesus Christ.[313] It is in this revelation, Pannenberg believes, that one is confronted with the three persons. Consequently, at the heart of Pannenberg's proposal for derivation of the Trinitarian doctrine is the reversal of the priority of the unity and the trinity of God so that the triune nature is primary.

Pannenberg is sympathetic to the position of the Reformation thinkers who argued that the doctrine of the Trinity had to be taken from the Scriptures rather than from speculative derivations. As a matter of fact, he writes that they "saw more clearly than many later theologians that as God reveals himself, so he is in his eternal deity."[314] The importance of the claim that God *is* as he is *revealed* ought not be underestimated. Consider Jesus' claim that "no one knows the Father except the Son and any one to whom the Son chooses to reveal him" (Matt 11:27). During the Last Supper, Jesus says to Philip that whoever has seen the Son has seen the Father (John 14:8–9). As we have already seen, the resurrection serves as the divine confirmation of the claims of Jesus during the course of his earthly ministry. Of course, the preceding quotations constitute two claims that express Jesus' revelatory work concerning the one whom Jesus called Father. If these claims of Jesus stand confirmed as a consequence of the resurrection, then it follows that the revelation of the Father, as contained in the message of Jesus, cannot be superseded and that God is in his eternal deity as he was revealed by the Son. The revelation in Christ cannot be superseded in light of the former claim, and the Father must be as he was revealed as a consequence of the latter. For these reasons, Pannenberg concludes that we must begin construction of the doctrine of the Trinity by examining the revelation of Christ.

---

311. Pannenberg, *Systematic Theology*, 1:298.
312. Ibid., 1:299.
313. This last phrase is from Pannenberg, *Systematic Theology*, vol. 1, chap. 5, section 3, subsection *a*, which reads, "The Revelation of God in Jesus Christ as the Starting Point, and the Traditional Terminology of the Doctrine of the Trinity."
314. Ibid., 1:300.

The Ultimacy of Christ's Revelation

Before proceeding, we need to examine the implications and origin of these claims. First, it was Karl Barth who argued that if the revelation of Jesus is to have ultimacy, in the sense noted above, then God in his eternity must be as he was revealed. Pannenberg expresses this as follows: "Karl Barth . . . argued that God in His eternal being must be conceived to be the same as He is in His historical revelation, since otherwise His revelation in Jesus Christ would not reveal Him like He is."[315] It was Karl Rahner who further developed this into the thesis that the immanent Trinity (God as he is in his eternal life) *is* the economic Trinity (God as revealed in salvation history).[316] The reason for Rahner's thesis was the concern that "the act of the incarnation cannot be considered to be something accidental in relation to the eternal life of God."[317] "Rahner's Rule," as it is now known, has implications for the present discussion, for if the economic "sendings" of the Son and Spirit into salvation history are representative of their inner-Trinitarian relations to the Father, then the biblical witness of salvation history gives us the means to affirm the inner-triune nature of God. If this is correct, "the concrete relation of Jesus to the Father must be the starting place for trinitarian reflection."[318]

There is some debate as to whether Rahner's Rule was intended by Rahner himself to be taken as far as Pannenberg and some of his contemporaries have done. Jenson raises this issue when he suggests that there is some question "whether, as Pannenberg says, Rahner did not succeed in drawing out the consequences of his own thesis, or Pannenberg and some others of us have adopted the verbal formula in a sense unintended by Rahner."[319] Jenson admits in a footnote to this quotation that he, Pannenberg, and others have "at *least* stretched it [Rahner's Rule] very far."[320] This would lead us to revisit the issue of the acceptability of the appropriation of Rahner's work by Pannenberg. However, at this point we are more concerned to understand the manner in which Pannenberg develops his position.

Even if we accept the primacy of the revelation in Christ for deriving the Trinitarian relations, there is an additional problem. As Pannenberg

---

315. Pannenberg, "Christian Vision of God," 29.

316. See, for example, K. Rahner, *The Trinity* (trans. J. Donceel; New York: Herd & Herd, 1970).

317. Pannenberg, "Christian Vision of God," 29.

318. Pannenberg, *Systematic Theology*, 1:307.

319. R. Jenson, "Jesus in the Trinity: Wolfhart Pannenberg's Christology and Doctrine of the Trinity," in Braaten and Clayton, *Theology of Wolfhart Pannenberg*, 197.

320. Ibid., 197 n. 23. In the balance of the citation, Jenson writes, "I must for honesty's sake record, however, that in my understanding Rahner intended *is* in his maxim analogically, so that our appropriations of it at *least* stretch it very far."

observes, there is no express formulation of the doctrine of the Trinity anywhere to be found "in the message of Jesus [or] the NT witnesses."[321] While the deity of the Son and the Spirit is, at least, suggested by the Scriptures, "it is not clear how the deity of the Son and Spirit relates to that of the Father."[322] Consequently, we must proceed with a systematic reconstruction of the doctrine from the biblical witness regarding the relations of the Son and the Spirit to the Father. This is the same path the Greek fathers took when they spoke of the Father as "origin" and "fount" of deity. Pannenberg affirms the appeal to revelation, though he holds that we must find a way to appropriate this revelation without slipping into either subordinationism or modalism.

Summary

In light of the historical problems reviewed by Pannenberg, his first revision to the traditional doctrine of God is a negative one: The Trinity cannot be derived from an abstract concept of the one God.[323] Second, Pannenberg is unwilling simply to dismiss the doctrine of the Trinity as a later Hellenization of Christianity. In fact, he argues that the Trinity will avoid being de-emphasized within the tradition only if it is essential to the explication of the one God, and he proposes to show that this is the case. Third, Pannenberg argues that the point of departure for derivation of the Trinitarian doctrine is the revelation of God in Jesus Christ, since as we have seen, if it truly reveals God, he is revealed as he is in his eternity. Finally, since the Scriptures contain no explicit Trinitarian formulation, the development of the doctrine must be by systematic reconstruction in light of explicit biblical references regarding the relations between the Father and the Son and the Spirit.

Pannenberg's Proposal for Conceptualizing the Inner-Trinitarian Relations

With the revelation in Christ as the point of departure, the next question is, what does that revelation demonstrate about the relations between the Father and the Son? Traditionally, passages such as John 1:18 and John 3:16 have been adduced. Obviously, the relation between Father and Son that one finds in these passages is "begottenness": The Father begets the Son. Thus, the Son is to be conceived as the one generated, and the Father as the one who generates but is himself ingenerate. However, as we have

---

321. Pannenberg, *Systematic Theology*, 1:301.
322. Ibid., 1:302.
323. The claim here is *not* that the form of derivation Pannenberg rejects is essential to the traditional view, but rather that, with notable exceptions, the tradition has generally proceeded in this manner.

seen, this one-way understanding of relations tends toward subordination of the Son to the Father, since the Son is conceived as dependent upon the Father, but the Father is conceived as having no such reciprocal dependence. In order to avoid ontological subordination, says Pannenberg, we have to be able to show that there is a mutuality of relations so that dependencies run in both directions. Hence, there are two questions: (1) Does the revelation in Christ provide grounds for other relations between Father and Son? (2) Are there grounds to support the mutual relations that Pannenberg proposes, so that not only is the Son dependent upon the Father for his deity, but the Father is also dependent upon the Son? In other words, can we reasonably conceive the relation between the Son and Father such that without the Son the Father could not be conceived as God? Of course, since the relation of begetting runs only in one direction, the sort of dependence that the Father has upon the Son—indeed, if such dependence is plausible—will be different.

The Principle of Self-Distinction

If we examine Jesus' language regarding the Father, we find that Jesus "distinguishes himself from God and sets himself as a creature below God as he asks his hearers to do."[324] Pannenberg points to the Johannine gospel wherein "Christ says that the Father is greater than he (14:28)" and wherein Jesus claims that the words he speaks are the Father's and not his own (14:24). In Mark, Jesus refuses to accept the title "Good Teacher" since only God is good.[325] Pannenberg gives yet other scriptural references, but the point is the same: Jesus—as opposed to the first Adam, who sought equality with God—differentiates himself from and submits himself to the Father. Here we must turn to a thesis from one of Pannenberg's earlier works: "Communion and unity with God increase in the same proportion as the modesty of the creature in distinguishing itself from God."[326] As Jesus differentiates himself from and submits himself to the Father, he fulfills the mission for which he was sent and, as a consequence, becomes "so at one with the Father that God in his eternity is Father only in relation to him."[327] Since God is Father only in relation to Jesus, "the Son shares [the Father's] deity as the eternal counterpart of the Father."[328] By Rahner's Rule,[329] this reflects an eternal, inner-Trinitarian relation between Father

---

324. W. Pannenberg, *Systematic Theology*, 1:309.
325. Ibid.
326. W. Pannenberg, *Christian Spirituality* (Philadelphia: Westminster, 1983), 82.
327. Pannenberg, *Systematic Theology*, 1:310.
328. Ibid.
329. See above, p. 144.

and Son. Of course, one must ask, what sort of oneness are we here affirming between the Father and the Son?

In order to grasp what Pannenberg intends, we must first recall the concept of person that he deploys, a concept that involves both relational and "absolute" elements. The "absolute" concept of person involves the unity of the "I" and the "self" within a given individual. In commenting on this understanding of person, Jenson remarks that it is the historical union of the "I" and the "self" that yields personal identity; however, the development of the unity of "I" and "self" does not occur in isolation but rather occurs in the interaction between individuals. In what way, then, can we speak of a oneness between Father and Son in light of this concept of person? Jenson summarizes:

> Given what a person is, it is clear that if one person's will were to be so directed to the will of another person as to be in "absolute practiced unity of will" with the other, achieved in "complete abandonment of self" to that other, *and* if that unity of will were confirmed by the other, this would amount to the reality of a personal being which is one for both persons, to a "personal union." In that the Father confirmed Jesus' self-abandonment to him, by raising him from the death in which it was actualized, Jesus and his Father are in this way one.[330]

In other words, when Jesus denies himself in order to be obedient to the call the Father places upon him and in so doing completely identifies himself with the will of the Father, then this unity of wills leads to the formation of the Son's "self" in complete submission to the Father. But this means that the Father and the Son would share a single personal being, to use Jenson's phrase. Then to speak of the oneness of the Father and the Son is to say that the Father and the Son share a personal being as a consequence of the self-abandonment of the Son in his submission to the Father and the corresponding acceptance of this self-abandonment by the Father. This, then, characterizes the unity of Son and Father.

When Jesus refuses to accept the title "good," and when he indicates that the work he is doing is the Father's, he demonstrates his self-distinctions from the Father. According to Pannenberg, it is precisely in this self-distinction and submission to the Father that Jesus is seen to be the Son of the Father. However, if in the act of self-distinction Jesus shows himself truly to be the Son, then the Father is to be understood only as the Father in relation to this Son. Pannenberg goes on to write that "this distin-

---

330. R. Jenson, "Jesus in the Trinity," 193.

guishes Jesus from all other human beings who follow his call or by his mediation share in his fellowship with the Father."[331] Pannenberg goes on to argue that this self-distinction of the Son from the Father is constitutive for the deity of the Son because in showing himself to be the Son, he shows that the Father is to be understood as Father *first and foremost in relation to him as Son.* Therefore, Jesus is seen to share in the deity of the Father by consequence of his being the Father's eternal correlate. The concept of self-distinction is central to Pannenberg's entire doctrine of the Trinity, for this is how he forges the mutual dependence and fully reciprocal relations that he believes are essential to avoiding subordination of the Son and the Spirit.

The Principle of Reciprocal Relations

From this discussion, we can already see a degree of mutuality in inner-Trinitarian relations, since the Father is only Father in relation to the Son. However, Pannenberg proceeds to examine whether a similar notion of self-distinction from the Son on the Father's side might apply. The Scriptures speak of the Father's handing over the kingdom to the Son.[332] In sending the Son into salvation history with his specific mission, the Father hands all authority over to the Son, who must execute that authority until he brings everything under his reign.[333] Then the Son hands back the kingdom to the Father and finally subjects himself to the Father's rule so "that God may be all in all."[334] Here, then, is a true mutuality of relations. The Father, by virtue of handing over the kingdom to the Son, makes himself dependent upon the Son for his own deity. Specifically, if the Son does not subject all things and hand the kingdom back over to the Father, it is hard to see how the Father could still be considered God.[335]

To some, this will no doubt sound odd initially. If God exists, how can his deity be called into question? However, we must remember Pannenberg's observation in the preceding chapter: While God need not create, once he does it would contradict his deity if he did not exercise lordship over creation. So if the Father's lordship over the world depends upon the Son's accomplishing his mission, then if the Son were to fail, the deity of the Father would be disproved. We need not consider whether it is possible

---

331. Pannenberg, *Systematic Theology*, 1:310.

332. Ibid., 1:312.

333. Consider, for example, Matt 9:1–8, where Jesus speaks of his authority to forgive sin.

334. Pannenberg, *Systematic Theology*, 1:312.

335. Some might argue that if the Father and Son are, in fact, God, their missions cannot fail. Consequently, one might continue, God's deity is never really challenged. But this misses Pannenberg's point. It is only as God's deity is worked out in the course of history that the hypothetical nature of claims concerning God's deity is demonstrated to be true.

that the Son should fail, for if he is God, he cannot. However, the point is that by depending upon the Son to accomplish his mission, the Father makes his deity dependent upon the Son. According to Pannenberg, this establishes a mutuality of relations that extends beyond mere one-way relations of origin. Hence, the Father's identity depends on the Son for deity, though not in exactly the same way as the Son's depends on the Father. Further, if we accept Rahner's Rule, the relation evident from the economic sending of the Son is definitive of an inner-Trinitarian relationship between the Father and the Son. Thus, there is in fact a mutual dependency between Father and Son for the deity of each.

With self-distinction as the principle for deriving reciprocal inner-Trinitarian relations, one must now ask how the concept relates to the deity of the Spirit. Pannenberg summarizes the Johannine record and its claims regarding the Spirit: "Precisely by not speaking of himself (John 16:23) but bearing witness of Jesus (15:26) and reminding us of his teaching (14:26), he shows himself to be the Spirit of truth."[336] The Spirit distinguishes himself from the Father and the Son, showing himself to be separate from both; by glorifying the Son and in him the Father, the Spirit shows himself to be one with the Father and the Son. Consequently, even though the reality of the Spirit's self-distinction and self-subjection is different than for the Son, it is still in this way that the Spirit shows himself to be distinct from the other two and yet one with them. By being one with them, he participates in the same divine essence and thus receives his deity.

To have a truly reciprocal relationship, the Father and the Son must also be dependent upon the Spirit for their deity. As the Spirit is the "condition and the medium of [the] fellowship [of the Father and Son]," the imparting of the Spirit brings believers into their fellowship.[337] Consequently, the Spirit participates in the realization of the kingdom among humans, and thus we see one way in which the rule/deity of the Father (and thus the Son) is dependent upon the Spirit. Of course, these discussions harken back to the connections between God's deity and his rule made in chapter 4. If, as Pannenberg claims, God's deity is his rule, then we can understand how these mutually reciprocal relations relate to the deity of the Trinitarian persons. To be more precise, the individual persons work together to realize the rule of the Father and thus to realize the Father's deity. Similarly, by participating in actions that actualize the reign of God, the Son and Spirit participate in the deity of the Godhead.

Pannenberg suggests that perhaps the best example of the mutual dependency of the Trinitarian persons is demonstrated in the crucifixion

---

336. Pannenberg, *Systematic Theology*, 1:315.
337. Ibid., 1:316; see also 281.

and resurrection of Jesus. At the crucifixion, asserts Pannenberg, the deity of all three members of the Trinity is brought into question. Pannenberg holds, citing Rom 1:4, that it is only by virtue of Jesus being raised from the dead that he is shown to be the Son. In fact, Pannenberg goes on to assert that should Jesus not have been raised, it would have been shown that he was not the Son. Further, if the Son had not been raised, he would not be able to subject all things and hand the kingdom back over to the Father, thus calling into question the deity of the Father. If the Spirit had not raised the Son, the Spirit's status as the giver of life would have been likewise questioned. Hence, in the events involved with the resurrection of Jesus, the deity of all Trinitarian members is challenged. Pannenberg claims that "decisive significance attaches, however, to the work of the Spirit as the creative origin of all life."[338] By recognizing the special significance of the work of the Spirit, we further amplify the dependence of the others upon the Spirit for their deity, since here it is secured by the Spirit's raising of Jesus.

Undoubtedly, many may find this line of argumentation puzzling. After all, how can the deity of God be seriously challenged? For example, if Jesus had not been raised, could we not merely say that God did not raise him, without any implications for the deity of either? However, one might ask in response, how could Jesus be divine if death defeats him? Further, if the Son is sent into salvation history to accomplish a particular task, would not his divinity be brought into question if he were to fail to accomplish the task, whatever it might have been? One might also challenge Pannenberg's argument by saying that this is all very interesting, but in reality no member of the Godhead can fail. However, Pannenberg's point is precisely that even though he need not have created, by creating a world, God, in a sense, stakes his deity on the outcome of the world. If God is God, he will prove his deity by successfully exercising lordship over the world of creatures. If he should not be successful, then this God could not have been God after all.

Pannenberg summarizes this argument by commenting that one may affirm the relations between the Father on the one hand and the Son and the Spirit on the other as relations of origin (the Son is begotten, the Spirit proceeds), but that seeing them *exclusively* as such leads to the problem of subordinationism. However, he continues, if the relations between the persons are such that they are fully reciprocal so that each is dependent on the others for his deity, ontological subordinationism is overcome. Similarly, the notion of self-distinction leads us beyond modalism, for we clearly have three persons and not merely one subject who

---

338. Ibid., 1:315.

simply appears in different modes. Hence, Pannenberg writes, "if the trinitarian relations among Father, Son, and Spirit have the form of mutual self-distinction, they must be understood not merely as different modes of being of the one divine subject but as living realizations of separate centers of action."[339]

The Unity of the Divine Essence

Once the threats of modalism and subordinationism are behind, the threat of tritheism returns. Consequently, we must now turn our attention to Pannenberg's demonstration that the three persons are only one God and that the "doctrine of the Trinity is in fact concrete monotheism."[340] Our discussion of the unity of the divine essence requires examination of four issues: (1) the relationship between the concepts of substance and accidents, (2) the importance of the monarchy of the Father, (3) the precise nature of the divine essence, and (4) the relationship between the economic Trinity and immanent Trinity.

The Implications of Substance/Accidents Metaphysics

In Aristotelian categories, relations were conceived as accidents that belonged to a substance that was ontologically prior. Implicit in the discussion so far is Pannenberg's reversal of this ordering so that substance is seen as subordinated to the category of relation. Rather than accidents conceived as attaching contingently to some prior substance, relations are conceived as constitutive for what a given thing is. As Ted Peters observes, "Now the concept of substance is subordinated to the idea of relation. The substance-accident relation now appears as a subspecies of the category of relation."[341] In agreement with Hegel, Pannenberg holds that a fundamental element of the logical structure of substance is its relatedness to another. So the divine essence must be defined relationally and not merely as an abstract "thing" lying behind the relations. To repeat, the relations are constitutive for the essence. Pannenberg argues as well that the relations are constitutive for the distinct persons. So the relationships between Father, Son, and Holy Spirit are also constitutive for their deity; they are each only God as they are related to each other in the divine life, which is mirrored in the Trinity as revealed in salvation history.[342]

---

339. Ibid., 1:319.
340. Ibid., 1:335.
341. T. Peters, "Trinity Talk," *Dialog* 26, no. 2 (1987): 136.
342. Pannenberg, *Systematic Theology*, 1:319–25.

The Monarchy of the Father

Given developments so far, Pannenberg must reject any notion of the monarchy of the Father that results in ontological subordination of the Son and/or Spirit. However, this does not mean rejection of the monarchy of the Father per se. As a matter of fact, Pannenberg argues that it is precisely the *self-subordination* of the Son and the Spirit in their acts of self-distinction that supports the monarchy of the Father without ontological subordination. We must combine this insight with that mentioned above regarding the constitutive nature of the relations. Is the monarchy of the Father threatened by the mutual dependence implied by the relations? Not at all, says Pannenberg. In fact, it means that the monarchy of the Father is mediated to him through the Son and the Spirit. As Pannenberg writes, "By their work the Son and the Spirit serve the monarchy of the Father. Yet the Father does not have his kingdom or monarchy without the Son and Spirit, but only through them."[343] The mutual goal (if we might speak in these terms) of the Trinitarian persons is the establishment of the monarchy of the Father over all creation. However, the Father's monarchy does not have logical precedence with regard to the Son and the Spirit, for this would lead us toward ontological subordination. Instead, the monarchy of the Father is the result of the "common operation of the three persons" and is, thus, "the seal of their unity."[344]

The Nature of the Divine Essence

The proposal Pannenberg advances to secure the unity of the Trinitarian persons relates to the precise nature (to the extent we can know it) of the divine nature. We know that it is constituted relationally and that it takes outward expression in the mutual cooperation of the three persons for whom the monarchy of the Father is a common goal. The question at this point is whether we can say more about the nature of the divine essence. The reversal of the ordering of the categories "substance" and "relation" allows one to overcome thinking of the divine essence as standing separated from relations. The older metaphysics that understood substance or essence as transcendent of relations led to a separation between the inner-Trinitarian relations and the divine attributes that God has in relation to the creation and the divine attributes that describe God's essence, the so-called omni-attributes.[345] However, with the ordering reversed, we can now think of essence as primarily constituted by relations, or as Pannenberg

---

343. Ibid., 1:324.
344. Ibid., 1:325.
345. See Jenson, "Jesus in the Trinity," 204

claims, "being" is most fundamentally a relational concept.[346] Also, we can now rethink the attributes in terms of their constitutive relations.

Pannenberg argues that the omni-attributes all "relate back to the concept of infinity."[347] He appropriates the Hegelian concept of the true infinite as that which overcomes the distinction between finite and infinite, becoming both transcendent to the finite as well as immanent to it. How might we describe a relation that has characteristics that correspond to the metaphysical concept of the infinite? Jenson writes that the "word for such a relation, where it is concretely realized . . . [is] 'love.'"[348] Consider the concept of the true infinite, which, by incorporating both transcendent and immanent elements, both allows the other to exist independently and yet invests its own being in the other. While it may not seem intuitive to think of the concretization of the true infinite as love, does it not seem reasonable to so conceive relationships characterized by the nature of the metaphysical infinite? To respect the distinct being of the other while investing ourselves in that other is consistent with the fundamental nature of engaging another in love. It is interesting that Gregory's argument for the infinity of the divine is based upon the idea of absolute perfection, which carries with it the idea of the Good. Surely, the notion of love is implied by such concepts. Pannenberg summarizes these points when he writes that "the phrase 'God is love' represents the concretization of the abstract structure of the concept of infinity."[349]

Finally, Pannenberg claims that love is not simply one divine attribute among others, but "according to 1 John 4:8, 16 love as the power that manifests itself in the mutual relations of the trinitarian persons is identical with the divine essence."[350] In other words, it is not simply that God, as a divine subject, has love so that he might then generate the others from himself; the very divine essence itself is love. The relations that have been discussed are all expressions of mutual love. Consequently, the claim "God is love" captures the fullness of the Trinitarian fellowship, and as Jenson summarizes, "the inner-triune fellowship *is* the one divine essence."[351] Further, if there is only one divine essence ("the relationally-structured love which unifies without obliterating distinctions"[352]), then there is only one God who, nonetheless, is concretely realized in three distinct persons: Father, Son, and Holy Spirit. Consequently, Pannenberg writes, "the doctrine of

---

346. W. Pannenberg, "Problems of a Trinitarian Concept of God," *Dialog* 26, no. 2 (1987): 254–56.
347. Pannenberg, "Problems," 256; quoted in Jenson, "Jesus in the Trinity," 204.
348. Ibid., 205.
349. Pannenberg, "Problems," 256.
350. Pannenberg, *Systematic Theology*, 1:427.
351. Jenson, "Jesus in the Trinity," 205.
352. Olson, "Wolfhart Pannenberg's Doctrine of the Trinity," 195.

the Trinity is in fact concrete monotheism in contrast to notions of an abstract transcendence of the one God and abstract notions of a divine unity that leave no place for plurality; so that the one God is in fact a mere correlate of the present world and the plurality of the finite."[353] In this fashion, Pannenberg believes that he has forged a doctrine of the Trinity that has the resources to overcome subordinationism and modalism on the one hand and tritheism on the other.

The Unity of the Economic Trinity and the Immanent Trinity

One additional aspect of Pannenberg's Trinitarian doctrine is the unity of the immanent and economic Trinities. We have already examined Rahner's Rule, which argues that the immanent Trinity *is* the economic Trinity, but I omitted critical analysis of the thesis itself as well as Pannenberg's deployment of it. At this juncture, we must return to the manner in which Pannenberg employs the principle to arrive at an understanding of the relation between the immanent and economic Trinities. Pannenberg is sympathetic to the concern of Kasper,[354] who pointed out that we must not let the equation of the immanent and economic Trinities result in the absorption of the immanent into the economic Trinity so that salvation history is necessary for God's eternal self-identity.[355] At the same time, of course, the strength of Rahner's proposal, if correct, is that it does away with the apparent independence of the economic and immanent Trinities that arose when early philosophical theology, guided by Hellenistic conceptions, viewed the divine essence as "untouched by the course of history on account of the eternity and immutability of God."[356] So an adequate Trinitarian conception of God must avoid either seeing salvation history as necessary to the divine essence on the one hand or conceiving the divine essence as being totally unaffected by salvation history on the other.

Consider the following points from previous discussions: (1) Pannenberg's claim that God's deity is his rule and (2) the observation that it would be a contradiction of God's deity to think a world could exist over which he does not exercise lordship. Pannenberg puts these two closely related notions together:

> Even in his deity, by the creation of the world and the sending of his Son and Spirit to work in it, he has made himself dependent upon the course of history. This results from the dependence of the trinitarian persons upon one

---

353. Pannenberg, *Systematic Theology*, 1:335–36.
354. Ibid., 1:330–31.
355. Ibid. See also Olson, "Wolfhart Pannenberg's Doctrine of the Trinity," 198–99.
356. Pannenberg, *Systematic Theology*, 1:332.

another as the kingdom is handed over and handed back in connection with the economy of salvation and the intervention of the Son and Spirit in the world and its history.[357]

Recall that Rahner's thesis regarding the identity of the economic and immanent Trinities was first worked out with regard to the incarnation of the Son. Specifically, the incarnation was not simply a mission appropriated to one of the Trinitarian persons who just happened to be the Son; instead, it was the salvation-history expression of an inner-Trinitarian relation among Son, Father, and Spirit such that should an incarnation be appropriate during the course of history, it was the Son who would become incarnate. Also, we have already seen that the crucifixion called into question the deity of all three persons of the Trinity. But if the immanent Trinity is the economic Trinity, it was in fact the immanent Trinity that was called into question in the events surrounding the crucifixion. Taking the next step, given that once God has created a world, his deity is only consistent with his ruling it, and given that his kingdom is not yet fully present in the world, Rahner's Rule suggests that "the immanent Trinity itself, the deity of the trinitarian God, is at issue in the events of history."[358] If Rahner's thesis is correct, it seems it must be taken at least this far.

To reiterate, the danger is that the immanent Trinity becomes so closely linked with the world's history that the economy of salvation becomes the means by which God develops into that which he is to be. This suggests that priority has to be given to the immanent Trinity so that God is who he is from "eternity to eternity." The question, of course, is how to reconcile the notion of eternal self-identity with the claim that God's deity is dependent, in some sense, upon the course of history. At this point Pannenberg deploys one of the claims examined in the previous chapter: the ontological priority of the future. Recall that the eschatological future (epistemically at least and ontologically according to Pannenberg) is the point where our sequentially experienced time and the undivided wholeness of the divine eternity correspond. However, at the eschaton we will see that God is who he has been all along. During the course of human history, from the perspective of the sequentially ordered experience of time, things such as the deity of God remain up in the air. Of course, if God does exist, once we experience his definitive appearance, it will be evident that he is who he was all along. This is why the immanent Trinity has priority in some sense, so that "the eschatological consummation is the only locus of the decision that the trinitarian God is always the true God from eternity to eternity."[359]

---

357. Ibid., 1:329.
358. Ibid., 1:330.
359. Ibid., 1:331.

Does this simply mean that our knowledge of God is made accurate by the coming of the kingdom, so that the apparent "dependence" of God upon the course of history is merely an epistemological matter? Pannenberg would answer this with a no. When a future state of affairs is necessary for a given thing or event to have its essence/meaning, the change resulting as a consequence of that future state of affairs is not epistemological but is truly constitutive for the essence of the thing or event. So if God's kingdom comes, then it will finally be decided, for all eternity, that God is. If the kingdom does not come, then God's deity is refuted, also with eternal implications. In Pannenberg's view, it is simply that the eschaton is "the locus of that decision." That this is Pannenberg's intent is clear from his comparison of the retroactive power of the eschatological consummation for God's deity with the retroactive power of the resurrection for the identity of Jesus as the Son. In summary, then, it is ultimately the ontological priority of the future that allows Pannenberg to conceive the relationship between the immanent Trinity and the economic Trinity such that God's existence in the world today is debatable, while at the same time maintaining the eternal self-identity of God so that the history of the world is not finally necessary for God's becoming who he is. In the end (quite literally), God will be shown to have been God all along.

The Application of the Concept of Infinity in the Doctrine of the Trinity

The fundamental requirement that the philosophical notion of the infinite imposes upon the doctrine of God is the requirement that God be conceived in such a way as to support the seemingly disparate notions of transcendence and immanence. Pannenberg has argued that a single, transcendent divine subject cannot be adequate for this reason. One must conceive the one God as differentiated in some way if the notions of transcendence and immanence are to be actual and not merely abstract. Pannenberg provides examples of the manner in which the doctrine of the Trinity manifests the true infinite. In a discussion of God's omnipresence and omnipotence, Pannenberg makes the connections explicit: "The doctrine of the Trinity made it possible so to link the transcendence of the Father in heaven with his presence in believers through the Son and Spirit that in virtue of the consubstantiality and perichoresis of the three persons the Father . . . could be viewed as present and close to believers through the Son and Spirit."[360] Now the pieces of Pannenberg's understanding of the relation of the Trinity to the concrete instantiation of the true infinite fall into place. The Father is tran-

---

360. Ibid., 1:415.

scendent, but the Son and Spirit, by being sent into the world, are present with the creatures in all their places. However, as a consequence of the unity of the divine essence, which means that we can truly say that there is only one God, we can affirm that the Father is also present with his creatures through the Son and the Spirit and, thus, that this one God is both transcendent to and immanent within the world. It only remains to make the connections explicit in the various omni-attributes.

As regards the divine omnipotence, Pannenberg argues that conceptions that merely see the divine power in opposition to all other powers is onesidedly transcendent. A proper account of God's omnipotence recognizes that the divine power also is present within and alongside the creatures, for example, in the act of self-distinction wherein the Son becomes a creature in order to rescue the creatures from their fall into nothingness resulting from their assertion of independence from God.[361] With regard to the divine eternity, it is again the incarnation of the Son that "sets aside the antithesis of eternity and time" so that the kingdom of the Father may be present through the appearing of the Son.[362] Finally, Pannenberg observes that the positive relation between the infinite and the finite as required by the philosophical concept of the true infinite, which appears insoluble in its logical form without loss of distinction between the two, is finally soluble with the Trinitarian conception of God. At this point, Pannenberg believes that he has shown the coherence of the reversal he proposed at the outset: To construct a coherent and adequate doctrine of the one God, the doctrine of the Trinity must be foundational to the whole concept of God. Only a Trinitarian conception of God, says Pannenberg, can do justice both to the regulative philosophical concepts and to the revelation in Christ. Further, he believes that the implications of a Trinitarian conception of God provide the resources for dealing with the attributes relating to the divine infinity. In light of these arguments, it becomes clear that the doctrine of the Trinity, which is the concrete expression of the metaphysical infinite, resides at the very center of Pannenberg's doctrine of God.[363]

---

361. Ibid., 1:420.

362. Ibid., 1:445–46.

363. Before we proceed directly to the assessment of certain issues that have arisen in the course of this chapter, it is appropriate to expand upon the discussion from chapter 2 concerning the nature of Pannenberg's method, particularly as it relates to his style of argumentation. I have argued that the two primary elements of Pannenberg's theory of truth are correspondence (propositions must correspond to the state of affairs they claim to be about) and coherence (sets of propositions must not violate the law of noncontradiction). Many individuals tend to argue in what may be rather loosely called a "foundationalist" fashion. By this, I mean that one proceeds from propositions that may be conceived as properly basic (leaving open the question of what constitutes a properly basic belief) to those that are supported (also left undefined here) by those basic beliefs. So there are two sorts of beliefs: (1) those in the foundation, which are properly basic, and (2) those that can be traced, using legitimate rules of support, back to the foundation. While we must be careful not to exaggerate the differences, Pannenberg's coherentism leads to a rather different approach.

(footnote 363 continued on page 158)

Critical Assessment

The four concerns that traditionally must be addressed in the articulation of a particular doctrine of the Trinity are those surrounding the issues of (1) subordinationism, (2) modalism, (3) tritheism, and (4) Monarchianism.

Subordinationism/Monarchianism

Does Pannenberg's doctrine of the Trinity avoid the charge of subordinationism in light of his emphasis upon the monarchy of the Father?[364] The question is whether the equal deity of the persons can be maintained if the Father is God in a special sense. Pannenberg argues that it is precisely the mutuality of relations and the *self*-subordination of the Son and Spirit to the Father that are intended to overcome any hint of ontological subordination. First, since he argues that the persons are mutually dependent upon each other for their deity, Pannenberg believes that the ontological status of the different persons is equivalent. He asserts that this stands in stark contrast to causal relations of origin, which directly suggest ontological distinction. Second, Pannenberg argues that self-subordination does not lead to ontological subordination. Olson is representative of those who, even with these distinctions, wonders if Pannenberg has escaped the charge of subordination of the Son and Spirit to the monarchy of the Father, though it would surely represent a unique sort of subordination.

To resolve the issue, we need to consider a pair of questions: (1) Does the tradition's affirmation of the equal deity of the persons imply more than ontological equality? (2) Do distinctions of "rank," as suggested by the notion of self-subordination, imply ontological inequality? As to the

---

(footnote 363 continued from page 157)

Characteristic of the arguments we have examined in this chapter are (1) an examination of the historical development of a doctrine in order to identify problem areas, (2) a search for plausible alternatives, and (3) consideration of the coherence of the alternative proposal. Rather than yielding something that has the appearance of a foundationalist structure, we have something that looks more like the "network" of beliefs of which the coherentist often speaks. One might even use the image of a puzzle where the puzzle-worker tries various possible pieces to determine the correct one for a particular location. In this case, the puzzle is the doctrine of the Trinity, the problems are pieces that do not fit, and Pannenberg's various proposals are his attempts to fit these pieces into the puzzle. Readers of Pannenberg often find themselves confused as to why Pannenberg makes a particular proposal at a particular point. For example, why does he deploy the concept of self-distinction within the members of the Trinity without a more detailed argument for the adequacy of the concept? However, for Pannenberg, the presentation of the doctrine of the Trinity, which includes showing how self-distinction is plausible and solves certain problems and that it is coherent with other claims in his doctrine of God *is itself* the argument for the truth of the concept. Given this, while it seems at times that Pannenberg takes for granted a particular position, it is not that he takes it for granted but rather that he believes by showing the plausibility of the proposal on the one hand and how it coherently fits within his overall doctrine of God on the other, he, at the same time, demonstrates the truthfulness (provisionally, of course) and adequacy of the position.

364. See, for example, Olson, "Wolfhart Pannenberg's Doctrine of the Trinity," 203ff.

first question, it seems reasonably clear that the church's creedal affirmations are focused upon ontological equivalence. Important phrases from certain of the early creeds include "very God of very God," "true light of true light," and "who with the Father and the Son is glorified, one God forever and ever." It certainly does not seem that this creed intends to affirm more than ontological equivalence; indeed, this seems precisely to be the point. Additionally, the tradition has generally recognized that the persons as they appear in salvation history have different roles, which in turn suggest that it has been generally accepted that ontological equality does not include indistinguishability. In fact, it is hard to know what becomes of the persons if they cannot be distinguished in some way. If we accept Pannenberg's construal of Rahner's Rule, then these roles in salvation history correspond to inner-Trinitarian distinctions. Hence, ontological equivalence of the persons must allow for certain kinds of distinctions.

At this point Pannenberg deploys the notion of self-subordination, which he believes implies distinctions of rank but *not* ontological distinction. Within human relationships, for example, even though we must affirm ontological equivalency, distinctions of rank are quite common. For example, the fact that one individual is the president of a company and others are subordinates does not mean that the individuals are ontologically unequal. The same is true of military organizations and, much more appropriately, of family relationships. The fact that a father is father to his son does not mean that he is ontologically superior to his son. However, we must recognize that each of these examples has a common weakness. The organizational subordination of the first two examples may include conflict, for the person in lower rank may not want to be subject to the other. In the case of the family, the father is temporally prior to his son. However, in Pannenberg's proposal, the Son and Spirit subordinate themselves to the monarchy of the Father. Additionally, Pannenberg gives priority to the constitution of the persons so that "the monarchy [of the Father] is not the presupposition but the result of the three persons' common activity."[365] Consequently, the persons freely choose to subordinate themselves to the task of realizing the kingdom of the Father. In other words, in the case of the Trinitarian persons, there is no conflict, nor is there anything external to the persons that results in this "ranking" among them. If one accepts that the tradition's concern over subordinationism is ontological subordination, then it is difficult to see how Pannenberg's doctrine of the Trinity is subordinationist, even if it contains something of the notion of "rank." On the other hand, if any sort of subordination is contrary to the tradition's denial of subordination, then the concept of "rank" would be problematic.

---

365. Olson, "Wolfhart Pannenberg's Doctrine of the Trinity," 194.

It seems, however, that Pannenberg is on safe ground, since his affirmation of non-ontological subordination derives, he says, directly from the biblical witness—for example, when the Son says the Father is greater, or when the Spirit's task is described as glorifying the Son and, in him, the Father.

As we have seen, it is precisely the monarchy of the Father that serves to ground the unity of the three persons. The tradition's concern with Monarchianism is closely related to subordinationism. Does the monarchy of the Father make the Son and Spirit inferior to the Father? According to Pannenberg, it is partially the mutually reciprocal relations that resolve the problem. In addition, Pannenberg believes that a proper understanding of the Father's monarchy provides a way around the concern. The monarchy of the Father does not result in the subjection of the Son and Spirit, but rather the Son and the Spirit subject themselves so that the common activity of the three persons has the monarchy of the Father as its goal. Olson summarizes the point succinctly: "Because [the kingdom's] fulfilment is dependent on the working of all three, the Father's monarchy does not mean his superiority over Son and Spirit. Instead, his monarchy, and therefore his deity, is *mediated* even to him through the other persons.[366] While this provides a unique understanding of the monarchy of the Father, it is not entirely clear that Pannenberg has resolved all concerns. Again, given that Pannenberg construes Rahner's Rule as he does, we must take the monarchy of the Father, which he believes is a part of the revelation of the economic Trinity, as indicative of an inner-Trinitarian relation. Can we then resolve the concern that the Father is God in a special sense by appealing to self-subjection? Would not the subjection itself be indicative of an inner-Trinitarian relationship? If so, have we yet fully escaped the concern expressed within the tradition? While it seems he has avoided ontological subordination, some concerns with Monarchianism still require resolution. We shall have to await further clarification from Pannenberg on this point.

Modalism

As we have seen, Pannenberg believes that the unity of God is secured by the manner in which he understands the divine essence (relationally structured love) and the common goal of the monarchy of the Father. In the final analysis, it is likely that the extent to which one accepts Pannenberg's doctrine of the Trinity will be related to the sympathy one has for social Trinitarian models. Interestingly, Pannenberg has expressed distrust of social analogies of the Trinity because there are no societies that would be

---

366. Ibid., 193.

truly analogous to the Trinitarian relations. All societies of which we know are made up of autonomous, independent beings who, at best, realize the bond of love only imperfectly. We know of no societies wherein members share the bond of love so perfectly that there is a mutual, unreserved self-giving of one to another. We know of societies wherein individuals struggle to be at the top, none wherein members willingly and totally submit themselves to the goal of realizing the monarchy of another. Consequently, from Pannenberg's perspective, social analogies are inadequate.

Nevertheless, his strong emphasis upon the distinctiveness of the persons coupled with the relational understanding of personhood strongly suggests that a social analogy is best suited for understanding Pannenberg's Trinitarian doctrine. Consequently, there is reason to believe that those who are generally sympathetic to social Trinitarian models will be sympathetic to Pannenberg's doctrine. This and the extent to which one affirms a relational definition of personhood will be the primary factors in one's assessment of whether Pannenberg avoids tritheism. Olson summarizes these points:

> Pannenberg's formulation of the doctrine of the Trinity will unquestionably be charged with Tritheism. Much of this criticism will come from those who are generally uncomfortable with *any* form of social analogy. The question they must deal with is how a doctrine of the Trinity which reduces the three persons to modes of being of a single divine Subject can overcome the danger of making the world appear as God's alter-ego.[367]

Olson comments that while there will likely be some questions about whether Pannenberg avoids tritheism, the good news is that, given Pannenberg's emphasis upon the threeness of God, there is little chance that his Trinitarian doctrine will be charged with modalism.

Tritheism

Any doctrine of the Trinity that takes seriously the distinction of the three persons likely will be charged with tritheism. From Pannenberg's perspective, we can perhaps reduce the issue to a pair of questions: (1) Can any doctrine of God that reduces the content of the Trinity to a single divine subject be philosophically and theologically adequate? (2) Does the reciprocity of relations as proposed by Pannenberg adequately establish that the three persons are one God? Clearly, Pannenberg believes that the answer to the first question is no, and we have already seen his reasons. To

---

367. Ibid., 202.

summarize those arguments: First, he argues that it is doubtful whether any meaningful notion of God remains if God cannot be conceived as personal. Second, personhood is a relational concept, so if we conceive God as personal, there must be something for him to stand over against. Third, this implies a concept of God wherein the relationality is internal, as in the Trinity, or something external becomes necessary for God to attain personhood. The latter alternative is not acceptable on account of the freedom and self-sufficiency of God; thus, the personhood of God is dependent upon his existing as a differentiated unity. Clearly, Pannenberg's defense of the unity of God depends upon the claim that personhood is defined by relationality, and the extent to which one finds this definition satisfactory will determine the extent to which the argument against a single divine subjectivity will be persuasive. On the second question, the mutuality of relations seems to show the mutual dependence of each Trinitarian person upon the others for their deity. In a very real sense, the three persons *only taken together* can be seen fully as God. Hence, the mutuality of relations serves to help rule out the idea of three independent gods, and this coupled with our previous discussions regarding Pannenberg's defense of the unity of God provides a strong defense against those charges of tritheism should they come.

Pannenberg's Concept of Personhood

We can be reasonably brief in assessing Pannenberg's deployment of a relational concept of personhood. First, of course, we must recognize that there is a range of positions about what constitutes a person, more than one of which seems plausible,[368] and it seems clear that the concept deployed by Pannenberg is, minimally, plausible. Second, the relational concept of personality as modified by Pannenberg is consistent with psychology's insights into the nature of ego development, which draws particular attention to the importance of external relations for the unfolding of the ego. Third, by also incorporating elements of what we called the "absolute" concept of personhood, Pannenberg's conception does not omit the important aspect of self-conscious agency. Finally, such a concept aligns particularly well with the differentiated unity necessary for the divine nature as implied by the doctrine of the Trinity. In light of these points, while we may not claim that Pannenberg has decisively refuted all alternative conceptions of personhood, it seems clear that his proposal can be plausibly and coherently deployed in the Christian doctrine of God.

---

368. Consider, for example, F. F. Centore, *Persons: A Comparative Account of Possible Theories* (Westport, CT: Greenwood, 1979).

Rahner's Rule

In addressing Pannenberg's deployment of Rahner's Rule, two questions need to be answered. First, is there adequate reason to believe that something like Rahner's Rule is true? Second, if so, is there adequate reason to believe that Pannenberg's deployment of it, extending it well beyond what many think Rahner himself intended, is plausible? Many of the theologians who have reemphasized the doctrine of the Trinity have accepted Rahner's Rule in some form—theologians including Moltmann, Jenson, Jüngel, and, of course, Pannenberg. It seems that the common concern of these theologians is to avoid the strong sense of immutability that resulted from adoption of Hellenistic conceptions and that tended to separate the being of God from salvation history. Rahner's Rule provides resources for overcoming this difficulty. As one might expect, there are arguments both for and against adopting Rahner's Rule. First, the Christian tradition has argued that the revelation of God in Christ is unsurpassable. If this is true in principle, not just in practice, then the revelation of Christ must reveal God as he is, which seems clearly to lead in the direction of something like Rahner's Rule. Of course, as we have already observed, the concern is that by connecting salvation history with the divine essence, we run the risk of seeming to make salvation history necessary for God's self-becoming. Consequently, it seems that something like Rahner's Rule is appropriate to the Christian doctrine of God, with the appropriate caution to avoid making the divine life dependent upon salvation history.

The second question is, in essence, whether Pannenberg overextends Rahner's thesis. Jenson believes that Pannenberg does extend it beyond what Rahner intended, but since Jenson admits he himself does so, one can infer that Jenson thinks some extension is justifiable. Pannenberg believes he can extend Rahner's thesis without endangering God's independence from salvation history as a consequence of (1) the ontological priority of the future, (2) a conception of the divine freedom that does not necessitate that God create a world, and (3) the doctrine of the Trinity, which provides internal relations that make personhood possible without the creation of an "other." Surely, Christians will want to affirm point 2, and even a majority of those who may not be entirely persuaded by Pannenberg's conception of person will want to affirm point 3. So as in the previous chapter, we are back to the plausibility of Pannenberg's thesis of the ontological priority of the future. Those who find this thesis plausible likely will find that his deployment of it helps avoid making the world the necessary correlate of God; those who do not likely will claim that Pannenberg has overextended Rahner's Rule.

It will be interesting over the next few years to see how the tradition responds to the calls for revision to the Christian doctrine of the Trinity, particularly so with the responses to Pannenberg's modifications. There can be no doubt that his proposals, whether entirely accepted or not, will fuel further exploration of the Trinitarian doctrine, which from a Christian perspective must be seen as a very positive contribution. With our examination of the details of his proposed doctrine of the Trinity behind us, we are ready to change our focus to the intersection of science and theology. In the next chapter, I will consider Pannenberg's provocative proposal that God be conceived as an infinite field of power.

CHAPTER 6

God as an Infinite Field of Power

ONE OF THE FREQUENT TERMS used to conceptualize God is "spirit." Of course, the term is applied both in relation to the Holy Spirit and in relation to the essence of God, as when the Scriptures record that "God is spirit." While "spirit" is a term used with great frequency within the tradition, the deployment of the term has not been always been clear. What does it mean to say that "God is spirit" or to claim that humans are composed of body and spirit? To make the difficulty explicit, consider the following thought experiment. Before you stand two rooms, say, room A and room B. The two rooms are exactly identical except that there is a spirit in room A and absolutely nothing in room B. Without simply using again the term "spirit," how can we explain the difference between the two rooms? Is there some analogy we can use to describe the difference? In other words, what exactly constitutes "spirit"?

In this chapter, I will focus my attention specifically upon how Pannenberg's modifications to the doctrine of God relate to an understanding of the concept of spirit. As one might expect in light of earlier comments, Pannenberg intends to offer correctives concerning both conceptual clarity (what does "spirit" mean?) and conceptual adequacy (are there better ways to conceptualize "spirit" than those currently employed?).

One of the first tasks to be undertaken as one develops the doctrine of God is a determination of the concepts, metaphors, and symbols that will be used to articulate it. For example, within the Christian tradition a wide range of terms and concepts has been used to articulate its doctrine of God.[369] Without attempting either to be exhaustive or to indicate which terms are to be taken metaphorically to a greater or lesser degree, some of the terms common to the Christian tradition include "Father," "Son," "Holy Spirit," "love," "mind," "wisdom," and "will." So far in our examination of Pannenberg's doctrine of God, we have seen that he employs a number of additional concepts: the true infinite, the power of the future, and the all-determining reality, among others. Once a particular set of terms and concepts has been established, the next step is identification of those that will be primary and those that will be secondary. Historically, according to Pannenberg, when the tradition has attempted to articulate its understanding of the divine nature, particularly as it relates to the notion of Spirit, two fundamental concepts are "mind" and "will." However, Pannenberg is concerned with the adequacy of these terms, since they bear traces of finitude as a result of their relation to human experience. As we might expect, he proposes something of a major conceptual shift.

While more than one of Pannenberg's proposed modifications to the doctrine of God may be termed "provocative" or "radical," it is likely that none can be characterized in these terms more than what he proposes here. In short, the essence of Pannenberg's proposal involves replacing the notions of mind and will with the concept of an infinite field of power.[370] A number of motivations drive Pannenberg's proposal, several of which I will examine in what follows. Perhaps the most significant motivation, one that has driven a good deal of Pannenberg's work, is the attempt to bridge the gap between theology and the physical sciences. It is precisely the idea of a "field" as deployed in modern physics that, Pannenberg believes, can be coupled with the biblical notion of God as spirit in such a way as to construct a doctrine of God that is coherent with models of the universe generally embraced by the scientific community. In this chapter we will consider the appropriateness of deploying the concept of an infinite field of power within the Christian doctrine of God. In conducting my analysis, I shall proceed as follows. First, I will consider the details of Pannenberg's proposal. Second, I will examine the motivations driving this proposed reconceptualization of the nature of God and whether the proposal satisfies these motivations. Third, I will analyze the proposal in light of a specific set of test questions and issues. Finally, I will summarize this assessment to determine the overall adequacy and desirability of this proposal.

---

369. I use this term for the sake of simplification, recognizing that it would be hard to identify a single "traditional doctrine of God" within Christianity.

370. As we shall see as our examination unfolds, however, he does not propose that the concepts of mind and will be discarded, but rather that they be treated as secondary to the concept of an infinite field of power.

The Proposal

God as an Infinite Field of Power

Pannenberg's proposal involves making the notions of mind and will, which have been primary concepts used to articulate the Christian doctrine of God, secondary to the concept of an infinite field of power where "field" roughly corresponds to the notion of field as used in modern physics. By this, Pannenberg means for the notion of a field to be used to give content to the biblical term "spirit." Just as the universal space-time-energy field is taken to be omnipresent throughout the cosmos, Pannenberg believes that the concept of field may be used to make intelligible the omnipresence of God with his creatures throughout all space. In fact, Pannenberg expresses it as follows: "The concept of a field of force could be used to make effective our understanding of the spiritual presence of God in natural phenomena."[371] To emphasize the promise he thinks this new conceptualization holds for theology, Pannenberg writes, "In contrast to the mechanical model of movement by push and pressure, the field concept could be celebrated as inauguration of a spiritual interpretation of nature."[372]

As is evident in the secondary literature, there is some uncertainty concerning the extent to which Pannenberg intends his proposal to be taken as a literal description of the essence of God. For example, Ted Peters writes, "Pannenberg rushes in where two-language angels have feared to tread. He does not say that spirit *is like* a force field. He says that spirit *is* a force field."[373] Here Peters claims that Pannenberg intends to be taken quite literally. However, Mark Worthing, who seems closer to the truth, quotes Pannenberg directly:

> To be sure, even a cosmic field conceived along the lines of Faraday's thought as a field of force would not be identified immediately with the dynamic activity of the divine Spirit in creation. In every case the different models of science remain approximations. . . . Therefore, theological assertions of field structure of the cosmic activity of the divine Spirit will remain different from field theories in physics.[374]

---

371. W. Pannenberg, *Toward a Theology of Nature* (ed. T. Peters; Louisville, KY: Westminster, 1993), 48. Here he means "field" in more than one sense, expanding now to include the idea of a "biological field."

372. Ibid., 40.

373. T. Peters, "Editor's Introduction: Pannenberg on Theology and Natural Science," in *Toward a Theology of Nature*, 14.

374. W. Pannenberg, *Toward a Theology of Nature*, 40.

In these divergent remarks, we see one of the difficulties: Pannenberg is not entirely clear as to how the scientific and theological uses of the field concept are similar and how they are different.

One way to think of Pannenberg's proposal is to return to our earlier thought experiment. There we imagined two rooms before us. In one room, there was absolutely nothing. In the other, there was a spirit. Our questions were these: What, exactly, is the difference between the two rooms? What does it mean to say there is a "spirit" in one and not in the other? Pannenberg proposes to answer this question by saying that claiming a spirit is present in the second room is, minimally, analogous to saying a field of power is present in the second room, a field not necessarily present to the five senses, but present and powerful nonetheless.

Motivations and Rationale for Reconceptualization

Including the desire to forge a closer connection between the natural sciences and theology, there are at least four motivations behind this proposal. First, Pannenberg intends to deal with the objection that nonembodied, intentional causation is not a coherent concept. Christians have overwhelmingly conceived God as an incorporeal entity, and this objection claims that the notion of such a God acting intentionally in the material world is incoherent. Obviously, if correct, this would have catastrophic consequences for belief in God. Second, Pannenberg is very concerned to show that the world that Christian theology claims is the creation of the one God is the very same one described by the theories of natural scientists, especially cosmologists and physicists. Third, Pannenberg believes that the Christian tradition's concept of God, which makes the notions of mind and will central, has resulted in an overly intellectualized, and therefore an overly anthropomorphic, doctrine of God. This has resulted, Pannenberg believes, in an obscuring of the proper relation between the divine Spirit and the material world and its process of creation.[375] Finally, and some will surely find this startling in light of the specifics of the proposal, there is the concern to return the doctrine of God to a more biblical basis. Pannenberg believes that the notions of mind and will diverge in important areas from the biblical concept of God, and, while helpful in some ways, he believes his proposal will serve to correct this divergence.

Nonembodied, Intentional Causality

The essential idea underlying the objection to nonembodied, intentional causality is the claim that it is incoherent (or unintelligible, depending

---

375. W. Pannenberg, *An Introduction to Systematic Theology* (Grand Rapids: Eerdmans, 1991), 44.

upon the objector) to assert that an incorporeal (i.e., nonembodied) entity can stand in a causal relation to the world. J. L. Mackie expresses the concern as follows:

> The key power [of such a God] . . . is that of fulfilling intentions *directly*, without any physical or causal mediation, without materials or instruments. There is nothing in our background knowledge that makes it comprehensible, let alone likely, that anything should have such a power. All our knowledge of intention-fulfilment is of *embodied* intentions being fulfilled *indirectly* by way of bodily changes and movements which are *causally* related to the intended result, and where the ability thus to fulfill intentions itself has a *causal history*, either of evolutionary development or of learning or both.[376]

The objection here is not so much a denial that incorporeal realities exist; for example, none of those who advance this objection would deny the reality of gravity or of magnetic fields. Instead, the objection claims that (1) all intentional causal activity is embodied and (2) all intentional causal activity is actualized indirectly (using Mackie's term), in other words, by means of the body of the causal agent in question.

In order to clarify further the point and to translate the language I have been using into that which Pannenberg employs, perhaps the objection ought to be modified to express the conviction that all causal activity, both agent (intentional) and nonagent (nonintentional), is traceable to embodied things. Agent causal activity, for example, would include the intentional choices of free agents, while nonagent causality would include mechanistic causes such as the causing of motion in one object by another. Hence, even the causal activity of fields would be traceable to the bodies to which those fields correspond. If we express the objection in this fashion, then the main content of the objection becomes evident: Bodies have priority over fields so that incorporeal realities, such as fields, are unintelligible apart from bodies.

An important focus of physics, in its attempt to generate adequate theories of motion and movement, is to "trace the concept of force back to that of body and the impulses that move it, and in this way to base all physics on the body and the relations between bodies."[377] Pannenberg comments upon the theological significance of such a project, should it prove successful:

---

376. J. L. Mackie, *The Miracle of Theism* (Oxford: Clarendon, 1982), 100.

377. W. Pannenberg, *Systematic Theology* (vol. 2; trans. G. W. Bromiley; Grand Rapids: Eerdmans, 1994), 79.

> The tendency on a certain line of the development of modern physics to reduce all forces to bodies or "masses" . . . had antitheological implications: If all forces would proceed from bodies or masses, then the understanding of nature would be so thoroughly separated from the idea of God—who is not a body—that theological language about a divine activity in the processes of the natural world would become simply unintelligible and absurd.[378]

In other words, if all forces were to be ultimately reducible to material bodies, what space would be left for a nonembodied agent—namely, God—in our causal explanations of phenomena? Since the Christian tradition and Scripture consistently conceive God as interacting in a causal fashion with the world, the implications would be devastating.

Pannenberg presents an interesting analysis of scientific developments that aimed to reduce all forces to prior bodies.[379] He begins the discussion by observing that Descartes attempted to account for the dynamics of interbody movements as the transfer of motion between bodies. Newton, on the other hand, considered some forces to be independent of bodies. In fact, he took the activity of the soul in causing bodily movement to be analogous to nonmaterial forces that move bodies. "One such force was gravity, which Newton viewed as an expression of the moving of the universe by God with space as his instrument."[380] Pannenberg questions whether the theological implications of such a concept drove the criticisms of physicists such as Mach and Hertz. In other words, did they want to avoid physical theories that seemed to imply God's activity? Whether or not this is so, physicists in the tradition of Mach and Hertz aimed to reduce forces to bodies or masses. If this attempt had been successful, Pannenberg believes that "theological talk about God's working in worldly events then becomes totally nonsensical."[381] Does this mean God's action would be literally impossible? Perhaps not, but it would leave us bereft of a conceptual foundation with any concrete analogues in the world.

At this point, we must return to Mackie's objection for more detail about the precise nature of the alleged problem. Some have argued that disembodied, intentional causation is unintelligible, but surely this statement of the problem is mistaken. Most if not all of the world's great religions affirm the existence of incorporeal entities, and surely we know what it *means* when we say that God (thereby implying an incorporeal agent) caused some event. In fact, Mackie seems to recognize this fact:

---

378. Pannenberg, *Toward a Theology of Nature*, 38.
379. See, for example, Pannenberg, *Systematic Theology*, 2:79ff.
380. Ibid., 2:79.
381. Ibid., 2:80.

We know, from our acquaintance with ourselves and other human beings, what a person is. . . . Although all the persons we are acquainted with have bodies, there is no great difficulty in conceiving what it would be for there to be a person without a body: for example, one can imagine oneself surviving without a body, and while at present one can act and produce results only by using one's limbs or one's speech organs, one can *imagine* having one's intentions fulfilled directly, without such physical means. Knowing what it is to be present in one place, we can form the concept of a spirit who is present everywhere.[382]

As is evident from Mackie's comments, the problem is not really conceptual intelligibility (we understand what it means to say a spirit moved an object). Some might suggest, then, that the real problem is that we cannot imagine *how* an incorporeal entity can be involved in intentional causality. As Mackie saw, the real problem is not intelligibility but rather that our absence of experience with nonembodied, intentional causality and our consequent inability to understand how such a form of causality might work lead some to conclude that it is exceedingly implausible that such a form of causality actually exists.

Initially, one is inclined to ask what sort of evidence or information would lead someone such as Mackie to withdraw the objection that nonembodied causation is very implausible. One suspects that, given Mackie's general commitment to scientific explanations of the world of nature, if there existed a broadly accepted scientific theory that, when properly applied, suggested that incorporeal entities can be intentional, causal agents, Mackie and other kindred spirits should be sympathetic. Fortunately for the theist, says Pannenberg, modern theoretical physics has provided resources to the defender of incorporeal, intentional causality. Prior to the field theories of Michael Faraday, physical scientists thought that our understanding of forces would eventually be reduced to forces that are exerted by bodies or masses. This meant that bodies were to be conceived as prior and that forces were to be conceived as manifested by masses or bodies. However, with Faraday, the priority of body and force was first reversed, so that modern field theories generally validate the belief that fields are prior to bodies. In fact, according to Faraday's vision, enduring physical bodies would be conceivable as the manifestation of the convergence of lines of force within overarching fields. Consequently, incorporeal fields would be seen as the primary "building blocks" of matter, and therefore, all physical causality in the natural universe would be traceable to incorporeal fields. Obviously, if it is true that fields are the fundamental

---

382. Mackie, *Miracle of Theism*, 1–2.

building blocks of all physical reality, then even human bodies must be conceived as the manifestation of prior fields. So it would not be the case that all fields would be traceable to bodies, but rather that all bodies would be traceable to fields, a major reversal of the manner in which the relationship between these realities had generally been conceived. In responding to Mackie's objection, I have extended somewhat beyond what is directly expressed in Pannenberg's writings, but the points are straightforward extrapolations. However, the main point for Pannenberg's argument is merely that all intentional causality of which we are aware must be seen, in this construal of the nature of the physical world, as manifestations of prior, incorporeal realities. Further, such a construal of the world of nature is invited, says Pannenberg, by the physical sciences themselves. Finally, since God is conceived as incorporeal, it seems clear that God could be conceived as an intentional, causal entity.

Those following in Mackie's tradition might not be inclined to give up so easily. In fact, they might continue to object by claiming that since every causal agent of which we have empirical sense data is embodied, perhaps fields must be embodied before they can become causal agents. Perhaps, but it is hard to see why one should feel constrained to believe that this is the case. First, by insisting upon an appeal to "empirical sense data" concerning our knowledge of nonembodied agents (who may not be subject to sense data), it seems the case is initially rather strongly biased against the theist. Second, if fields underlie all bodies, as the theories Pannenberg cites propose, humans themselves, as we have just seen, are most fundamentally incorporeal *so that even human intentional causality is plausibly traceable to incorporeal fields*. Third, we know that physical movement does not require physical contact but rather can be caused by the interaction of fields (gravity and magnetism are but two examples). At a minimum, it seems that these factors make incorporeal, intentional causality eminently plausible.

At this point, it is appropriate to pause and make more explicit the connections between these arguments and Pannenberg's proposal that God be conceived as an infinite field of power. The discussions of this objection to theistic belief have two very closely related elements:

1. the claim that human experience makes it exceedingly implausible that nonembodied *causality* is instantiated in the world, and
2. the claim that human experience makes it exceedingly implausible that nonembodied *intentionality* is instantiated in the world.

The implications of the two together, Pannenberg claims, are significant for Christian theology, since God is conceived as a nonembodied, intentional causal agent. While it is debatable whether Pannenberg's stronger claim is justified (that theological language about God's activity in the world would become unintelligible and absurd), it seems clear that he is correct in claiming that the implications of elements 1 and 2 would be the opening up of a significant separation between scientific understandings of nature and the concept of an incorporeal, intentional God. Since Pannenberg's standard is plausibility (rather than mere logical possibility), the question would then become whether the activity of such a God could be conceived as plausible.

By proposing that God be conceived along the lines of an infinite field of power, Pannenberg is attempting to take advantage of modern scientific theories of the natural world to resolve these difficulties. The primary point, of course, is that the reversal of the priority between fields and bodies argues that incorporeal fields are more fundamental than bodies. Consequently, it is evident that the effort to reduce all forces to bodies fails. Further, to the extent it is reasonable to conceive God in terms of a field of power, the activity of God is clearly coherent and plausible. It is coherent with what is understood of the world of human experience, and there is no doubt of its plausibility in light of the fact that the arguments above show that Pannenberg's proposal, at least initially, seems to offer a plausible account of nonembodied causation. The bottom line is this: If it is appropriate to conceive God along the lines of a field of power, then at a minimum, objection to nonembodied causation is rendered ineffective. Of course, a good deal of discussion remains before we can draw a conclusion about the appropriateness of deploying the concept of an infinite field of power within the Christian doctrine of God.

The Relation between Science and Religion

Pannenberg is generally unsympathetic to those who embrace a "two-language" theory of the relation between science and theology; rather, he emphasizes the importance of recognizing that both disciplines, in the final analysis, speak of the same universe. More specifically, Pannenberg would not be sympathetic to a compartmentalization model of the relation between science and religion wherein the two fields are seen as employing entirely different aims, objects, and methods.[383] Rather, he is committed to the belief that the systematic reconstructions of the theologian must remain in dialogue with the sciences and incorporate their insights wherever possible and appropriate. Consequently, he holds that if God is to be conceived as Creator, the concept of God is essential to an exhaustive understanding of the natural world. This is evident in the following comment:

---

383. Consider, for example, Pannenberg's essay "The Crisis of the Scripture Principle," in W. Pannenberg, *Basic Questions in Theology* (vol. 1; trans. G. H. Kehm; Philadelphia: Westminster, 1971), 1–14.

No finite reality can be understood in its depth without reference to God. . . . If talk of God has any claim to truth, however, it must be possible to show that secular descriptions of reality are indeed abstracting from the fullness of its nature. . . . It must be possible to point to traces of dependence upon God, if that is indeed constitutive of the nature and existence of an entity.[384]

Of course, Pannenberg is not proposing that no knowledge of the cosmos is possible unless we show the relation of that aspect of the cosmos to God. Such a claim would be clearly mistaken. Rather, he is arguing that if God is Creator, then the creaturely status of all created entities is an essential part of their makeup. Consequently, if we are to grasp any and all aspects of reality in fullest detail, we must be able to show the creation's relation to God. Pannenberg goes on to claim that if it should turn out that no reference to God is necessary for nature's thorough explanation, it would follow that God, as understood by the Christian tradition, does not exist. In short, if nontheistic, scientific explanation should prove fully adequate, no room is left for God. Scientific claims, then, are of vital concern to the theologian.

One way to proceed would be to show that a properly articulated conception of the Christian God contains elements that plausibly correspond to elements of modern understandings of the nature of the physical universe.[385] It is precisely the step of connecting the theories of physicists concerning the constitution of the cosmos and the priority of fields over bodies and masses with the biblical concept of God as spirit that Pannenberg intends to take. Again, Pannenberg's proposal asserts that spirit, when applied to God, should be understood in such a way that, at a minimum, a field of power can be taken for spirit.[386] Albert Einstein, as part of his theory of relativity, presented the essential nature of the universe as a space-time-energy field. Pannenberg's proposal does not suggest that God is *this* field; if he did, of course, the threat of pantheism would be very serious. Rather, Pannenberg proposes that the infinite field of power that God is *underlies* and *gives rise to* the universal space-time-energy continuum.[387]

There is a second way in which Pannenberg believes that theological implications follow from the utilization of the field concept. As it is the universal field that underlies and gives rise to all finite realities, one can argue

---

384. Pannenberg, *Introduction to Systematic Theology*, 9–10.

385. One must proceed cautiously, for this step in itself would not be adequate. However, it opens the way to conceive the theories of modern science as having a degree of correspondence with what Christians say about the one God.

386. At this point I allow the minimum for "field" as a metaphor for "spirit," since as we have seen, there is some disagreement as to the extent Pannenberg intends to be taken literally or metaphorically on this issue.

387. Again, this point is not entirely clear within Pannenberg's written corpus or in the secondary literature. However, I have confirmed this intent in personal conversation.

that field theories give priority to the whole over against the parts so that the parts cannot be fully grasped without reference to the underlying whole. Similarly, as God must be conceived as the unifying ground that underlies all the created order, God corresponds to the whole, which has priority over the individual parts. If this is correct, it supports Pannenberg's earlier contention that no creaturely reality can be fully grasped without reference to the one God. Since both of these points would represent commonalities between Pannenberg's Christian conception of God and modern scientific theories about the nature of the universe, this proposal would represent a positive connection between theology and the natural sciences.

Anthropomorphic Concepts

Another motivation for Pannenberg's proposal is his concern to avoid overly anthropomorphic concepts. Specifically, he is concerned that the traditionally emphasized concepts of mind and will, because of the connection with human self-experience, are so tinged with finitude as to be inadequate when applied to God. At the root of this concern is Pannenberg's belief that to apply the notions of mind and will to God requires so many modifications in our basic understanding of these words and their associated phenomena that they can tend to be more misleading than helpful when predicated of God. In order to better grasp the precise nature of Pannenberg's concerns, we will have to consider in some detail his views about the inadequacy of each term. Assessment of his concerns with the concept of mind must begin with consideration of two other closely related notions: (1) the concept of knowledge and (2) what, for the lack of a better term, I will call the reasoning process.

Knowledge may come from various sources: direct experience (for example, I am now working on this chapter) or memory (I remember having salad for dinner) or inference (it is 3:00 here, so it must be 9:00 in Germany) or some combination of these or other means. If these beliefs are true and warranted for me, these things are examples of propositions that I know. Now, Pannenberg proposes, let us consider what it means to say that God knows something. First, since he does not have sense organs, it would be false to say that God knows anything by direct sensory experience, such as when humans use one or more of their five senses. Next, in view of God's eternity as the presence of the totality of life in undivided wholeness,[388] he need know nothing by memory. And, of course, by virtue of his omnipresence, God need not infer the sorts of things given in the example

---

388. In fact, one need not fully endorse Pannenberg's doctrine of the divine eternity to reach the conclusion noted in the text, which follows directly from the limiting speed of light and God's omniscience. See chapter 4.

above. Since the doctrine of God's omniscience claims that God knows all true propositions, it is clear that God need not infer at all to have knowledge about various things.

In speaking of God's knowledge, Pannenberg writes, "When we speak of God's knowledge we mean that nothing in all his creation escapes him. All things are present to him and are kept by him in his presence."[389] Perhaps it is best simply to say that what God knows, he knows "directly," without the mediation of sense experience, inference, and the like. The point, of course, is not what we call this sort of knowing, but rather that it is radically different from the manner in which knowledge is gained by humans, and thus, the divine mode of knowing radically stretches our concept of knowledge and of coming to knowledge. Of course, Pannenberg is by no means denying that God has knowledge, nor is he suggesting that the process by which God knows has an impact upon the knowledge itself. Rather, his point is that to the extent that coming to knowledge is part of what it means to be "mind," the radically different senses of "coming to know" imply radically different senses of what it means to be a "mind." All of this impacts the degree to which and the manner in which the term "mind" can be applied to God.

By now the reader may be able to guess the nature of the problem Pannenberg would see with attributing the "reasoning process" to God. When we say that humans gain knowledge by "reasoning" through some data, we generally mean that they use various forms of mental manipulation— deductive arguments, inductive arguments, syllogisms, for example—as the means of gaining that knowledge.[390] Yet everything that God knows he knows "directly," without the mediation of an inferential or reasoning process. God does not weigh evidence to come to the right conclusion, nor must he traverse the steps of some sound and valid argument before he knows the answer to some question or problem. Here the difficulties seem even greater than with the notion of knowledge, for there does not seem to be anything analogous to a reasoning process that we can posit of God.[391] Hence, once again we are far removed from common notions of "mind" when we speak of the "mind of God."

With regard to the concept of will, Pannenberg finds similar problems. He argues that the idea of will or willing implies a goal that is willed by a

---

389. W. Pannenberg, *Systematic Theology* (vol. 1; trans. G. W. Bromiley; Grand Rapids: Eerdmans, 1991), 379–80.

390. The intent of breaking "mind" down into the two constitutive elements of "knowledge" and "reasoning process" is simply to emphasize the nature of the problems Pannenberg believes exist between applying these notions to humans, their normal domain, and applying them to God. In my critical analysis, I shall ask the question whether so characterizing "mind" does not already prejudice the outcome of the discussion and whether such a construal masks other equally or more important characteristics of "mind."

391. In my subsequent analysis, I will address the aspects of "knowledge" that must be retained.

given subject. Thus, as Pannenberg writes, "the concept of a goal presupposes that there is a difference between the object of the will and its fulfillment."[392] In actualizing a particular goal, then, a given human subject selects means appropriate to the goal and the existing conditions wherein the goal is to be realized, which means that the willing subject is limited by both the goal and existing circumstances. If the subject could realize the goal directly so that there is no difference between willing and achieving, how much would remain of the concept of will? Pannenberg suggests that the answer is "not much." However, this is precisely the nature of God's actions. God brings about what he chooses, whenever he chooses, without being limited by either the goal or existing circumstances. We must recognize, of course, that God may choose to limit himself (as when he allows humans a degree of autonomy). The point here is that God, in himself, is not limited by an external set of circumstances. Further, Pannenberg does not deny that God "chooses" to act or that God does, in fact, act; rather, the concern is with the notion of will and its seemingly inevitable connection with human finitude.

Biblical Concepts of the Divine Nature

Much of Pannenberg's evaluation of the "biblical concept of God" centers on the proper way to understand such terms as *ruah* (Hebrew) and *pneuma* (Greek), specifically the extent to which these terms ought to be taken as synonymous with *nous*.[393] We have seen already that Pannenberg believes there are philosophical/theological reasons for devaluing the concepts of mind and will in the Christian doctrine of God. Here he proposes that there are also strong biblical justifications.

The essence of Pannenberg's argument may be briefly summarized in the following points:

1. The oldest strands of the biblical tradition, which use the term *ruah* (often translated "spirit") as in *ruah Elohim*, clearly do not take *ruah* to mean "mind." Instead, *ruah* is better translated as "wind" or "breath."

2. Similarly, the New Testament tradition's use of *pneuma* (again, often translated "spirit") is generally not intended to mean *nous* ("mind"). Again, the better translation would be "wind" or "breath," as in John 3:8.

3. It was primarily in response to the Stoic doctrine of the divine nature (wherein the divine *pneuma* is understood as a "tenuous

---

392. Pannenberg, *Systematic Theology*, 1:380.
393. Whether this is an adequate means of assessing these issues will await a later critique.

thinking gas"[394]) that Origen set the Christian tradition on the track of taking *pneuma* to mean "incorporeal reason." Origen's concern was to make sure that the Christian use of *pneuma* avoided the materialistic consequences of the Stoic doctrine.

The fundamental question underlying Pannenberg's thought at this juncture is the extent to which the biblical use of the term "spirit" is intended to imply incorporeal reason. Pannenberg argues that the move to conceive "spirit" in this fashion was relatively late and that the notions of wind and breath as life-giving phenomena are much closer to the biblical intent. Pannenberg cites numerous texts in his effort to make his case, including Ps 104:30; Job 33:4; Ezek 37:9–10; and Eccl 12:7. It can hardly be debated that Pannenberg is correct in pointing out that the words translated as "spirit" in the Old and New Testaments are not generally intended to be synonymous with "mind" or "incorporeal reason." His analysis seems plausible, but an important question remains: Is there adequate reason to think that the concept of "field" is closer to what is intended by the term "spirit"?

Critical Assessment of Pannenberg's Proposal

The Issues

To focus our critical assessment of Pannenberg's proposal, the following five questions will serve as points of departure:

1. What has the Christian tradition generally intended by the term "spirit" when the term is applied to God?
2. To what extent should we be concerned with anthropomorphic language concerning God?
3. What are the consequences of making the concepts of mind and will secondary within the doctrine of God?
4. What are the essential elements of personhood, especially when applied to God?
5. The proposal to conceive God as an infinite field of power will seem to many to have pantheistic implications. Does Pannenberg successfully defend his proposal against the charge of pantheism?

Only as we answer the challenge implied by each of these questions will we be able to make a determination as to the adequacy and appropriateness of Pannenberg's proposal. After addressing these five questions, we will turn our attention to the question of the acceptability of this proposal from the

394. C. Stead, *Divine Substance* (Oxford: Clarendon, 1977), 175.

perspective of those who advance and employ the field concepts Pannenberg appropriates. Specifically, we will consider scientific criticism of Pannenberg's appropriation of the field concept.

The Meaning of "Spirit"

Within the Christian tradition, we must make a distinction between the claim that the divine essence is spirit and the identification of the third person of the Trinity as the Holy Spirit. My concern here is with the former use of the word. While it is by no means decisive, it is at least worth initially considering the manner in which "spirit" is taken in the beginning of the twenty-first century. One popular dictionary lists thirteen definitions for the noun form, of which the first five are of interest to our examination:

1. The vital essence or animating force in living organisms, esp. man, often considered divine in origin.
2. The part of a human being characterized by intelligence, personality, self-consciousness, and will; the mind.
3. The substance or universal aspect of reality, regarded as opposed to matter.
4. In the Bible, the creative, animating power of God.
5. A supernatural or immaterial being, as an angel, ghost, specter, etc.

These definitions do not explicitly connect the concept of spirit with the nature of God, though in definition 4 spirit is seen as a power *of* God. However, connections to the divine are implicit in all but definition 2. The points particularly worth noting are that spirit is

1. a vital, life-giving force;
2. an incorporeal or immaterial reality;
3. those things attributable to mind; and
4. the underlying, universal aspect of the cosmos.

With this as background, let us turn to the manner in which the concept of spirit was taken in ancient Hebrew culture as well as during the period around the writing of the New Testament.

In the Old Testament, the Hebrew word underlying "spirit" is generally *ruah*. While the later strands of the Old Testament tradition sometimes connect spirit with mind or intellect,[395] the earliest strands more frequently seem to equate *ruah* with wind; breath; vital, life-giving force; or the like. In fact, Pannenberg explains that in ancient Hebrew thought the "term for

---

395. Stead observes, "The 'spirit' assigned to Sophia by the Wisdom writer (7:22ff) represents an important landmark in this process" of detaching the concept from its original basis in physical theory. Stead, *Divine Substance*, 177.

'spirit' (*ruah*) does not mean reason or consciousness. Rational thinking and judgment are located in the 'heart.'"[396] He goes on to write that "*ruah* is described as a mysteriously invisible force which declares itself especially in the movement of the wind."[397] In addition, he cites Wolff's work in support of the claim that the Old Testament seldom takes spirit as it was often taken in the later Christian tradition, namely, as thinking consciousness.[398]

Recall that Pannenberg is not attempting to show that the concepts of mind and/or thinking consciousness are entirely unjustified as concepts that may be used to give content to *ruah*. Rather, he is seeking to show that the much more common meaning, and therefore the meaning that has *prima facie* priority, is that of a mysterious, invisible force. Of course, this is a meaning he thinks is given content by the concept of a field of power.

Moving forward to the beginning of Greek philosophy and proceeding through the early Christian period, the Greek term *pneuma* replaced *ruah* as the word underlying the English "spirit." In the Greek world, according to Kittel's *Theological Dictionary of the New Testament*, "*pneuma* means the elemental and natural force" that has "the basic idea of energy."[399] Its meanings include "wind," "breath," "life," "soul," and "spirit." While in some contexts it is justifiable to interpret both *pneuma* and *nous* as "spirit,"

> two basically different forms of the being and action of the spirit are expressed by the two words *pneuma* and *nous*. They are as different as the unmoving and calm medium of light, which for the pure and remote contemplation of the eye presents things statically as they are in truth, differs from the much more material and powerful movement of air, which by nature fills, permeates, seizes and embraces either beholder or object with elemental force, catching him up into tension or movement.[400]

Interestingly, while the later Christian tradition moved to equate "spirit" with *nous*, *pneuma* is the word of choice in the New Testament.

Contemporary with the writing of the New Testament, the Stoics understood *pneuma* to be that which underlies physical reality, and *pneuma* was itself understood to be a material substance underlying the four elements rather than constituting a fifth. As Kittel explains, "Invisibly fine corporeality, air-like form, the bearing of warmth or fire, spontaneous movement, and tension make *pneuma* the mighty substance which permeates, inte-

---

396. Pannenberg, *Systematic Theology*, 1:373.
397. Ibid.
398. Ibid. Pannenberg is citing here H. W. Wolff, *Anthropology of the Old Testament* (trans. M. Kohl; Philadelphia: Fortress, 1974).
399. G. Kittel and G. Friedrich, eds., *Theological Dictionary of the New Testament* (trans. G. W. Bromiley; Grand Rapids: Eerdmans, 1968), 334–35.
400. Ibid., 338.

grates, moves, vivifies, and gives soul to all reality in all its forms."[401] Stead attributes Drummond with characterizing the Stoic doctrine as conceiving God as a "tenuous thinking gas."[402] Further, Stead reports that at least some of the early church fathers accepted the material consequences of the Stoic concept of *pneuma*.[403] The Stoic *pneuma* doctrine, so it seems, was seen by some within the Christian tradition as a live option.

Stead offers support to Pannenberg's assigning Origen a central place in the rejection of a corporeal understanding of *pneuma* in favor of the older "Platonic concept of intelligible reality."[404] In fact, Origen recognized the degree to which *pneuma* had been understood materially when he noted that "the description of God as *pneuma* is only a figurative attempt to explain the nature of spiritual essence with the words taken from the sphere of sense."[405] Finally, it is worth noting that in Greek thought *pneuma* was always conceived as a thing rather than as a person.[406] Interestingly, Pannenberg has often said that *pneuma* (even when applied to God) as such is impersonal and only becomes personal in the three concrete persons of the Trinity. In some sense, then, Pannenberg allows that *pneuma* is to be understood as impersonal.[407] The challenge for Pannenberg is whether it is even plausible to conceive *pneuma* along the lines of a field of power and as personal.

In the course of the Old Testament, God is certainly portrayed as an intentional, personal agent. This is not inconsequential, for it seems clear that the Scripture writers considered this a central aspect of their conception of God. Consequently, even if Pannenberg's assessment of the early uses of spirit are correct (that notions of, for example, wind and breath are closer to the biblical intent), and even if the concept of field can be used in some way for spirit, it seems the field concept can be adequate for deployment in the Christian doctrine of God only if it can be conceived as a personal, intentional agent. So before this chapter ends, we must undertake the matter of whether the field concept, when deployed in the Christian doctrine of God, can plausibly support both the personhood and the intentionality of God.

In addition to the development of these concepts and terms in the Scriptures as well as in Hellenistic thought, Pannenberg gives considerable weight to the study of field theories and their antecedents carried out by

---

401. Ibid., 344.

402. Stead, *Divine Substance* (Oxford: Clarendon, 1977), 175. Stead believes this phrase was initially put forward by James Drummond.

403. Ibid., 178–79. Stead cites Tertullian as one example.

404. Ibid., 177.

405. Kittel and Friedrich, *Theological Dictionary of the New Testament*, 358.

406. Ibid., 359.

407. See, for example, Pannenberg, *Systematic Theology*, 1:383ff.

Max Jammer.[408] Jammer's work is a lengthy examination of the historical developments underlying the field theories of modern physics. Jammer believes there is an intimate connection between the notions of field and spirit. In fact, he "thinks that the Stoic doctrine of the divine *pneuma* was actually the direct precursor of the modern field concept."[409] In the course of deploying the field concept within the Christian doctrine of God, Pannenberg is keenly aware of the potential objection that he is illegitimately co-opting a scientific concept. Scientists have often raised such an objection, arguing that theologians do not properly understand the concepts they borrow and that they co-opt scientific concepts and theories without proper justification. Pannenberg believes Jammer's work plausibly demonstrates that, in fact, science has deployed a concept that is rooted in early metaphysical reflections upon the nature of the divine. If this is so, there is a sense in which Pannenberg is merely reclaiming a concept that began within theology and philosophy. If Jammer is correct, such an objection of this sort from the scientific community would not carry much weight. Of course, even if Jammer's thesis is correct, it does not constitute a theological justification for Pannenberg's proposal but rather serves to establish that there exists a rationale, internal to the history of field theories, for seeing a positive relationship between the concept of field and that of the divine origin of the world.

At this point, we can summarize our findings and draw initial conclusions:

1. Neither in the Old Testament nor in the New Testament is the idea of incorporeal reason predominant when the terms underlying the English "spirit" are used.

2. One of the primary reasons for the adoption of *pneuma* = *nous* was to reject materialist pneumatic theories, such as those held by the Stoics.

3. With the advent of modern field theories and the reversal of the priority between fields and bodies, the materialist implications of the earlier conceptions of *pneuma* are reversed. Consequently, conceiving God as *pneuma* no longer need have materialist consequences.

4. There are reasons, internal to the development of field theories, that justify connecting field theories with the concept of God. In other words, if Jammer's thesis is correct that the Stoic doctrine was the precursor of modern field theories, then we see that those field theories have developed out of the Stoic inquiry into the divine.

---

408. M. Jammer, "Feld," in *Historisches Wörterbuch der Philosophie* (1972): 2:923.
409. Pannenberg, *Systematic Theology*, 2:81.

Pannenberg's analysis establishes at least these points. Let us turn our attention now to the conclusions we can draw from these discussions.

The fundamental issue in these discussions is the essential nature of "spirit," particularly as it relates to the claim "God is spirit." Clearly, to say that God is spirit is not intended to mean that God is nothing. As we saw earlier in this chapter, there must be a real distinction between saying "Nothing is present" and saying "A spirit is present." The question is, what exactly is the difference? Pannenberg's proposal asserts that where a spirit is present, something analogous to a field of force is present. A field may be a good way to conceive an incorporeal presence; at a minimum, it seems a useful analogy. Further, it seems reasonably clear from our examination of the use of various terms within the scriptural witness that merely to equate "spirit" with incorporeal reason is too simplistic. Several of the passages cited in the preceding discussion suggest other concepts, such as vital, life-giving force and animating power so that something more than simply incorporeal reason must be inferred. The notion of field seems to have the conceptual richness to capture a broad range of these ideas. The challenge, which I shall take up subsequently, is whether a field of power can adequately account for the notions that are central to Christian conceptions of God, namely, the notions of personhood, intentionality, and agency.

Anthropomorphic Language

Pannenberg takes overly anthropomorphic language to be a very serious concern and one in need of correction: "Though the constructive theories of modern atheists and the details of the arguments they developed to establish their point were not particularly strong, the underlying criticism of the classical concept of God contained important elements of truth. Therefore, a revision of the classical theological and metaphysical language about God is inevitable."[410] Some of those underlying criticisms that contained elements of truth, says Pannenberg, resulted from the application of overly anthropomorphic concepts to God. As we have seen, his specific concern is that notions derived from human self-experience are inevitably tinged with finitude so that to apply them directly to the infinite God is problematic. Pannenberg often cites Fichte's objection that the personhood of God stands in contradiction to his infinity as an example of the sorts of problems that arise when overly anthropomorphic concepts are applied to God.[411]

---

410. Pannenberg, *Introduction to Systematic Theology*, 23.

411. Pannenberg, *Systematic Theology*, 1:376. Specifically, Fichte had argued that God, as the infinite, must include all, but as person, he must stand over against something else.

Of course, the claim that humans conceptualize God in categories derived from human self-experience is at least as old as Xenophanes' claim that horses would conceive God as a horse.[412] However, the extent to which we ought to be concerned is a subject of serious debate among scholars. There are those who, siding with Pannenberg, see this to be a very serious objection indeed. On the other hand, there are those who take the objection as predominantly specious. Those in the latter camp often suggest that we cannot really conceptualize nonhuman entities apart from some level of anthropomorphism; it is merely the manner in which we conceptualize living beings. When we talk of God, whom even the Scriptures affirm is related to man as original to image, can we altogether avoid anthropomorphisms? The seriousness with which one is likely to treat this issue is directly related to one's concern with objections such as the projection thesis advanced in the tradition of Fichte, Feuerbach, and Freud. Fichte, in the atheism controversy of 1798 and 1799, argued "that the idea[s] of God as substance and person are projections of finite relations into his essence."[413] Within the Christian tradition, attempts to describe the divine attributes were often carried out by transference of creaturely attributes to God. Pannenberg describes subsequent moves:

> The divine qualities were deduced from the human experience of dependence which points beyond as well as embraces worldly objects. . . . The critical description of this procedure as projection gained force once the resultant concept of God was seen not to be unified but contradictory, since the qualities that are ascribed to God still bear traces of finitude (in opposition to God's infinity) along with anthropomorphic features. Psychological motivation was all that we needed, then, for the human imagination to project ideas of God which would ascribe to the divine essence qualities analogous to those of human and finite things. The premise of this type of criticism, of course, is the inappropriateness of such features in view of the infinity of the divine essence.[414]

Pannenberg claims that the discovery of the alleged contradiction between the divine infinity and attributes derived in this way opened the Christian concept of God to the charge of incoherence. Then as psychologists began

---

412. See J. Barnes, ed. and trans., *Early Greek Philosophy* (London: Penguin, 1987), 95, where Xenophanes is cited as follows:

But if cows and horses or lions had hands
or could draw with their hands and make the things men can make,
then horses would draw the forms of the gods like horses,
cows like cows, and they would make their bodies
similar in shape to those which each had themselves.

413. Pannenberg, *Systematic Theology*, 1:363.
414. Ibid., 1:363–64.

to understand in more detail the nature of human insecurities and fears, it became plausible to argue that the whole idea of God was merely a wishful projection grounded in human finitude. According to Pannenberg, even if the constructive atheistic proposal that resulted was not all that strong, the criticism that pointed out this alleged contradiction requires resolution. Deployment of a less anthropomorphic concept of God represents one possible resolution.

These discussions outline the basis for the concern Pannenberg expresses with regard to overly anthropomorphic language. The question, of course, is whether these concerns justify the revision of the doctrine of God proposed by Pannenberg. While it is certainly true that it is important to maintain a strong distinction between God and the creatures, the matter here runs deeper than that. As we have just seen, the real issues are the objections raised by Fichte, Feuerbach, and Freud, which seem to bring to the surface contradictions hidden within the Christian doctrine of God. It seems clear that the concept of an infinite field of power is a nonanthropomorphic concept, but does it really help resolve these concerns? There are two reasons to believe that it does. While it is plausible that the concepts of mind and will first arose in human self-experience and were then transferred and applied to the concept of God, it is extremely difficult to see how it could be claimed that the field concept has been transferred from humans to God. Consequently, the projection thesis would be undermined from the start. Second, the idea of an infinite field avoids those problematic hints of finitude, which inevitably accompany concepts derived from human self-experience. Further, it is important to recall from chapter 3 Pannenberg's argument that the infinite is a positive concept, which means that one does not derive it from negation of human finitude. According to this line of reasoning, just as we have argued that the concept of field is not transferred from humans to God, neither is the concept of the infinite transferred, by negation, from humans. Therefore, it is clear that, should Pannenberg's proposal prove to be plausible, the projection thesis is decisively refuted. It seems clear that Pannenberg's proposal results in a less anthropomorphic concept of God, but does it, at the same time, put too much at risk?

When we say that Pannenberg proposes that the concepts of mind and will be made secondary to that of an infinite field of power, the first question is one of clarification: What exactly does this mean? Clearly, he does not mean to discard them completely, given that he has commented that such a change in the doctrine of God "does not mean, of course, that the idea [of either mind or will] is meaningless or dispensable."[415] However, Pannenberg believes that both mind and will must be conceived in a man-

---

415. Ibid., 1:379.

ner so as to purge them of the hints of finitude arising from their relation to human self-experience. While one can get some sense of what they mean when applied to God, it must be recognized that both are radically different from their application to humans. Nevertheless, even if they are made secondary, one need only casually peruse Pannenberg's writings to see the extent to which God's knowledge and his freedom are deployed, though with modification.

In the latter stages of volume 1 of his *Systematic Theology*, Pannenberg offers a different basis upon which to construct the concepts of mind (or, more specifically, knowledge) and will. As to the former, he grounds God's knowledge in his omnipresence, God's presence with all of his creatures in all of their places. Concerning will, Pannenberg makes use of the notion of a transcendent power that impinges upon human experience:

> There is another starting point, however, for the idea of will. This does not lie in our human experience. It does not lie, then, in the relation of willing to a lack, or to the idea of seeking an end. It is to be found in the experience of a reality which presses in upon us, or seems to do so, even though what it wants is not very precise. This is an idea that has constantly impressed itself upon people in very different cultures.[416]

Here the notion of will does not have the tinges of human finitude as in the sense of willing toward a goal. Instead, this notion of will connects with God's expression of his intentions regarding human action and behavior. In both cases, Pannenberg does not so much delete mind and will as he tries to purge them of elements of finitude.

As a consequence, one is inclined to ask whether there might be a better term or phrase to capture what mind and will were intended to capture in their application to God without carrying the same anthropomorphic concerns. I believe the answer to that is yes, and that the better phrase is "an intentional agent." In the first place, there can be no question but that Pannenberg conceives God as a God who acts. Further, it is not at all clear that the notion of God's acting derives, either metaphorically or analogically, from human self-experience that is then transferred to God. In the second place, not only does Pannenberg conceive God as an acting God, but he also believes that God's acts issue forth in the results that he intends. As before, it is not clear that the notion of intention has the same finite limitation as implied by the concept of will; in other words, God's intentions are actualized by virtue of his power. Finally, Pannenberg affirms God's freedom in the strongest sense, and it is extremely hard to see how one makes

---

416. Ibid.

sense of the notion of freedom apart from that of intention. Consequently, while Pannenberg does not address these issues using these terms, there are reasons to believe that he would accept conceiving God as an intentional agent. By making this modification, I would characterize God in such a way as to overcome the difficulties inherent in the concepts of mind and will while maintaining those elements of mind and will that seem indispensable, namely, the notions of action, knowledge, and intentionality.

Personhood

More than once so far I have expressed concern regarding whether this proposal can adequately preserve the claim that God is personal. In fact, I have implied that if Pannenberg's proposal could not satisfactorily account for the personhood of God, that would be sufficient reason to judge it inadequate. Furthermore, that Pannenberg would agree with this assessment is evident when he argues that little remains of the concept of God if God cannot be conceived in some sense as personal.[417] Nevertheless, Pannenberg also admits the problematic nature of applying the concept of person to God: "If I see the matter correctly, the crisis of the idea of God since the eighteenth century is connected chiefly with the problem of how the power that determines all reality can be thought of as a person."[418] In order to determine the adequacy of Pannenberg's proposal in this regard, we will consider three questions: (1) What constitutes an adequate conception of personhood? (2) Is Pannenberg's concept of personhood adequate? (3) Can an infinite field of power plausibly be conceived as personal?

A Definition of Person

Conceptions of personhood vary widely. On the one hand, there are conceptions that emphasize individuality and autonomy. On the other hand, there are those that focus more upon the relational aspect of personhood to the extent that relationality is essential to conceiving something as person. In the modern era, the former conception is often associated with the Kantian tradition, while the latter is associated more with Hegel. The former (which Pannenberg calls the "absolute" concept of personhood) focuses upon the person as an expression of an independent (at least relatively) sphere of action, while the latter focuses upon the person as in relation with things or persons. Notwithstanding the variety of notions of personhood that have been proposed, for the purposes of this examination,

---

417. See, for example, W. Pannenberg, *Basic Questions in Theology* (vol. 2; trans. G. H. Kehm; Philadelphia: Westminster, 1971), 227ff., for a discussion of the importance of the personhood of God.
418. Ibid.

I shall take the following as a normative definition of personhood such that Pannenberg's proposal will be judged adequate only if it can meet the requirements laid down: "To say that God is *personal* is to say at least the following things: God has *knowledge and awareness*, God *performs actions*, God is *free* in the actions he performs, and God can *enter into relationships* with persons other than himself."[419] The notions of individuality and autonomy are captured in the requirement of freedom, and that of relationality appears in the last part of the definition.

Pannenberg's Concept of Person

To begin, let us expand upon Pannenberg's earlier judgment that the primary problem concerning the doctrine of God has to do with how to conceive him as personal. Why is it such a problem? The answer relates closely to our earlier discussions concerning anthropomorphic language. Specifically, the problem is that, in general, a concept of personhood was allegedly developed from humanity's self-experience, and then that concept was transferred to God. All such efforts, says Pannenberg, are vulnerable to Fichte's criticism that "every concept of 'person' conceived in this way includes within itself the finitude of man as a constitutive element, and therefore is unfit as a designation of the infinite power that determines all reality."[420]

Obviously, one way to remedy this situation would be to show that the concept of person could be plausibly understood as originating with God (or at least in the religious realm) and then transferred to humans. Consequently, Pannenberg asks, "Was not the personality of man originally thought of as a participation in the inviolable majesty of God, just as the ancient commandment against murder in Israel was motivated by man's being in the image of God?"[421] Next he argues that many modern concepts of personhood are rooted in Christian theology, specifically in the Trinitarian debates of the early church. Again, the idea of person is transferred from the religious sphere to humanity. Ultimately, Pannenberg believes that the origin of the concept of person is to be found in the religious experiences of primitive humans who found themselves confronted with a power that can be characterized as nonmanipulable but that also "makes a concrete claim upon man."[422] Of course, the concept of a personal *power* is not anthropomorphic.

The four elements of personhood, according to the definition cited above, are that a person (1) possesses knowledge and self-awareness,

---

419. D. Basinger et al., *Reason and Religious Belief* (New York: Oxford University Press, 1991), 54.
420. Pannenberg, *Basic Questions in Theology*, 2:227.
421. Ibid., 2:229.
422. Ibid.

(2) performs intentional actions, (3) is free, and (4) is capable of entering relationships. Would a "person," along the lines proposed by Pannenberg (which are focused primarily upon how a power could be personal[423]), meet these four conditions? In the first place, the personal power that Pannenberg conceives, by virtue of its nonmanipulable character coupled with its activity, must be seen as free and autonomous; it makes claims, for example, rather than submitting to them. Since making a claim and expressing that claim to humans must be seen as an act, this power engages in acts, which, as a consequence of its freedom, must be conceived as intentional. While in the passages above Pannenberg makes no explicit reference to knowledge and awareness, it seems to follow from the nature of the acts described that knowledge and awareness would be an integral part of the reality of this power. Further, as we saw in our discussion of concepts of mind and will and the discussions of chapters 4–5, Pannenberg affirms the traditional divine attribute of omniscience, which means God has something analogous to knowledge even if it is gained in a mysterious fashion. The issue is that when knowledge is predicated of God, it has a radically different sense than when applied to humans. Finally, the concept of the interaction between this power and humans seems clearly to describe a relationship. Consequently, while the concept that Pannenberg lays out of a power as a person is rather different from what we normally expect, there seems to be no clear reason to deny that the power he describes could be conceived as personal in the sense I have taken as definitive.

A Field as Person

Recall briefly the previous discussion concerning the developments in elementary physics whereby the priority between fields and bodies has been reversed so that fields are now conceived as primary. While fields were once conceived as manifestations of prior bodies, fields are now seen as basic reality and bodies as manifestations of those fields. More specifically, theories advanced by today's physicists conceive enduring material objects as the results of the convergence of lines of force within overarching fields. This means that all material objects are composed of fields, including human beings. Consequently, all human persons, who actualize those characteristics constitutive of personhood, are manifestations of prior fields. Can fields be personal? If these field theories are correct, it seems the answer is yes.

---

423. I make this distinction here not in order to repudiate the definition deployed in chapter 5 in discussion of the doctrine of the Trinity, but rather to focus upon the issues relating to his argument intending to develop the idea of a personal power.

There is one other group of experiences to which one might make appeal in attempting to show that it is plausible that fields of force may be personal. Consider the evidence from reported near-death experiences.[424] It is a very common element of such experiences that the one near death describes an encounter with a "being of light." This being of light is, psychologically anyway, always described in personal terms, which might include feelings of love, expressions of judgment, and the like. However, even though the being is described in such personal terms, the descriptions of the nature of the physical encounter make it seem more like an encounter with a field of some sort. There is generally no body or other physicality involved in the description of the "being"; rather, it is simply characterized as a "presence" that is described as existing simply in the form of a bright light. Does not such a description lead one to something like the concept of a field of energy? If God is correctly characterized as an infinite field of power, then construing experiences of this sort as interaction between God and the "soul" of the individual seems entirely plausible. We need not hang too much upon this admittedly slender evidence, but it is some evidence nonetheless, and it suggests that the notion of personhood and realities that may be conceptualized as a field are coherent with each other.[425]

The preceding discussion has looked at whether Pannenberg's proposal can adequately maintain the affirmation that God is personal. I have concluded that Pannenberg's concept of person is adequate and that in light of current theories, it is plausible to conceive a field of force as personal. Of course, this by no means demonstrates decisively that God is a field of force or that a field of force is personal. Nevertheless, this suggests one issue that will require subsequent treatment: How much confusion will be generated by the fact that most "commonsense" intuitions will find the concept of field, particularly as deployed in the natural sciences, difficult to conceive in personal terms? This concern does not provide philosophical or theological reasons to reject Pannenberg's proposal; after all, initial intuitions may be mistaken. However, it does suggest that this reconceptualization might invite misunderstanding. Preventing such misunderstanding will be an important aspect of the articulation of this doctrine of God should it become widely accepted.

---

424. Some may find the evidence of near-death experiences to be of a very speculative nature. However, there is a great deal of commonality in these experiences, and a large number of them has been reported by now. Consequently, it would be intellectual snobbery to dismiss them out of hand. Here I consider certain elements important for my argument.

425. Some will undoubtedly object that surely such a field as present in these experiences is not an *infinite* field, but Pannenberg argues that God need not manifest his infinity to manifest himself to humans.

Pantheism

There can be no question but that Pannenberg overtly rejects pantheistic conceptions of God, and this is frequently evident in his writings.[426] Consequently, the question requiring attention is not whether Pannenberg is a pantheist, but whether his proposal to conceive God along the lines of an infinite field of power has pantheism as its consequence, or at least as a likely implication. In order to assess this matter properly, it will be necessary to consider the relation between this proposal and the doctrine of creation. Specifically, how is God, understood as a field of power, related to the initial act of creation and the subsequent sustaining of that creation?

Given that fields are conceived as prior to bodies so that lines of force in overarching fields give rise to bodies and since in this proposal God is conceived as an infinite field, is it plausible to understand the big bang as God's initial creative act whereby that initial space-time-energy field (perhaps once or twice removed from the divine field) gave rise to independent, material bodies? To date, Pannenberg has not explicitly made such a proposal.[427] However, it is a question that must inevitably arise in the course of further development of his proposed reconceptualization of God.

First, there is a similarity between this extension of Pannenberg's position as described above and Karl Rahner's claim that when God wills to be not God, human beings come into existence. In Rahner's statement, there seems at least the suggestion that God's creation of humanity, while not from some antecedent material or substance or even from God's own substance, is somehow to be understood as from the fullness of God's own being. Rahner's claim is not that everything is divine, for he clearly states that humanity corresponds to "not God." At the same time, however, there is most certainly implied a very close relationship between humanity and its creator.

Second, Pannenberg makes it clear that he intends to distinguish between the infinite field that corresponds to the divine essence and the space-time-energy field that constitutes the background field of the physical universe. He does not deny that the latter is dependent upon the former; however, this distinction is part of his explicit attempt to avoid the charge of pantheism. Recall the quotation earlier in this chapter: "Even a cosmic field conceived along the lines of Faraday's thought as a field of force would not be identified immediately with the dynamic activity of the divine Spirit in creation."[428]

---

426. Consider, for example, *Systematic Theology*, 1:443–44, or *Systematic Theology*, 2:89. In addition, Pannenberg confirmed his explicit rejection of pantheism in private conversation.

427. In private conversation, however, he did not reject the idea.

428. Pannenberg, *Toward a Theology of Nature*, 40.

Third, it is rather unfortunate, but nevertheless I think true, that the tradition has not been as clear as one would have liked with regard to the exact intent of the doctrine of *creatio ex nihilo*. Specifically, is the nothingness from which God creates nothingness in the absolute, undialectical sense? Or is it to be taken in the relatively weaker sense of nothing apart from the fullness of God's own being? Worthing believes that the tradition has intended the latter:

> This is not to say that the Christian doctrine of *creatio ex nihilo* is to be understood in the most radical sense of a creation from absolute nothingness. "Nothing" means simply no material substance or principle apart from the fullness of God's own being. Thus Democritus' ancient philosophical dictum, *ex nihilo nihil fit* (nothing comes out of nothing), is not in conflict with a correctly understood doctrine of *creatio ex nihilo* which asserts that God created out of nothing other than God's own "fullness of being."[429]

Pannenberg seems largely in agreement with the claims that the primary intent of the doctrine of *creatio ex nihilo* was to deny another material substrate or principle that limited the freedom of the Creator with regard to his creative act.[430] That Pannenberg sees the creatures God created as other than God is clear when he writes that the creatures "are an expression of the love of the Creator, who willed that his creatures should be free and independent."[431]

Unfortunately, the distinctions made in the quote from Worthing are not altogether satisfactory in helping bring the clarifications necessary for this discussion. Even if the intent of *creatio ex nihilo* is to indicate that God created from nothing other than the "fullness of God's own being," what exactly does that mean? Worthing believes that to claim God creates from his own "substance" results in pantheism. However, Worthing is not at all clear on what distinguishes "God's own 'substance'" from "the fullness of God's own being." This is particularly problematic in light of the fact that substance within the philosophical/theological tradition can be taken immaterially (e.g., intelligible substance) as well as materially. If God is to be conceived as an infinite field of power, is this field best described as the "divine substance" or as "the fullness of God's own being"? How are we to decide the issue of the pantheistic implications of Pannenberg's proposal?

Consider a possible resolution along the following lines. Let us say that God's initial creative act was that of giving rise to the space-time-energy field, which, while separate from, is nonetheless utterly dependent upon the

---

429. Worthing, *God, Creation, and Contemporary Physics*, 75.
430. See, for example, *Systematic Theology*, 2:13–17.
431. Ibid., 2:16.

field of power that corresponds to the divine essence. And to maintain continuity with our last discussion, let us say that this is creation from the fullness of God's own being. The creation of enduring physical objects came about when God willed the convergence of lines of force within the overarching field so that these enduring physical objects "ride" upon the underlying field. God's continuing interaction with the cosmic field initially brought about the big bang and, subsequently through his omnipotence and omnipresence, guided the formation and evolution of the physical universe so that eventually stars, planets, living creatures, and human beings came into existence. Does such a construal avoid pantheism?

In the first place, much will hinge upon further determination of exactly what the distinction between God's substance and the fullness of God's own being means and whether the construal of creation indicated above would count as creation from the fullness of God's own being. There are other reasons to conclude that Pannenberg's proposal does not lead to pantheism. First, just as it is the case that while fields give rise to enduring physical objects, the physical objects are not those fields, it seems that one can argue that even if the field of power to which God corresponds gives rise to physical objects, those physical objects are not a part of God. Second, Pannenberg seeks to distance himself from pantheism by arguing that the cosmic space-time-energy field is already once removed from God's field of power. Third, Pannenberg affirms the independence (relative, not absolute, of course) and autonomy of the creatures, again seeking to distinguish them from God's own "substance." These considerations seem at a minimum to show that Pannenberg's proposal does not necessarily imply pantheism but rather that a plausible denial of pantheistic consequences can be given. If this is correct, Pannenberg's proposal could provide a profound sense of meaning to the claim that God is the unifying ground of all creation and that creation is sustained from moment to moment by God's active involvement.

Scientific Criticism of Pannenberg's Appropriation of the Field Concept

Having completed our examination of Pannenberg's proposal from a theological perspective, we now turn our attention to assessment of his appropriation of the field concept. More specifically, the issue is whether his proposal correctly and fairly uses the notion of field or whether it is merely another case of theology engaging in pseudoscience. While it is not surprising that atheistic scientists would be critical of attempts by theologians to make use of scientific concepts for theological purposes, it seems that even theistic scientists are often more critical than they might be. In what follows, our examination will consider two issues: (1) whether Jammer's work supports Pannenberg's proposal and (2) whether the field concept has been justifiably deployed.

Pannenberg summarizes the thrust of Jammer's work as follows:

> The claim that the switch in modern physics to increasingly comprehensive field theories of natural occurrence is of theological relevance finds support in the metaphysical origin of the field concept. The idea of the field of force goes back by way of Stoicism to pre-Socratic philosophy, namely, to the teaching of Anaximenes that air is the *arche* and that all things originated as compressions of air. Max Jammer thinks that the Stoic doctrine of the divine *pneuma* was actually the direct precursor of the modern field concept.[432]

The claim here is that the origin of the field theories of modern physics is to be located in the Stoic metaphysical inquiry into the divine origin of the cosmos. Consequently, one can argue that rather than theology appropriating a concept from the natural sciences, in actuality the natural sciences appropriated and developed a philosophical/theological concept. While this alone does not prove that the field concept has been deployed properly by Pannenberg, it seems to provide *prima facie* justification for attempting to establish the sorts of connections outlined in his proposal.

Of course, even if the field theories of modern physics are traceable to the philosophical inquiry into the nature of the divine as Jammer thinks, this does not mean that the scientific and theological uses of the concept are identical:

> The principal differences between the ways of describing reality in physics and in theology prohibit us from offering a direct theological interpretation of the field theories of physics. In accordance with the nature of scientific perceptions, these theories can be seen only as approximations to the reality that is also the subject of theological statements about creation. We see that the reality is the same because theological statements about the working of the Spirit of God in creation historically go back to the same philosophical root that by mathematical formalizing is also the source of the field theories of physics, and the different theories give evidence of the same emphases that we find in the underlying metaphysical intuitions.[433]

Again, the emphasis is upon the common historical antecedent, not the manner in which the concepts are deployed. Also, we must remember that

---

432. Pannenberg, *Systematic Theology*, 2:81.
433. Ibid.

the point of Pannenberg's drawing attention to Jammer's work is to show that this is not merely another case of theologians blindly adopting concepts from the natural sciences because they appear to be applicable to some problem in theology. Instead, Pannenberg wishes to establish that there are good reasons for applying the concept of field to God's nature, and one good reason is that modern field theories, if Jammer is correct, actually derived from the early Greeks' meditations upon the nature of the divine.

Finally, Pannenberg goes one step further in that he denies that theology may simply adopt the field concept for its own use unless there are reasons internal to theology that justify that move:

> The relation, of course, is not merely an external one. If it were, we would simply have bad apologetics. Theology has to have its own material reasons for applying a basic scientific concept like field theory to its own philosophical rather than scientific explanation. Only then is it justified in developing such concepts in a way appropriate to its own themes and independently of scientific usage. Reasons for introducing the field concept into theology have been given already in the context of the doctrine of God, namely, in interpreting the traditional description of God as Spirit.[434]

It is, according to Pannenberg, precisely the difficulties associated with conceiving God as *nous* that leads us to conclude that it is more appropriate to understand the claim that God is spirit to mean "a dynamic field that is structured in a trinitarian fashion."[435] Jammer's work, it seems, provides support for Pannenberg's appropriation of the field concept.

Up to this point, we have largely assumed that Pannenberg's understanding of the field concept and his articulation of it are essentially correct from the standpoint of the underlying physics. However, scientists who feel this is not the case have advanced some criticisms. In fact, Jeffrey Wicken has argued that Pannenberg does not adequately distinguish between the different senses in which the field concept can be used and that his arguments misconstrue much of the underlying science.[436]

There are two issues in Pannenberg's use of the field concept that require attention: (1) whether he intends field to be taken literally, analogically, or metaphorically and (2) which of the several field concepts he intends to deploy theologically. On the first issue, Worthing says, "The analogical character of the field concept, especially within quantum physics, must not be overlooked. . . . Words such as 'field' and 'force' are analogies

---

434. Ibid.
435. Ibid.
436. J. Wicken, "Theology and Science in the Evolving Cosmos: A Need for Dialogue," *Zygon* 23, no. 1 (March 1988): 48, 51; cited in Worthing, *God, Creation, and Contemporary Physics*, 124.

that help us comprehend physical reality, they are not themselves reality—
unless perhaps they be understood as mathematical reality."[437] In other
words, fields are themselves conceptual tools that help us understand the
cosmos; they are not to be taken as more than that. Interestingly, Faraday
himself decided to use the term "field" to describe the phenomenon he had
in mind upon observing the lines in the earth caused by a farmer's plowing
his field. These lines in the earth seemed to Faraday to be a good analogy of
what "lines of force" might look like if they were visible. Clearly, then,
"field," even when used in science, is intended to be something of a
metaphor. Additionally, Worthing cites physicist James Jean: "Before man
appeared on the scene there were neither wave nor electrical nor magnetic
forces; these were not created by God, but by Huyghens, Fresnel, Faraday
and Maxwell."[438] By this Jean intends to point out the metaphorical nature
of the field concept, saying that God did not create *these ideas* (which he
certainly would have if fields constituted reality), but rather humans created them as conceptual aids. All of this suggests that Pannenberg's use of
the field concept should be taken as no more than metaphorical, though it
often seems to be more than a model or paradigm. Pannenberg's desire to
bring the sciences more closely together with theology leads him to expend
"great effort to show the connections to the use of field theory in physics,"
and consequently, "it is not always easy to distinguish whether he means a
field in the theological or physical sense."[439] At a minimum, Pannenberg
needs to say more in order to clear up these ambiguities.[440]

Closely related to the question of whether Pannenberg is using the field
concept literally, analogically, or metaphorically is the fact that "there are a
number of field theories in the natural sciences, biological as well as physical. Within physics alone there are classical and quantum field theories of
different types."[441] Unfortunately, so the criticism goes, Pannenberg does
not distinguish between these different sorts of fields. Instead, he builds his
proposal to conceive God as an infinite field of power upon the general
concept of fields of force, depending most heavily upon Faraday's original
ideas. Worthing notes three problems with this. First, Faraday is hardly a
twenty-first-century physicist. In fact, while some aspects of Faraday's original vision seem confirmed by later developments, in other aspects he has

---

437. Worthing, *God, Creation, and Contemporary Physics*, 118–19.

438. J. Jean, *Physics and Philosophy* (Cambridge: Cambridge University Press, 1944), 234; cited in Worthing, *God, Creation, and Contemporary Physics*, 120.

439. Worthing, *God, Creation, and Contemporary Physics*, 121.

440. I discussed these issues in private conversation with Pannenberg in October 1999. He indicated that
his primary concern in using the field concept in theology is not so much to insist upon its literal use but to
argue that it be taken as seriously in theology as it is in the natural sciences. This seems to help clear up this
point, and we can say that Pannenberg accepts a metaphorical usage of the term—as long as we at the same
time point out that it is similarly used in science.

441. Worthing, *God, Creation, and Contemporary Physics*, 123.

been proven wrong. So to the extent Pannenberg's proposal is tied to Faraday's theory, there is some reason for concern. Second, concerning one specific aspect of Faraday's theory, while he envisioned one overarching, universal field as the foundation of reality, modern physics has largely abandoned hope that such a unified field will be discovered. Finally, Wicken suggests that if God is to be conceived literally as the field that physicists propose, one wonders why the notion of God is still needed. Under such conditions, physics would adequately describe the cosmos without reference to God.

While these criticisms are substantial and require response, it is not at all clear that they refute Pannenberg's proposal. In fact, and Worthing seems to agree, many of the problems highlighted above would tend to be resolved if Pannenberg were to make it clear that he intends the use of fields to be a model, a conceptual tool aimed at aiding our understanding of what it means to say God is spirit. This would obviate the concern that Pannenberg takes the field concept too seriously, and it would obviously clear up the ambiguity concerning the manner in which he intends the field concept to be used. Of course, the more analogically the field concept is taken, the looser the bonds with the theories of the natural sciences. However, many consider this an advantage rather than a disadvantage, since it would not make the theological claims subject to the need for revision if the fine details of the field concept are modified in future versions. Further, the more the field concept is taken analogically, the freer one is to deal with the differences between theological and scientific uses of the field concept.

As to the "misconstrual" that arises from Pannenberg's failure to distinguish between the various types of fields, it is not clear but that Pannenberg's proposal already contains the resources necessary to respond. As we saw earlier, Pannenberg argues that the space-time-energy field is already once removed from the underlying, unifying field that corresponds to God. The fact that there are various fields (quantum fields, electrical fields, for example) seems quite unproblematic. Why could not the divine, unifying field give rise to various higher-order fields, just as I argued that it gives rise to a variety of material objects? Clearly, Pannenberg's primary concern is with what he takes to be the underlying divine field; consequently, it is not entirely surprising that he does not distinguish between the higher-order fields.

Summary and Conclusions

Throughout the course of this assessment, the focus has been primarily upon whether Pannenberg's proposal can be reasonably defended against the sorts of objections that have been (or surely will be) raised. The analyses in this process have indicated that such a defense can be reasonably given. We have seen that Pannenberg's proposal has the potential to alleviate many of the concerns that Pannenberg has with regard to the traditional doctrine of God. For example, it appears that the arguments involved with the defense of this proposal provide more than adequate rebuttal of the objection that nonembodied causation is incoherent; certainly Pannenberg's proposal would reduce the concern with the use of overly anthropomorphic concepts in the doctrine of God; to the extent the field analogy is acceptable, the natural sciences and theology are brought closer together; and this proposal clearly goes a long way toward overcoming the tendency to divinize reason. However, concern remains in some areas; for example, the proposal that a field can be personal seems to violate commonsense perceptions of personhood, especially in the mind of the nonexpert. Likewise, it seems that the notions of God's love and compassion are intimately connected with the concepts of thought and mind. Consequently, even those generally sympathetic toward Pannenberg's proposal are likely to be reticent about allowing the concepts of mind and will to wander too far from center stage.

Given that a reasonable defense of this proposal seems possible, is it a desirable reconceptualization of the Christian doctrine of God? Surely this is an important question, for the grounds for such a radical revision to the doctrine of God must be more than that the new proposal can be rationally defended. Instead, one must judge the extent to which the new proposal is an advance over preceding conceptions. Pannenberg argues that his proposal does constitute such an advance because he believes it resolves a number of issues, most of which I have identified along the way. However, I suspect that individuals will be inclined to accept Pannenberg's proposed revision to the extent that they believe refutation of Fichte, Feuerbach, and Freud, for example, and the bringing closer of the natural sciences and theology are worth the risks to conceptual clarity regarding God's personhood and his intentional activity.

Perhaps the most significant objection that Pannenberg's proposal will face is the extent to which personhood can be asserted of God conceived as an infinite field of power. Notwithstanding the sorts of arguments that were deployed on behalf of Pannenberg's proposal in our earlier discussions, intuitions likely will be divided on a number of the details. Consequently, the issue of whether a field of power can be conceived as personal is likely to persist for some time. There are some areas of scholarly inquiry where research is being done that might prove helpful in addressing this issue. Unfortunately, at the present, some are likely to consider the field of paranormal research to be quasi-scholarly and, therefore, not adequately "scientific" to provide much useful data. However, Christians have been some of the first to point out that one cannot merely apply the epistemic standards of sense perception to forms of perception that are not based upon sense perception.[442] Consequently, we ought not dismiss paranormal research out of hand; rather, it seems entirely plausible to argue that paranormal research and the corresponding experiences provide *prima facie* justification for belief in certain nonphysical realities, specifically, nonembodied causal agents. Further, we ought to remember that such research tends to affirm the existence of some of the same entities that Christians have traditionally affirmed, such as the reality of angels and demons, which are examples of those nonphysical, intentional agents. In fact, language highly suggestive of a "field of power" is quite common in paranormal research, and frequently the entities described in such research would easily meet the requirements for personhood that we identified earlier.[443] As with our earlier consideration of the evidence that might be available from near-death experiences, perhaps one ought not hang too much on the evidence available from the paranormal at present. Nevertheless, neither should we entirely ignore such evidence. All of this suggests that, initial intuitions to the contrary, there are reasons to believe that conceiving fields of power in terms indicative of personhood may well be appropriate. Consequently, in spite of the initial problems with conceiving a field of power as personal, there simply is not adequate reason to believe that such a proposal has been refuted, nor for that matter are there adequate reasons for arguing that it is implausible. So my conclusion that Pannenberg has demonstrated the plausibility of his proposal maintaining the personhood of God stands.

While objections concerning the manner in which Pannenberg appropriates the field theories proposed in the natural sciences are likely to continue, my examination has tended to show that these objections often read more into Pannenberg's appropriation than he intends. For example, while in places Pannenberg has said that he intends the concept of field to be

---

442. One might consider, for example, William Alston, *Perceiving God* (Ithaca, NY: Cornell University Press, 1991), wherein Alston distinguishes between sense perception and mystical perception, the latter being a form of perception that Alston proposes for perceiving nonphysical realities. He calls epistemic imperialism an attempt to deny mystical perception on the grounds that it cannot meet the standards of sense perceptual faculties. He goes on to defend mystical perception by trying to show that attempts to defend it are no less circular than those defending sense perceptive faculties. Richard Swinburne, in *The Existence of God* (Oxford: Clarendon, 1979), has argued for the principles of testimony and credulity. In short, Swinburne argues that in the absence of special circumstances, one should find the testimony of others trustworthy. Swinburne argues that if some state of affairs seems to obtain to some subject in the absence of special circumstances, then most likely that state of affairs does obtain. One can relate this to the present argument by cautiously suggesting that paranormal research provides *prima facie* justification for believing that extraphysical realities, specifically nonembodied agents, exist.

443. Such entities are generally described as invisible and immaterial, and yet they are conceived as able to cause physical objects to move. Further, these nonphysical entities are generally conceived as wanting something or attempting to communicate something to humans. References to fields of energy also are quite frequent.

applied to God literally, he also observes that the deployment of the concept will be different in theological applications from that in, for example, the applications of physicists. I believe that what Pannenberg means by these two comments is that he intends for the general concept of field, most basically as an energy gradient over an expanse of space, to be applied literally to explain what it means to say God is spirit. However, he does not intend that any specific field affirmed by physicists be applied literally to God. In this case, the objectors owe us a more detailed analysis of this understanding of Pannenberg's position. In the meantime, I maintain the position that Pannenberg's appropriation of the concept meets reasonable requirements.

I have identified moves that Pannenberg could undertake that have the potential to noticeably strengthen his proposal. First, he should admit that the concept of field is intended merely as an analogy or a model for conceptualizing spirit. This would most likely loosen the bonds he seeks to forge between science and theology. However, it could be argued that in the long run, the proposal so clarified would no longer so clearly bind it to the details of a particular scientific theory. Second, it seems clear that this proposal, notwithstanding our various arguments, needs a better accounting of personal, intentional agency. Even if one agrees with the need to resolve the issues involving the use of anthropomorphic language in the doctrine of God, one is likely to wish that Pannenberg had provided explicit address to the question of God's intentions and intentional actions. Again, it is abundantly clear that Pannenberg affirms both the intentionality and the personhood of God; however, more explicit attention to these issues in the context of his deployment of the field concept might be helpful.

Even with these few shortcomings, Pannenberg's proposal for reconceptualization of God as an infinite field of power is a fascinating, and I believe promising, proposal for revising the Christian doctrine of God. It will be interesting to see how the interaction between critics and supporters will result either in the widespread acceptance of the proposal, possibly with appropriate modifications, or in the rejection of the proposal. I have examined Pannenberg's doctrine of God over the course of the last several chapters, and the focus has been more on the inner being of God. With the next chapter, I change the focus to examine the divine attributes, which as one might expect, Pannenberg also proposes to revise in important ways.

CHAPTER 7

The Doctrine of the Divine Attributes

UP TO THIS POINT, our examination has proceeded along the lines of an inquiry into four of the central themes of Pannenberg's proposed revision to the Christian doctrine of God: (1) the elevation of the concept of the infinite to primacy within the doctrine of God; (2) the claim that God is the power of the future that determines everything that exists; (3) the centrality of the claim that the one God exists as a differentiated unity, specifically, a Trinity of Father, Son, and Holy Spirit; and (4) the reconceptualization of God as an infinite field of power. I have undertaken these topics in the preceding four chapters, and in each case, I have found Pannenberg's proposal plausible, coherent, and defensible. At the same time, I have recognized that intuitions are deeply divided at several points so that even in light of plausible and coherent arguments, Pannenberg's doctrine of God will undoubtedly face a number of challenges, the most significant of which we have considered.

Several issues relating to the divine essence and the attributes that reveal it have arisen as they were relevant to the issue then at hand. For example, an important element of our discussion of God as the power of the future was Pannenberg's articulation of the divine eternity. While examining the doctrine of the Trinity, I commented briefly on such attributes as omnipotence and omnipresence. In particular, I attempted to show how the doctrine of the Trinity informs our understanding of these. Finally, in the last chapter, I examined Pannenberg's proposal that the concept of a field of force be deployed to help give content to the "spiritual" nature of the divine essence. So far, then, I have dealt with the divine attributes only to the extent necessary and have refrained from addressing matters related directly to the attributes as such and the unity of the attributes. However, in this chapter, I turn my attention directly to the divine attributes, with particular attention to how a particular conception of the divine essence instructs derivation of the divine attributes.

Pannenberg has indicated that he believes the chapter in his *Systematic Theology* that deals with the divine attributes is the most difficult chapter in volume 1. He takes up two closely related topics in that chapter, and both are suggested by its title: "The Unity and Attributes of the Divine Essence." While we have discussed the unity of the divine essence in relation to Pannenberg's Trinitarian doctrine, here we shall see how that unity impacts our understanding of the attributes. I will proceed as follows. First, I will consider what the tradition has intended when it has spoken of the mystery of the divine essence, particularly regarding the seemingly contradictory claims that the essence exists as a unity but also exists concretely as three persons. Second, to develop a proper understanding of the relation between the essence and its attributes, I will discuss the relationship between the concepts of existence and essence. Next I will consider how God's actions influence our ability to derive the attributes, precisely as attributes that reveal the essence. After these preliminary but necessary discussions, I will undertake an examination of the individual attributes as Pannenberg understands them. Finally, I will critically examine the proposal for his doctrine of the attributes in total, considering its conceptual adequacy, coherence, and plausibility.

Three yet One: The Mystery of the Divine Essence

At the beginning of volume 1 of *Systematic Theology*, Pannenberg asserts that if God is to be known, then he must reveal himself:

> The founding of theology on divine revelation is not a determination that is foreign to its nature, as the later distinction between natural and revealed theology might seem to imply. Instead, the knowledge of God that is made possible by God, and therefore by revelation, is one of the basic conditions of the concept of theology as such. Otherwise the possibility of the knowledge of God is logically inconceivable; it would contradict the very idea of God.[444]

---

444. W. Pannenberg, *Systematic Theology* (vol. 1; trans. G. W. Bromiley; Grand Rapids: Eerdmans, 1991), 2.

I believe we must be careful in drawing out the implications of what Pannenberg is suggesting here. He certainly does not intend these assertions to stand in contradiction to his earlier claim that, for example, the creatureliness of humans cannot be hidden from them.[445] And, of course, if one's creatureliness cannot be hidden, it is a very short inference from there to the proposal that a Creator exists. Pannenberg's claim here is that the existence of something that can be conceptualized as creature presupposes something that must be conceptualized as Creator. So Pannenberg's claim that God can only be known if he should give himself to be known does not contradict his earlier claim that a vague, quasi-inferential knowledge of God is innate in humans. Rather, the point is that to move beyond this innate knowledge of God to more detailed and explicit knowledge requires God's self-revelatory acts. Otherwise, the vague, fuzzy intuition would receive little concrete content.

So if knowledge of God hinges upon God's revelation, the next issue concerns whether God has, in fact, given himself to be known. If the answer is affirmative, then we must ask where he has given himself to be known. We have already seen Pannenberg's answer in our discussions concerning the doctrine of the Trinity: "No one knows the Father except the Son and any one to whom the Son chooses to reveal him" (Matt 11:27).[446] Similarly, from John 1:18: "No one has ever seen God; the only Son, who is in the bosom of the Father, he has made him known" (339). Hence, we see that God has given himself to be known and unsurpassably so in the revelation in Jesus Christ so that "the essence of the otherwise incomprehensible God is disclosed" (340).[447] Momentarily, I shall have more to say about Pannenberg's claim that the essence of God is known in this revelation, but first I will comment further upon his reference to God as the one who is "incomprehensible."

Pannenberg calls Gregory of Nyssa's incorporation of the concept of infinity as central to his whole concept of God an epochal contribution to reflections on the divine. In chapter 3 we examined Gregory's argument for the divine infinity. In the course of the Arian controversy, there were those—Eunomius and his school in particular—who denied the incomprehensibility of God. Gregory of Nazianzus argued against the Arians for the incomprehensibility of the divine essence, and Gregory of Nyssa, agreeing with his fellow Cappadocian, based the incomprehensibility of the essence upon the divine infinity. As Pannenberg writes, "If God is infinite, [Gregory] said, it

---

445. Here, "creatureliness" should be taken to mean something like "contingent" or "finite."

446. Pannenberg, *Systematic Theology*, 1:264. The remaining citations in this chapter from volume 1 of *Systematic Theology* are in parentheses in the text.

447. Of course, this is not to deny God's revelatory acts preceding Christ but rather to focus upon Christ as the revelation of God par excellence.

follows that we cannot ultimately define his essence, for it is indescribable"
(342). This same set of sentiments guides Pannenberg when, at the outset of
his discussion of the divine attributes, he writes that all talk of God "must
begin and end with confession of the inconceivable majesty of God which
transcends all our concepts" (337). According to these arguments, the divine
essence cannot be exhaustively comprehended, and yet God can be known
in some sense since he gives himself to be known. Consequently, the question
that becomes important for our analysis is, what can be known about God?

It has generally been the unity of the one God that has been conceived
as knowable by means of philosophical or rational inquiry, and the Trinitarian nature of the divine essence has been taken as that which is hidden.
However, it is at this point that Pannenberg proposes to reverse our understanding of what is hidden and revealed so that it is the Trinitarian nature
of the divine essence that is revealed. Specifically, it is revealed in the concrete actions of the Father, Son, and Spirit in the course of salvation history.
It is the unity of God, says Pannenberg, that is hidden:

> In the contradictions of historical experience the unity of God is hidden, the
> unity of God who works in world history and the God whose love is
> revealed in Jesus Christ. . . . The trinitarian distinctions of Father, Son, and
> Spirit are not hidden. They characterize the divine reality that discloses itself
> in the event of revelation. What is hidden is the unity of the divine essence in
> these distinctions. (340–41)

In essence, Pannenberg is claiming that if we take the revelation in Christ
seriously, we must deal with the references to Father and Spirit in addition
to the Son, even if there is no explicit statement of the Trinitarian relations
in Scripture. Once we accept the Trinitarian consequences of the revelation
in Christ, then the problem becomes how to understand the unity of the
three divine persons. In other words, how is it that these three divine persons are one God? Consequently, it is the unity of the divine essence, not its
Trinitarian nature, that is hidden.

Pannenberg makes two other points. First, he comments briefly upon
the development of the apophatic tradition, that portion of the tradition
that attempts to speak of God by saying what he is not. Pannenberg's primary point is simply this: Even by speaking in terms of what God is not,
those engaging in apophatic predication are still expressing *something*
about the divine essence. Even by saying what God is not, one presupposes
at least a preliminary conception of God's nature. Apophaticism may not
yet say what God is, but by precluding certain predicates, one begins to nar-
row what the term "God" could mean. I will unpack this more in our discussion of the relationship between the concepts of existence and essence.

The second point deals with the tradition's attempt to speak of God by combining general terms with distinguishing terms. The general terms, which can be conceived as something of a preliminary definition, may come from different sources, such as the concept of God as spirit or as first cause of the world. The distinguishing terms are generally related to the divine infinity. Here the details are less important for our analysis than merely observing that one begins with a preliminary concept of God that one develops into a doctrine of God including the divine attributes.

Existence and Essence

Historical Development and Analysis

Pannenberg begins his analysis of the concepts of existence and essence with the work of Aristotle. On the one hand, he tends to reject Aristotle's identification of essence with substance. On the other hand, he rejects certain philosophical criticisms of the Aristotelian notion of essence. In the first place, he argues that the concept of essence is necessary for the identification of a given existent's "whatness," and it is precisely the older concept of essence in Aristotle that serves the function of allowing existents to be distinguished from each other. Next Pannenberg observes that the traditional ordering of the relation between existence and essence has been that one *first* observes that a given thing exists and *then* moves to define the essence of that existent. However, Pannenberg argues that the ordering between the two concepts is more complex and, therefore, requires subtler analysis.

At the beginning of the section entitled "The Distinction between God's Essence and Existence," Pannenberg writes, "The thesis that God's essence is incomprehensible did not stop the fathers from maintaining that we may know God's existence" (347). So while they tended to argue that the divine essence could not be comprehended, in the sense of fully grasped, the Fathers believed one could know that God exists. Further, Pannenberg claims that many of the early Fathers believed that *some* understanding of the divine nature went along with the knowledge of God and of God's existence. At this stage, Pannenberg's concern is not yet the ordering of the concepts but rather the very close way in which they are related.

Pannenberg writes that "Aquinas made the most impressive attempt to derive all his statements about what God is from the proof of his mere existence as first cause of the world" (348). However, in subsequent generations, this sort of move from God's existence as first cause to his defining characteristics became more tenuous so that, in fact, the concepts of essence and existence drifted further apart. At first glance, Pannenberg argues, this separation seems to continue in Luther, who "argued that there is a great difference between knowing that there is a God and knowing what or who God is" (348). By reason, one may know that God is, but not who he is. However, Luther had accepted the argument of Augustine concerning an "intuitive knowledge of God [that] precedes all rational argument" (348). Consequently, Luther's distinction between essence and existence is not as severe as it might seem at first. In fact, Pannenberg observes that Luther and the older Protestant tradition tended to see more clearly that "the question of the existence of a thing (*an sit*) cannot be totally independent of some idea of what the thing is (*quid sit*)" (349).

One need only consider the various arguments for God's existence to see something of what Pannenberg means here. To deploy the cosmological argument for God's existence is to presuppose that proving the existence of a Creator (or first cause) means proving that God exists. To deploy the teleological argument is to presuppose that the order apparent in the cosmos requires explanation and that the existence of a designer or orderer proves the existence of God. Finally, to deploy the ontological argument is to argue that proving the existence of a necessary being or a perfect being or the metaphysical infinite (depending upon the form) proves the existence of God. In each case, one presupposes something of what it means to be God *before* one engages the question of the existence of that particular being. While, as with Aquinas, much of the tradition has tended to favor derivations that are based upon conceiving God as first cause, Pannenberg is skeptical: "It is thus a dubious procedure to try to derive from the idea of a first cause more concrete statements about God in his distinction from creatures and his relation to the world, and even more so to try to argue that the resultant statements are materially congruent with the biblical witness to God" (349). If the idea of God as first cause is a "dubious" basis for developing an understanding of God's essence, then what idea might we use? As one might guess, given Pannenberg's proposal to make the concept of infinity central to the whole doctrine of God, it is the concept of the infinite that he proposes as the basis for deriving the divine attributes.

During the ensuing discussion, Pannenberg begins with Gregory of Nyssa's contribution to the Christian doctrine of God, namely, his claim that God, rather than being conceived as the ingenerate One, should be conceived as the infinite.[448] Next Pannenberg points to Duns Scotus, who argued that the concept of the infinite "has basic significance for the whole concept of God" (349). Pannenberg believes Descartes was one of the more significant contributors to the evaluation of the concept of infinity. Descartes regarded the infinite as "the first intuition of the intellect on

---

448. In what follows, there will be some repetition of material covered earlier. I have repeated it here because of the novelty of Pannenberg's proposal and to help keep these matters freshly before the reader.

which all knowledge of other things depends" (350). However, the intuition of the infinite that precedes all finite conceptions, Pannenberg argues, is a very vague and unclear intuition, so much so that it cannot be initially identified with God. This was Pannenberg's primary criticism of Descartes' argument. Upon initial presentation of Descartes' position, Pannenberg makes the following important observation: "With its revival of the ontological argument, Descartes' grounding of philosophical theology seems to me to have reversed the traditional order of the questions whether God is and what he is. The idea of God as infinite and perfect being comes first and existence follows from it" (352). Once again, we see the central role that the concept of the infinite and its priority over all finite perceptions plays in Pannenberg's theology. Because conceptualization of God as infinite precedes affirmation of God's existence, Pannenberg proposes reversing the traditional ordering of essence and existence. At this point we have gathered the necessary puzzle pieces; now we must assemble them.

Pannenberg's Critical Appropriation

First, Pannenberg argues that this initially vague intuition of the infinite cannot be directly equated with the idea of God. Instead, one must justify those connections. In other words, a defense must be provided for the claim that this vague something that stands before us is God. So if this vague awareness of the infinite turns out upon further reflection to be an awareness of God, has Pannenberg not argued that an awareness of God's existence has, in fact, preceded awareness of his essence (which is not to reverse the traditional ordering after all)? The answer must be no, for this vague awareness of God is initially not an awareness of *God as such* but merely an awareness of the bare existence of the infinite, as yet without any definitive essence. Pannenberg clarifies this claim as follows:

> The question of the essence (the *ti estin*) of a thing presupposes its existence even though it has not yet been determined what it is, or whose or what's existence is at issue. . . . [However,] when not defined, the thing simply exists. We grasp it only when we say what it is. . . . The concept of essence is thus relative to that of existence, which is grasped as something definite and distinct when we see *what (ti)* it is. (354)

Now we see why Pannenberg suggests that the relation between existence and essence is rather complicated. The point that he intends with these distinctions is twofold. First, the initial identification of an existent *something* may be, as with the intuition of the infinite, a vague awareness of the presence of that something that as yet has no defined essence; therefore, we have no specific concept of what it is but merely recognize that it is. So we cannot say *x* is before us but rather only that *something indefinite* is before us. In this case, we may rightly say that existence precedes essence. However, to move from the vague awareness of something to a more specific, even if not exhaustive, awareness of *x* presupposes some conception of the essence of *x*. In this case, then, we must be able to say something of what *x* is before we can affirm that this existent is, in fact, *x*, and here we rightly say that essence precedes existence.

Perhaps the implications are by now obvious. The structure of the awareness of the infinite matches Pannenberg's conception of the structure of our awareness of God. In other words, God's presence is here in the world for us "as the undefined infinite which is formed by the primal intuition of our awareness of reality, as the horizon within which we comprehend all else by limitations" (356). However, his presence does not overwhelm us but rather remains the mysterious presence of one who confronts us at every turn. This presence, though, is not initially for us an awareness of God but only an awareness of something not yet defined. How do we make the transition from this vague awareness of a mysterious *something* to identification of that something as God? We do this within the history of the religious traditions as they attempt to give content and identification to that mysterious presence. We assess those various proposals, throughout the march of history, in order to determine their adequacy, and only as they give definition to God can we say that the initial mysterious presence was already an awareness of God. Pannenberg summarizes the implications: "In this way the traditional problem of whether God exists disappears and instead the issue is how that primordial mysterious (and vague) presence is to be identified. Only with reference to specific conceptualizations of God's nature [does] it make sense to ask whether *such* a God exists."[449] For now, let us say that this is the fashion in which the concepts of essence and existence are related. We must now turn our attention to the question of how we are able to gain an awareness of the essence so that we may know something about it. To give a preview of the answer: We learn about the essence of God by virtue of his manifestation in the world, specifically by exhibiting a specific set of attributes in his interactions with the world.

God's Actions in the World

If, as Pannenberg argues, the divine essence is manifested in God's specific interactions with the world, the essence must become apparent in the working of God's power. In other words, by the actions God undertakes

---

449. Pannenberg, in personal correspondence to the author, July 13, 1994.

in the world, his essence would be revealed. Pannenberg articulates the point as follows: "The essence of things comes to manifestation in existence as a specific essence which is distinct from others. It distinguishes itself from others by its attributes. Thus God finds manifestation in the working of his power, and we know the distinctiveness of his essence, and differentiate it from others, by the characteristics of his working" (359). Therefore, if the attributes or qualities that derive from the working of God's power are truly to reveal the divine essence, then they must in fact be the attributes or qualities that are definitive of the essence. Yet, as is evident from the scriptural record of God's actions in the world, there is a multiplicity of divine works and actions that are, in fact, undertaken by three distinct persons. One of the related questions that has challenged the tradition is how the multiplicity of divine qualities manifested in the variety of works that God undertakes in the world can express the unity of the divine essence.

Generally speaking, there have been two ways of dealing with this challenge. On the one hand, there are those who have made a real distinction between the various attributes and the divine essence. On the other hand, some have made only a conceptual distinction between the essence and the attributes. Pannenberg believes that both solutions are problematic.[450] In the first case, to make a real distinction between the essence and the attributes is to separate the essence from the attributes in such a way that the essence is not constituted or defined by those attributes. Consequently, we would not know the essence as it truly is by appealing to such attributes. Of course, by ascribing the attributes to the essence, as it seems we must, the unity of the essence seems to disappear. In the second case, to make the distinction merely conceptual seems to result in an undefined unity.

The Council of Reims in 1148 attempted to solve the problem by tying the multiplicity of attributes to the multiplicity of the divine relations to the world. Pannenberg summarizes: "The attributes of God do not in fact differ either from the divine essence or indeed among themselves. Their multiplicity only expresses the multiplicity of God's *relations* to the world."[451] However, as long as one abides by the Aristotelian notion of essence as relationless and transcendent, conceiving the attributes as merely expressing the relation of God to the world means that "these attributes cannot belong properly to God in the same way as he is himself in his essence."[452] D. F. Strauss explicitly identified the contradiction lurking in this position: God is no different from his attributes but is somehow different from the

---

450. For more detail on what follows, see Pannenberg, *Systematic Theology*, 1:360ff.

451. W. Pannenberg, "Problems of a Trinitarian Concept of God," trans. P. Clayton, *Dialog* 26 (1987): 254.

452. Ibid.

"cosmic functions which form the material of these attributes."[453] In essence, then, the doctrine of God so conceived claimed that God is both the same as and, at the same time, different from his attributes. With the contradiction now explicit, Pannenberg points out that it was an easy matter to consider the divine attributes as nothing more than projections of human wants and needs. After all, if Christian theology itself seemed to say that the relations are not really constitutive for God, is it not possible that the attributes ascribed to God are merely expressions of the human desire for a "God"? Of course, when the attributes ascribed to God also had traces of finitude, and when Feuerbach later proposed a psychological motivation for projection, the plausibility of this whole line of argument was only amplified.

The next step, says Pannenberg, is atheism, and it was formally taken by Feuerbach. As a student of Hegel, Feuerbach was persuaded by Hegel's claim that the logical structure of essence requires that it be related to another. In fact, under this construal of essence, if there are no attributes and therefore no relations, there is no essence. Once reason had been given to believe that the attributes were merely projections, Feuerbach could deny the existence of the essence. Thus, as Pannenberg writes, "if there are no qualities, there is no divine essence to bear them. If the cloak falls, the duke falls with it" (364). Of course, it was precisely the Aristotelian understanding of essence as transcendent and relationless that led to these difficulties. If essence had been understood as relationally structured from the beginning, these problems would have been avoided, for the relations would have been seen as constitutive for the essence. However, in Aristotelian categories, essence was conceived in terms of substance, specifically "as that which remains the same beneath all change" (359). Substances were conceived as ontologically independent of appearances, changes, and relations. Consequently, Aristotle had to conceive relations and attributes as belonging to the category of accidents. This simple ordering of relation and essence led directly to these difficulties. Pannenberg uses the relation between Father and Son as an example of the difficulties that arise when relations are viewed as accidents of a prior substance. Specifically, the relations between Father and Son had to be viewed as two relations: one of Father to Son and another of Son to Father. However, is this not really a single relationship, even if it may be viewed from either side? If this is correct, Pannenberg argues that the Aristotelian ordering must be reversed: "Instead of being the accident of a substance, ordered to the substance, the concept of relation is now above that of substance, since we can speak meaningfully of substances only in relation to accidents" (366). Kant

---

453. Ibid.

explicitly recognized this new ordering in *Critique of Pure Reason*, in which in his table of categories, the overarching category is listed as relation and the substance-accident relation is listed as a subspecies of that category.

Pannenberg's Proposed Modifications

Briefly stated, Pannenberg's historical analysis claims that the roots of this reversal are to be found in the way Descartes and the pioneers of modern physics came to describe nature in geometrical terms. Clearly, the relation represented by the line that connects two points, A and B, say, is a single relation, being the same whether one starts at A or B. As this "spatial" view of nature became more prevalent, the importance of relations as descriptors became more obvious. Finally, Pannenberg asserts, substance came to be understood as relationally constituted. "It is certainly startling to hear that a thing simply consists of relations," he comments, but such a view "helps us to understand Kant's view of things as pure phenomena" (366). Hegel develops in more detail the relationships between the concepts of essence, substance, and accidents. He argues that essence is relationally structured so that any essence requires an "other" over against which to stand relationally. According to Hegel, the primary other of essence is existence. So discussions of essence apart from existence are mere abstractions. Of course, any actual essence has, in addition to its relation to existence, other concrete relations that define it.

Does this reversal of ordering have consequences for the doctrine of God? It does, for as I suggested earlier, the divine essence can no longer be conceived merely as transcendent and relationless outside the world. Instead, the divine essence must be conceived precisely in its relatedness to the world. Consequently, we must look at God's concrete relations to the world if we are to discover anything about the divine essence. Those relations are, Pannenberg believes, primarily manifested in God's acts. However, two questions remain: (1) What actions (or other manifestation-related concepts) best disclose the essence? (2) To what extent may we be confident that these particular actions or concepts truly reveal God as he is?

In dealing with these questions, Pannenberg critically appropriates the work of Hermann Cremer, *Die christliche Lehre von den eigenschaften Gottes*. There are two distinct lines of argument deployed by Cremer with the intention of getting at the divine attributes. The first one makes use of the concept of God's acts. Cremer bases this argument upon the historical revelation of God and uses the concept of purposeful action. While Cremer is not entirely clear on the rationale for his use of the concept of purposeful action, Pannenberg observes that the one who chooses a particular activity, by the selection of an end, "identifies himself or herself with the chosen end by accepting it as his or her own" (366). However, there is an irremediable weakness involved with this approach. As Pannenberg points out, "The one who acts might reveal by the action only one part of his or her essence, which is not specific enough. This is because the chosen goal might be exchangeable at will with another one, so that it does not characterize the one who acts" (369). In other words, if we are to gain access to the divine essence by way of the actions chosen by God, we must have some reason to believe that the activity we examine is such that it is expressive of the divine essence. As a consequence of this shortcoming, Pannenberg turns his attention to Cremer's second argument.

I have examined Pannenberg's claim that the divine essence is relationally constituted love and have found this to be consistent with the nature of the inner-Trinitarian relations as well as the scriptural claim that God is love. Cremer, Pannenberg observes, builds upon these insights and argues that the "central content of the divine action" is characterized by "the love of God as it is manifested in Jesus Christ" (369). However, if the love that God shows toward us is infinite love, as I have already argued that it is, then God engages himself wholly in the actions that manifest his love in the world so that "he keeps nothing back" (369). If God holds nothing back in the loving acts he undertakes on our behalf, then the divine essence is fully present in those acts, and God is thereby revealed. Therefore, the qualities manifested in that revelation are precisely the qualities of the divine essence. If this God, into whose attributes we inquire, is an effective presence in the world, then a basis exists for determination of the divine attributes. However, at this point Pannenberg raises an important question: How reasonable is it to apply the concept of action to God? Does the idea of action imply mind and will? If so, we have already seen that Pannenberg proposes significant modifications to the application of these concepts to God. At the same time, I have argued that Pannenberg's work clearly sees God as an intentional, acting agent.

In discussing the application of the concept of action to God, Pannenberg asserts, "The idea of a God who acts purposefully presupposes that God has intellect and will and that he works out ideas of his intellect in relation to the goals of his action as in the case of human persons" (370). Of course, this is precisely Pannenberg's concern, for it seems to finitize God, or at least use concepts in describing God that have traces of finitude. These traces of finitude arise when concepts appropriate for finite creatures are applied to God, and, Pannenberg claims, this opens Christian theology to the criticisms flowing from Fichte and the tradition that followed after him.

Pannenberg argues that the early church's adoption of Platonism led it generally to equate *pneuma* and *nous* so that God came to be conceived as incorporeal reason. Pannenberg believes this was a move away from the biblical conception:

> The penetration of the narrower view of *pneuma* as rational soul and consciousness into Christian theology is connected with the rise of the Platonic school in the 3rd century and the decision of Christian theology in favor of the Platonic transcendental view of God rather than Stoic pantheism. . . . Nevertheless, the identifying of *pneuma* and *nous* put theology on a path that is alien to the biblical view of God. (374)

So the tradition set itself up for the criticisms from Fichte and Feuerbach. Consequently, in attempting to avoid the material implications of Stoicism, the tradition adopted the concepts of mind and consciousness, concepts Pannenberg believes are overly anthropomorphic.

Pannenberg believes that we cannot merely dismiss the concepts of mind and will but rather that we must recognize their limitations when applied to God. He summarizes the concerns with the application of the notion of intellect to God: "Those who are aware of the difficulties will have to agree with the verdict of Spinoza that it is just as metaphorical to speak of the intellect of God as to call God the 'rock' of our salvation (2 Sam. 22:32, cf. v. 2) or the 'light' of our path (Ps. 119:105), or to speak of the Word of God (cf. Ps. 27:1, etc.)" (379). Pannenberg proposes that we conceive God as an infinite field of power. At the end of his analysis, Pannenberg, while believing this conceptualization of God resolves the anthropomorphisms, asks whether we can still make sense of the concept of a divine action: "If the living essence of God as Spirit has more the nature of a force field than a subject, how can we justify speaking of God's action, and how can we read off the attributes of the one God from his action?" (384).

Of course, one of the difficulties of applying the concept of action to God is that "the concept of action demands an acting subject" (384). However, we cannot apply the action directly to the divine essence, for as we have seen, the impersonal aspect of the divine nature is the spiritual essence. Consequently, "only the three persons are the direct subjects of the divine action" (384), so that the actions must be attributed to the Trinitarian persons. However, we must proceed cautiously, says Pannenberg, for as one develops a strong sense of distinction between the persons of the Trinity, the threat of tritheism arises again. I have argued that the unity of the divine essence is derived from the fact that all three persons are wholly committed to the monarchy of the Father. Pannenberg summarizes how this relates to the identification of the attributes of the one divine essence from the acts of the one God:

> The monarchy of the Father is God's absolute lordship. . . . But the monarchy of the Father is mediated by the Son, who prepares the way for it by winning form for it in the life of creatures, and also by the Spirit, who enables creatures to honor God as their Creator by letting them share in the relation of the Son to the Father. . . . Only herein is the one God the acting God as even before he is already the living God in the fellowship of Father, Son, and Spirit. . . . The action of Father, Son, and Spirit in the world is thus ascribed not merely to the three persons of the Trinity but also to the one divine essence. (389)

If, then, the actions of the one God, even though properly speaking they are the acts of the Trinitarian persons, are ascribable to the divine essence, we may know that the attributes revealed in salvation history are the attributes of God's nature. Consequently, the actions of God, so conceived, open the way to the essential attributes of the one God.

Pannenberg argues that the actions of God as revealed in the course of salvation history are those of the in-breaking of God's lordship into the world of creatures. By this he means that the acts of the Trinitarian persons are those acts undertaken in order to realize the monarchy of the Father. The Father's monarchy is the common goal of the three persons and is, therefore, the seal of the unity of the divine essence. This justifies our reading the divine attributes, as the essential attributes of God, off the actions of the divine persons in the world. Consequently, Pannenberg writes that "these attributes may be seen equally in the divine works of creation, reconciliation, and redemption, though they are articulated differently" (391). These arguments, then, are intended to demonstrate the validity of deriving the divine attributes from the revealed acts of the Trinitarian God in salvation history and to take those attributes as those actually belonging to the divine essence.

The Divine Attributes

As we begin to speak of the divine attributes that are evident from God's relation to the world, we notice that such speech has the form of "God is *x*" where *x* might be "gracious," "merciful," "good," and the like. Such statements have two elements that are set in relation to each other: "God" is the subject of the statement, and *x* is the attribute predicated of that subject. Pannenberg points out that in order to make meaningful statements about God, we must have some prior sense of what is intended by the word. Here we see again Pannenberg's claim that an initial awareness of essence precedes the definitive discovery of the attributes of that essence. Consequently, before we can say "God is *x*," we must have some prior conception of who God is, even if that prior conception provides little more than a means of pointing to God. Pannenberg argues, for reasons outlined previously, that the concept of the true infinite is our fundamental concept.

Pannenberg argues that there are two types of attributes that must be used in conjunction in describing the divine essence; however, they are by no means independent but rather are mutually dependent. In the first place, says Pannenberg, there are those that are presupposed as part of the very concept of God itself. More specifically, Pannenberg writes that "the answer lies in terms that explain the word 'God' as such, e.g., terms like infinite, omnipresent, omniscient, eternal, and omnipotent."[454] In addition to these terms that define what is meant by the word "God" as such, there are those that describe the relations evident from God's working within the world.[455] Again, Pannenberg believes that Cremer has captured this correctly when he describes qualities "contained in the very concept of God" as distinguished from those "which are disclosed in revelation."[456]

Before we proceed to an articulation of the specific attributes of God, it is appropriate to pause and connect this discussion with my analysis from earlier in this chapter of Pannenberg's understanding of the relation between the concepts of existence, essence, and attribute. One of the fundamental points of this series of arguments was to establish that before one can inquire into the existence of God, one must have some prior conception of what it means to be God. Consequently, Pannenberg argues that, contrary to a good deal of the tradition, essence precedes existence. However, he observes that it is possible to be aware of a vague existent that is present merely as a mysterious *something* prior to any conception of its essence. So to inquire into God's existence, we must presuppose something of what it means to be God; however, God may be present to us in the world as a mysterious presence *prior* to recognition that this mysterious presence is, in fact, God. In the latter case, existence precedes essence, though it would be wrong to say that the existence of *God* precedes a concept of his essence, since as that mysterious presence he is not yet known as God. This does not change the fact that to inquire into the existence of God *as God* requires presupposing some concept of God.

Next we observed that a good deal of the Christian tradition presupposed the essence of God to be that of first cause of the world. However, Pannenberg argues that this conception, while it must be affirmed if we

---

454. W. Pannenberg, *Systematic Theology* (vol. 1; trans. G. W. Bromiley; Grand Rapids: Eerdmans, 1991), 392.

455. These two "types" of terms or attributes correspond to the two mentioned earlier in this chapter. The ones that aid in defining the term "God" correspond to those referenced as distinctive terms—those that distinguish God from man. The ones that capture the concrete effects of his presence in the world correspond to the general terms—i.e., those that might also be applied to humans.

456. Pannenberg, *Systematic Theology*, 1:392.

are to maintain the idea of God as Creator, is not the most fruitful. Rather, he argues that the concept of the metaphysical infinite, with its implied notions of perfection, wholeness, and self-sufficiency, is much more fruitful. Pannenberg argues, appropriating certain ideas from Descartes, that an intuition of the infinite precedes all finite contents of awareness. Further, while this intuition, due to its vague and confused nature, cannot be initially equated with the idea of God, it turns out to be an intuitive awareness of God following mediation through the religious traditions. As we can see, the structure of the awareness of this mysterious presence of God and the intuitive awareness of the infinite correspond in that Pannenberg argues that humans experience the mysterious presence of a transcendent Other in the world before we learn to call him God, just as the experience of the intuition of the infinite precedes reflective awareness that the infinite precedes all intuitions of finitude. Consequently, in both cases, a vague awareness of the existence of *something* (now God, now the infinite) precedes our definition of the essence of that something. However, to inquire reflectively into the existence of God or of the infinite presupposes that we know something of what these concepts mean. Since the religious traditions have used the concept of the infinite to give content to what it means to be God, and because of the correspondence we find here between the structure of the awareness of the infinite and that of the awareness of God, Pannenberg believes this reinforces his argument for the primacy of the category of the infinite in the doctrine of God. It is not that the concept of first cause is mistaken but rather that the concept of the infinite yields much richer conclusions about the nature of God and correlates more closely with the human experience of the mysterious presence of God in the world. Now we can return to the earlier point: There are two types of mutually dependent qualities that we may ascribe to the divine essence: (1) those that define what it means to be God, and for the reasons given above, these derive from the concept of infinity; and (2) those that may be directly read off the working of God in salvation history.

The Attributes and Infinity

If, as Pannenberg argues, infinity is the primary aspect of the general concept of God, then it is obvious that the set of qualities that accompanies this would relate the idea of God as infinite to, for example, the concepts of time, power, space, and knowledge. These, of course, constitute the omni-attributes: eternity, omnipotence, omnipresence, and omniscience. Additionally, the attribute of immutability has generally been conceived as one of the qualities that derives from the divine infinity. Recall Pannenberg's statement that "in the concept of infinity freedom from limitation is not the primary point"; rather, the primary point is its "antithesis to the finite as such."[457] However, the truly infinite cannot be conceived as merely opposed to the finite but rather must also overcome the opposition between itself and the finite. Pannenberg concludes that if God is to be conceived as truly infinite, then God must be conceived both as opposed to the finite (the created world and its creatures) and as overcoming that opposition. In other words, God must be both transcendent to the finite world and immanent in it. Consequently, this series of attributes that derives from application of the concept of the true infinite to God must exhibit this structure.

Eternity

Our analysis of the divine attributes that relate to the infinity of God may move quickly now. Let us consider first the notion of God's eternity, which is God's infinity as it relates to time. Pannenberg holds that the divine eternity is to be conceived as the powerful presence of God to all times in undivided wholeness. As such, there is no past that fades away from God nor any future to which he looks forward; rather, God holds the totality of life present to himself in undivided perfection. Earlier I characterized the divine eternity as "temporal omnipresence" and called this mode of experiencing "superlatively temporal" since it is an expression of God's infinite presence to time. We have also seen that Pannenberg argues that the eternity of God, so understood, opens the way to a theological interpretation of time since the divine eternity would then be conceived as constitutive for time. Pannenberg believes it is precisely the doctrine of the Trinity that makes it possible to conceive the divine eternity in a fashion consistent with the true infinite. More specifically, it is the Father who remains transcendent in the mode of his eternity, while it is in the Son that the kingdom of God makes an appearance in time. Further, it is the Holy Spirit who indwells believers in time and thereby mediates participation in the kingdom to those believers. In short, God's eternity is the concrete expression of the infinity of God with respect to time, and it is the doctrine of the Trinity that makes it possible to conceive the divine eternity in such a way as to satisfy the requirements imposed by the concept of the true infinite.

Omnipresence

Let us consider next the attribute of omnipresence, which is the expression of God's infinity as it relates to the concept of space. Just as Pannenberg argues that the concept of the divine eternity opens a way to a theological

---

457. Pannenberg, *Systematic Theology*, 1:397.

interpretation of time, he argues that the divine omnipresence opens the way to a theological interpretation of space, since the concept of infinite and undivided space, as the presence of the divine immensity, is the precondition for all concepts of finite space. Pannenberg distinguishes between God's eternity and his omnipresence in that the former speaks of all things as present to God while the latter emphasizes God's presence to the creatures in their own places.[458] According to Pannenberg, the divine omnipresence is an essential presence, not just a presence of his power, since he argues that "no distinction can be made between the essence and power of God."[459] Further, this essential presence is not to be understood as an extension of the divine essence through space but rather as a presence that fills all things. And since the divine essence is not to be conceived as a body, nothing precludes the presence of other things in the same space simultaneously, just as the presence of a gravitational field does not preclude the simultaneous presence of celestial bodies.

Consistent with the structure of the true infinite, God's omnipresence both transcends and is immanent to the spaces of the creatures. In the first place, God transcends all creaturely spaces by virtue of the divine immensity, which fills them all, yet his presence to all creatures in their places demonstrates his immanence. As with the attribute of eternity, the divine omnipresence is made conformable to the true infinite by virtue of the Trinitarian structure of the divine essence. Once again, it is the Father who remains transcendent in "heaven," while the Son and Spirit are sent into the economy of salvation with the mission of actualizing the kingdom of the Father.

Omnipotence

Pannenberg finds a close connection between the attributes of omnipotence, omnipresence, and eternity. He writes that "as all things are present to God in his eternity, and he is present to them, so he has power over all things."[460] Further, since only a power that is present may produce effects, "omnipresence is thus a condition of omnipotence."[461] Pannenberg supports the traditional notion of omnipotence as meaning that God's power knows no limits "except for the requirement of consistency with his own divine nature,"[462] and he cites such biblical references as Job 42:2: "I know that thou canst do all things, and that no purpose of thine can be thwarted (416)."

---

458. Ibid., 1:410.
459. Ibid., 1:411.
460. Ibid., 1:415.
461. Ibid.
462. W. Pannenberg, *An Introduction to Systematic Theology* (Grand Rapids: Eerdmans, 1991), 9.

However, Pannenberg cautions that we should not allow unlimited power to be misunderstood as tyrannical power, and he asserts that a proper recognition of the implications of God's role as Creator provides the insights necessary to avoid such an error. Why? Because "as Creator, God wills the existence of his creatures. Hence his omnipotence cannot be totally opposed to them if he is to be identical with himself in his acts and to show himself therein to be the one God" (416). By virtue of the very fact that God wills the existence of a world of relatively independent creatures, God's omnipotence cannot be seen merely as standing over against the creatures. Rather, the divine omnipotence must also serve as the ground of whatever power the creatures themselves might have. One might argue, against Pannenberg, that there is no logical inconsistency in the concept of a God who is tyrannical and that, therefore, one cannot so easily dismiss this concern. However, infinity implies perfection, wholeness, and thereby goodness. Consequently, the combination of God as Creator and God as infinite suggests that, while initially a logical possibility, the idea of a tyrannical God ends up being inconsistent with fundamental elements of the divine nature. The combination of these factors (along with the subsequent discussion relating omnipotence to the true infinite), Pannenberg believes, yields a proper understanding of the divine omnipotence and avoids the purely transcendent, tyrannical conception of omnipotence.

In this, we can see elements of the structure of the divine omnipotence that correspond to the structure of the true infinite, for by serving as the causal ground of the power of the creatures, God's power is both within and over against the power of the creatures. Interestingly, Pannenberg calls "the incarnation of the Son . . . the supreme expression of the omnipotence of God" (421).Why does he make this judgment? Because the incarnation is the supreme example of the divine power appearing on the side of the creatures, even the rebellious creatures. As Pannenberg observes, the Creator's intent that the creatures should have life is expressed in the very act of creation. However, if the rebellious act of the creatures results inevitably in their death, with no possibility of rescue, Pannenberg argues that the impotence rather than the omnipotence of the Creator is demonstrated. Consequently, when the creatures' rebellion and sin lead to their fall into nothingness, the Son becomes a creature in order to exercise the divine omnipotence on their behalf in order to rescue them. So God's omnipotence does not merely stand opposed to even the fallen creatures but rather undertakes the task of their redemption and restoration. Further, the Trinitarian structure of the divine essence makes possible this construal of the divine omnipotence, for it is the Son's self-distinction from the Father and his entry into salvation history that makes the Son immanent to the creatures (along with the Spirit who mediates a share in the divine life to the creatures), while the Father remains transcendent to the creatures.

Omniscience

As eternity expresses infinite temporal presence, as omnipresence expresses infinite spatial presence, as omnipotence expresses infinite power, so omniscience expresses infinite or unlimited knowledge. If there is any question that God's knowledge is actually infinite, consider that omniscience entails that he knows all true propositions. Let us say that one of those propositions is "God knows p." Implied directly by this proposition is the question of whether God knows that he knows p; of course he does, since he knows all true propositions. However, this raises the question of whether God knows that he knows that he knows p, and this process goes on forever, so that directly implied by God's knowing p is the fact that God's knowledge actually contains infinite propositions. As we might expect, Pannenberg's assessment of the divine omniscience is less abstract, for he sees God's omniscience as closely related to his eternity and his omnipresence, since when we speak of God's omniscience, "we mean that nothing in all of creation escapes him. All things are present to him and are kept by him in his presence" (379–80).When we speak of God "knowing" something, we mean that he knows it directly without the mediation of memory, anticipation, or the normal processes that humans go through when they come to know a thing. Since both God's eternity and his omnipresence conform to the structure of the true infinite by virtue of his Trinitarian structure, and since God's omniscience follows from his eternity and his omnipresence, it is clear that God's omniscience conforms to the structure of the true infinite as well.

It is important to draw attention to the fact that each of these discussions regarding the omni-attributes has reinforced the conclusions of chapter 5, namely, that it is only by virtue of God's Trinitarian nature that the doctrine of God can be shown to satisfy the conditions imposed by the concept of the true infinite. This, of course, further lends credence to Pannenberg's claim that a coherent doctrine of God can be constructed only if based upon a notion of a differentiated unity within the Godhead, such as we have in the doctrine of the Trinity.

Infinity as Holiness

The first section in which Pannenberg presents the attributes that correspond to the divine infinity is entitled "The Infinity and Holiness of God." In fact, Pannenberg finds important linkages between the metaphysical infinite and the biblical notion of holiness: "The confession of God's holiness is also closely related to the thought of his infinity, so closely, indeed, that the thought of infinity as *God's* infinity needs the statement of his holiness for its elucidation" (397). Pannenberg observes that "the basic meaning of holiness is separateness from everything profane" (398). However, the idea of holiness also implies the notion of judgment, for when the holy contacts the profane, death is the result. This becomes a very present threat of judgment to the profane since the holy God "does not remain a totally otherworldly God but manifests his deity in the human world" (398). God calls his people to separate themselves from all that is profane so that they may dwell safely in his presence. However, God's holy presence with his people brings close the threat of judgment for all those who in rebellion turn away from God.

This is not, however, the final word, for "beyond every threat of judgement the holiness of God also means hope of new and definitive salvation" (399). Thus, Pannenberg summarizes the correspondence between the true infinite and the divine holiness: "The Infinite is truly infinite only when it transcends its own antithesis to the finite. In this sense the holiness of God is truly infinite, for it is opposed to the profane, yet it also enters the profane world, penetrates it, and makes it holy" (400). This is an interesting construal of the concept of the divine holiness. Pannenberg is surely correct that the elemental notion implied by holiness is separation from that which is not holy, or that which is profane. Similarly, as we learn throughout the course of salvation history, God calls those whom he chooses to become holy themselves. However, the problem is how the creatures are to become holy, and God's answer to that seems clearly to be the indwelling of the Holy Spirit. In this way, the divine holiness does, in fact, stand opposed to the profane, but at the same time, through the Holy Spirit the profane is transformed so that it is made holy. Consequently, Pannenberg's claim that the divine holiness demonstrates the structure of the true infinite seems correct.

Attributes Derived from Salvation History

In the earlier presentation and analysis of Pannenberg's doctrine of the Trinity, we saw arguments that the divine essence is the relationally structured love that exists between the three persons of the Trinity. These arguments were based on the revelation of God in salvation history; consequently, we should expect that the analysis here also would lead to the conclusion that the divine essence is, in fact, love. In the last section of volume 1 of *Systematic Theology*, Pannenberg examines the love of God, and he does so in three distinct steps: (1) "Love and Trinity," (2) "Attrib-

utes of the Divine Love," and (3) "The Unity of God." Because the subject
of the third section was addressed in chapter 5, we need here to consider
only the other two.

The Love of God

In undertaking to develop the theme of the Trinitarian nature of the divine
love, Pannenberg, consistent with his earlier methodological commitment
concerning statements about the Trinitarian persons, moves directly to the
revelation in Christ. He begins by mentioning that the "essential content of
the history of Jesus" is the expression of God's love for the world (422).
Why did the Father send the Son into the world? In order to seek and to
save that which was lost; consequently, Pannenberg, citing the evidence of
the divine purpose expressed in the parables of Jesus, writes, "The parables
portray God as the one who seeks what is lost and who in so doing displays
the self-attesting love of the Father. They also show that the search which
reveals the divine love takes place through the work and message of Jesus"
(423). Jesus is the emissary of the Father who, by entering salvation history,
exemplifies the love of the Father; or to use more scriptural language, Jesus
is the good shepherd who seeks out the lost sheep on behalf of the Father.

However, it is not simply that Jesus expresses the love of the Father;
rather, his own love for the creatures is likewise expressed in his message.
Pannenberg observes Paul's clear connection between the love of God and
the love of Christ: "Paul goes a step further when he also calls the love of
God that is expressed in the sending of the Son (Rom. 8:39; cf. 8:3) the love
of Christ himself (8:35; cf. Gal. 2:20). Here Christ, too, is the subject of the
loving address. One and the same event has two different subjects" (423).
Finally, Pannenberg argues that in addition to the love of the Father and of
the Son, the work of the Holy Spirit in salvation history reveals his love for
the creatures in the seeking to save those who have become lost. Here Pannenberg draws our attention to Rom 5, where Paul explains that the love of
God is shed abroad in the hearts of believers. If, as Pannenberg argues, this
construction in Romans is a subjective genitive, "then we must assume that
the Spirit of God who is at work in our hearts is the subject of this love and
remains so even insofar as it is at work in us and through us" (424). In this
way, Pannenberg believes that the salvation-historical revelation of Father,
Son, and Holy Spirit makes it clear that all are subjects who actualize the
love of God in the world.

However, the issue is not merely whether the Trinitarian persons are
subjects of the divine love, but rather how the concept of love relates to the
divine essence. Here Pannenberg finds the expressions by the Apostle John
in his first pastoral letter to be decisive, specifically those passages that

assert that God is love. But what exactly does John mean by this? Pannenberg believes that the work of Regin Prenter captures the intended meaning: "God is love. Why not simply: God has loved us? That is also said. Why not simply: God, because he so loved us, has an infinite love for us? Why not simply: God is loving? Why: God is love?"[463] Consequently, Pannenberg concurs with Prenter's conclusion: "The Johannine saying is not describing a quality of God but his essence or nature as love" (424). This interpretation, of course, hangs on the particular grammatical construction from 1 John, though such an exegetical approach is at least plausible so that the metaphysical interpretation given the passage here is also plausible. However, Pannenberg gives additional reasons for believing that the metaphysical claim is correct.

In the first place, Pannenberg expresses concern that if we merely ascribe love as a quality or attribute to the divine essence so that "love is not itself a substance or essence there 'lurks in the background' a subject that might exist without it" (425). At this point, one might object to Pannenberg's line of reasoning by asserting that it is possible, at least in the broadly logical sense, to conceive God without love; perhaps an evil, nonloving deity is a logical possibility. However, an entirely plausible line of defense against such an objection might begin by observing that the very concept of God implies the epitome of all perfections. Further, love itself surely must be conceived as a perfection; consequently, God, if he exists, must embody the perfection of love. Such a line of argument, of course, trades upon the tradition's frequent assertion that the ontological status of goodness and love is fundamentally positive, while the opposites are merely a deprivation of goodness and love. If love becomes expressive of the divine nature so that the divine nature cannot be conceived apart from love, does not love become constitutive for the essence? Consequently, are we not led to concur with Prenter and Pannenberg that love cannot merely be conceived as an attribute of God but must be conceived rather as descriptive of the very essence itself?

Pannenberg makes two other interesting connections in this series of arguments that we must note briefly before moving on to the attributes that are expressive of the divine essence conceived as love. First, he suggests that if we so conceive the divine essence, the doctrine of the Trinity is implied. How so? In the first place, if God were conceived as a single person, then the generation of an other would be necessary for the actualization of that love.[464] Likewise, if God were conceived as a biunity, it is difficult to see

---

463. R. Prenter, "Der Gott, der Liebe ist: Das Verhältnis der Gotteslehre zur Christologie," *Theologische Literaturzeitung* 96 (1971): 403.

464. I use the term "person" in this case very loosely, for it is hard to see how, if a relational conception of personality is correct, a single entity could be loving.

how we could be certain of a relationship characterized by unselfish love. Consequently, a third is necessary for the actualization of perfectly self-giving love, and thus a Trinity of persons within the Godhead is implied if we are to assert that the divine essence is constituted by perfect love.[465]

The second connection Pannenberg makes brings to bear the proposal examined in chapter 6: that the concept of an infinite field of power be used to give content to what it means to say God is spirit. Pannenberg writes that the "two statements 'God is Spirit' and 'God is love' denote the same unity of essence by which Father, Son, and Spirit are united in the fellowship of the one God" (427). Subsequently, he writes that the "essence of the Godhead is indeed Spirit. It is Spirit as a dynamic field" (429). The concept of spirit, Pannenberg believes, is given content by the field concept, and the divine essence is constituted by the relationally structured love shared by the three Trinitarian persons. In this way, then, Pannenberg argues that the divine essence is an infinite field of power constituted and characterized by the reality of perfectly selfless love. Consequently, we may draw the following conclusions from Pannenberg's arguments. First, the general concept that is most fruitful for articulating the doctrine of God is the concept of the metaphysical infinite. Second, from salvation history, we learn that the divine essence is constituted by perfect love. Third, the concept of God as spirit is given content by the field concept. Consequently, the divine essence, bringing these various points together, is to be conceived as infinite love, which has a Trinitarian structure and which is to be seen actualized as a dynamic field. If this is correct, the specific attributes we read of God's interactions in the world must be conceivable as concrete expressions of the infinite love of God.

The Attributes of God's Love

Goodness

In addressing the notion of God's goodness, Pannenberg reminds us that the Father whom Jesus proclaimed was alone to be characterized as the one who is good (Mark 10:18). In this particular passage, Jesus refuses the title "Good Teacher" for himself, indicating that the term "good" can only be predicated of God. The early church fathers tended to argue that by such statements Jesus was distinguishing between his divinity and his humanity, so that according to his humanity, Jesus could not accept the title "good," since it was reserved for God alone.[466] Of course, the affirmation that God

---

465. See p. 141.

466. See Hanson's instructive discussion of Athanasius's appeal to the distinction between Christ's humanity and divinity in dealing with such scriptural passages, in R. P. C. Hanson, *The Search for the Christian Doctrine of God* (Edinburgh: T&T Clark, 1988), 446–58.

is good raises the question of what precisely is being affirmed; in other words, what does it mean to say that God is good? Pannenberg draws our attention to such passages as Matt 5:45, where God is presented as the one who causes the sun to shine upon the evil and the good; Matt 6:30, where God is described as watching over all his creatures and where God is described as extending his gracious mercy to all who are needy and helpless (432–33). Perhaps one of the central aspects of God's gracious goodness is his blessing without regard to merit. In addition to the term "good," the Scriptures communicate the divine goodness with the notions of mercy, grace, and favor. Such a constellation of concepts is conceivable as the concrete manifestations of the infinite love of God.

Righteousness

In addition to goodness, the biblical data speak of God's righteousness. Pannenberg believes it unfortunate but true that the bulk of the Christian tradition from the Fathers to the modern age has tended to conceive God's righteousness as penal righteousness, that is, the sort of righteousness that makes sure that individuals get what they deserve (the guilty, punishment; the good, reward). However, as we have just seen, God's goodness is perhaps most fundamentally characterized by blessing apart from merit. Consequently, Pannenberg argues that a penal conception of righteousness is hard to reconcile with the divine goodness. He further questions whether this is an appropriate understanding in light of the biblical witness of both the Old and New Testaments. Pannenberg believes that a better conception of the divine righteousness is the concept of covenant righteousness, which is a righteousness that is fundamentally characterized by God's faithfulness to rescue and save his people. Thus, he writes:

> In his covenant righteousness God shows himself to be righteous (Rom. 3:3–5) even though he lets his chosen people fall into disobedience (11:30ff), for he orients his covenant righteousness to the atoning death of Jesus Christ (3:21–26) in order to have mercy not only on Israel but on all (11:32), i.e., on all who in faith appropriate his saving work in Jesus Christ (3:22, 26). (434)

God's righteousness finds expression not in the punishment of the wicked and the blessing of the good, but rather in the divine will to save and to bestow righteousness upon all who enter into relationship with God. With such an understanding of the divine righteousness, we can see how consistency can be maintained between the divine righteousness and the divine goodness understood as mercy.

At this point, one might reasonably ask whether Pannenberg's conception of the divine righteousness does away with the concepts of condemnation and punishment. The short answer to the question is no. While the will of the Creator is oriented toward the salvation of the creatures, that same will intends the creatures to have their degree of autonomy. Consequently, the creatures may reject the Creator's covenant righteousness and thereby refuse to be saved. The outworking of this we would call condemnation and punishment. However, I believe that Pannenberg would see these merely as the expression of the fact that the creatures cannot, as it were, rise above God in order to find fulfillment apart from God. The ultimate rejection of the divine will to save is the creature's expression to be his or her own god. Consequently, the creatures must fall into nothingness as a consequence of their own impotence, which, from the creature's perspective, would appear to be condemnation and punishment.[467] Clearly, the divine righteousness understood as the will to save can be seen as a concrete expression of the divine love. Further, I would argue that even when the creatures turn away from God, God expresses his love for them in that he takes their own autonomy seriously and does not override their wills.

Faithfulness

As it turns out, the notion of God's faithfulness is closely related to this notion of God's righteousness, for it is to be understood as related to the "consistency of the eternal God in his turning in love to his creatures" (436). God's faithfulness, then, is precisely his faithfulness to the covenant righteousness that finds expression in God's will to save his creatures. In exploring this point, Pannenberg finds several Old Testament texts that deny that God changes his mind as do humans. Yet he finds corresponding texts that indicate that God does, in fact, change his mind. These cases, Pannenberg observes, have specifically to do with God changing his mind with regard to some intended judgment or punishment of sin. This amplifies the point that God's faithfulness is expressed in the constancy of his love. Thus, Pannenberg concludes that "in the story of Israel, however, it becomes increasingly apparent that [God] does not change his mind about his will to save" (437). We see the ultimate manifestation of God's will to save in the sacrifice of his Son upon the cross.

Pannenberg believes that too frequently the notion of God's faithfulness has been taken as immutability in the sense advanced in the philosophical concept of God developed by the early Greek philosophers. Such an under-

---

467. By this language, Pannenberg does not intend to imply annihilationism but rather is merely recognizing that for humans to exist apart from their Creator is, essentially, to fall into nothingness.

standing overly emphasizes the transcendence of God and appears to make him unmoved by the course of human history. This has frequently led to the interpretation of various doctrines (most notably the doctrine of the atonement) such that any apparent change in the relationship between God and creatures has to be conceived as coming from the side of the creatures. The passion of the Son cannot be conceived as affecting the Father, and salvation is understood as satisfaction made by Christ through his human nature. In short, no change whatsoever can be understood as occurring in God. However, as Pannenberg claims, the notion of God's faithfulness does not carry such stringent implications for the historicity of God. Instead, it allows for historicity and change. How so? Pannenberg argues that "if eternity and time coincide only in the eschatological consummation of history, then . . . there is room for becoming in God himself, namely, in the relation of the immanent and the economic Trinity" (438). Consequently, genuine becoming in God can be reconciled with the unity of his eternal self-identity by virtue of the priority of the future in God's eternity. In the eschatological consummation, all historical change in the economic Trinity will be absorbed into the immanent Trinity so that, with retroactive power, that consummation will reveal that the eternal God is precisely who he has always been. The rethinking of the divine immutability in terms of God's faithfulness is an important insight that Pannenberg advances as part of his doctrine of God.[468]

Patience

The attribute of patience, says Pannenberg, is also closely related to the notion of God's faithfulness. Both, he goes on to say, have to do with the idea of remaining constant through the passage of time. However, Pannenberg distinguishes righteousness and faithfulness, which have God's saving purpose as their content, from patience, which has its orientation toward the creatures, specifically with regard to their conduct. "God is patient with them because of his saving purpose" (438). Pannenberg points to the contrast between those who are "patient" because of their impotence and God, who, by virtue of his omnipotence, can allow the creatures space for their own development while not fearing the consequences that may arise during that development. In other words, God may patiently bear the inappropriate behavior of his creatures so that they may yet repent and be restored.

---

468. One need not go all the way over to the position of those who deny the divine immutability, however. See my essay "Does God Change? In Defense of the Divine Immutability," in *God under Fire* (ed. E. Johnson and D. Huffman; Grand Rapids: Zondervan, 2002), 231–52.

Patience is evident in the history of Israel in that God extended grace to those who had sinned and thereby violated their covenant with God. God's patience in this case took form in delaying judgment in light of their disobedience as well as in providing the opportunity to begin afresh after judgment. Pannenberg comments, however, that "the people realized that it was dangerous to abuse this divine overlooking" (439). This is because the very concept of patience implies a forestalling—specifically, a forestalling of judgment and the attendant punishment, and it directly implies a time when the forestalling will come to an end. When God's patience, construed in this way, has expired, the working of his wrath becomes a reality. Once again, it seems entirely plausible to see the divine patience as one more concrete expression of the divine love toward God's creatures.

Wrath?

Pannenberg argues that "wrath is not an attribute of God. His acts are not in general determined by it" (439). To defend the point, Pannenberg cites passages wherein it is implied or stated that God's wrath is "a sudden emotional outburst" or that "it burns" at the scorning of the divine holiness, especially when those whom he has called to holiness fall away (439). Instead of being a divine attribute, Pannenberg asserts, wrath is the result of the contact of the holiness of God with that which is profane and has remained profane (or fallen away from holiness) through the refusal to take proper advantage of the opportunity to repent afforded as a consequence of the divine patience. However, as the Scriptures show again and again, God is ever willing to turn from his wrath in order to be gracious. While it is true that wrath is not an attribute of God per se, the exercise of the divine wrath is just as real for those who despise God's patience as is reconciliation for those who appropriate the divine patience as an opportunity to repent. The holiness of God will not be restrained from contact with the creatures indefinitely.

Wisdom

Interestingly, Pannenberg associates the divine wisdom with the notion of patience, particularly as it relates to the question of how God governs the world he has created. Pannenberg cites passages wherein the biblical data refer to God's founding of the world (e.g., Job 28:25ff.), to his sending of the prophets (Luke 11:4), and to his sending of the Son into the world to die upon the cross (1 Cor 2:7–8) (440–41). Further, God's wisdom reaches expression in the bringing together of world occurrences that are oriented toward the salvation of the creatures. In other words, God's wisdom is concretely manifested in salvation history as the manner in which his will to save works within the world history of contingent events so as to bring about the reconciliation of the creatures and, thereby, overcome their sin and perdition. Thus, Pannenberg connects God's wisdom with "the power of love over the march of history" (441). As in each case before, we see that a specific divine attribute can be understood properly as the concrete expression of the infinite, divine love.

Summary and Conclusions

First of all, it seems that Pannenberg's treatment of the divine attributes is fairly straightforward, and while he proposes some modifications, these proposals do not seem to be particularly problematic. In fact, it seems that his attempt to revise the concept of the divine immutability so that it is to be understood as an expression of God's faithfulness is a significant step forward. Increasingly, theologians are seeing the difficulties that arise from appropriating the concept of immutability from Platonism. The proposal Pannenberg makes seems to preserve the intent of the Scriptures while not retaining the problems suggested by the older conception. Pannenberg's intent to subsume change in the divine under his rubric of the "ontological priority of the future" will seem plausible to the extent one finds the arguments for the ontological priority of the future persuasive. Those who are unpersuaded will have to find some other way of overcoming the concerns that have arisen within the tradition concerning immutability taken in the Platonic sense. Some may object to Pannenberg's treatment of the divine wrath as merely the outworking of the divine holiness rather than as a separate attribute in itself. However, the effect of God's wrath in the world seems no different than if it were conceived as a separate attribute, but the difficulty in seeing wrath as a manifestation of the very same essence as, say, mercy is overcome by Pannenberg's construal. As we have seen in each case, it seems that Pannenberg has given us adequate reason to believe that, at a minimum, the claim that the divine essence is constituted of love is a plausible account.

One remaining question concerns the manner in which we are to bring together Pannenberg's various comments concerning the divine essence. In some places, Pannenberg refers to the divine essence as spirit, where spirit is to be taken as an infinite field of power. In other places, he suggests that the essence of God is power. Recall his comment that a God without power is no God at all. Consequently, it seems we must conceive the divine essence as somehow characterized by power so that, should God not have any, he would not be God. In yet other places, Pannenberg argues that God's being is his rule. And, of course, in this chapter we have seen that Pannenberg holds the divine essence to be infinite love. So the question is, can all of these concepts be brought together in a straightforward and consistent manner? I believe that Pannenberg would argue that it is the concept of infinite love that brings these different notions together in a coherent fashion. To say that the divine essence is love is to say what kind of power God has, namely, the power of love. To say that God's being is his rule is to express how the power of love acts in the world—specifically, it rules it, but in a way that is consistent with God's love for his creatures. Finally, the concept of a field of power or a field of force is intended to give content to what it means to describe God as spirit or as an incorporeal entity. This can be brought together in the following statement: The divine essence is constituted by the relationally structured love shared by the three Trinitarian persons, the incorporeality of whom can be characterized as an infinite field of force and who are active in the world even as they exercise lordship over the world of creatures in a way consistent with its characterization as infinite love.

Finally, there can be no doubt but that the concept of the infinite as a metaphysical reality and the distinction between the spurious and true infinites are once again at center stage. Pannenberg's philosophical justification for arguing for the necessity of a Trinitarian conception of God (or, minimally, for a concept of God as a differentiated unity) is what he believes are the normative requirements imposed upon theology by the philosophical concept of the true infinite. At the beginning of this chapter, we saw how he attempts to forge connections between the arguments concerning the essence and existence of God as they relate to the divine attributes with the methodological commitments outlined in chapter 2. There we saw that one of the justifications for engaging in talk about God in the first place is the vague intuition of the infinite that Pannenberg argues underlies all finite perceptions. Pannenberg contends that initially the awareness of the infinite is a nonthematic intuition of an encompassing all that is not yet an awareness of God. It can be called "God" only later by mediation through the religious traditions. Similarly, I have noted Pannenberg's claim that a vague awareness of a mysterious presence, which initially is without specific content, is a fundamental datum of human experience. Only later, however, when we begin to conceptualize and give content to that mysterious presence are we able to determine whether that presence is, in fact, God. To begin this latter task, one must have a general concept of what it means to be God, since only with that in mind may we ask whether the initial, mysterious presence can be reasonably shown to be the presence of God. Where does one obtain a general concept of God? From the religious traditions, of course.

Once Pannenberg begins his explicit articulation of the divine attributes, he again and again uses the concept of the infinite to show how, first, the general concept of God is to be understood in terms of the true infinite. Subsequently, he uses the balanced view of transcendence and immanence, which derives from the true infinite, to argue how the various attributes are the concrete expression of the infinite love of God in Trinitarian structure. Of course, Pannenberg gives a very good argument for why, if the infinite is to be taken metaphysically, it must correspond to the one God whose actual existence has a Trinitarian structure. On the whole it seems clear that the proposal that Pannenberg lays out is a plausible and coherent account of the divine attributes and of the divine essence. After all, Pannenberg's methodology (particularly the debatability of God's existence throughout the march of human history and the provisional nature of all truth claims) suggests that a plausible and coherent account of the doctrine of God is the best we can hope for during human history.

CHAPTER 8

Conclusion

THERE IS A SENSE in which one might characterize the history of theology, and an important part of philosophy as well, as the attempt to articulate an adequate concept of the Ultimate. Certainly this has been a major task of the majority of the world's great religious traditions. However, as the history of philosophy and theology as well as the history of religious traditions demonstrate, finding such an articulation is not an easy task. Why this is the case is, no doubt, the subject of some debate, though surely the hiddenness of God and the incomprehensibility of the divine nature are major contributors. Once one recognizes the complexity and difficulty of the task, it should come as no surprise that virtually every generation has found reason to argue for modifications or corrections to the prevailing understanding of the divine. Consequently, the fact that a contemporary systematic theologian such as Wolfhart Pannenberg should find the need for what he has called a "rather radical revision" to the Christian doctrine of God is not surprising. The question that has appeared more than once in the course of this study, and that must now be finally given an answer, is whether the proposed "radical revision" yields improvements to the Christian doctrine of God adequate to justify its acceptance. Before we move directly to the set of issues that will enable us to draw our conclusions on the matter, a summary is in order.

Our examination of Pannenberg's doctrine of God has proceeded along the lines of four different aspects of that doctrine. However, before we could examine these areas of Pannenberg's theology, we began with a consideration of his theological method. Also, in light of the centrality of the concept of the infinite to Pannenberg's overall theological enterprise, we investigated the historical development of the concept of the infinite as well as the manner in which Pannenberg appropriates and deploys the concept within his theology. Then we examined the claim that God is the power of the future that determines everything. This provided access to a number of important aspects of Pannenberg's work, not the least of which were his doctrine of the divine eternity and his proposal for the ontological priority of the future. Afterward, we examined his doctrine of the Trinity. The latter half of the twentieth century saw a resurgence of attention to the Trinitarian doctrine, and Pannenberg has taken it so seriously that he argues a coherent doctrine of God is not possible apart from it. If he is correct, the Trinitarian doctrine becomes the centerpiece of the entire Christian doctrine of God. Next we analyzed his proposal to import the field concept from physics and to use it to give content to what it means to say God is spirit. More specifically, Pannenberg argues that God should be conceived as an infinite field of power. Finally, we examined Pannenberg's proposed doctrine of the divine attributes, particularly regarding the unity of the attributes as well as the unity of the divine essence. During the course of this study, we have considered a number of provocative proposals. I have drawn preliminary conclusions in light of the critiques provided in particular chapters. Now it is time to draw final conclusions. Let us begin by considering Pannenberg's methodology.

Pannenberg's work is most generally characterized as rationalist, and this seems a fair assessment overall. His appropriation of Scripture is generally through the lens of the historical-critical method. He does not presuppose the truthfulness of the Scriptures but rather asserts that one must weigh the appropriate evidence in order to determine the truthfulness of what the Scriptures claim. Further, he seems to hold something of an evidentialist position with regard to belief in God, which is to say that one must have adequate evidence in order rationally to affirm the existence of God.[469] Consequently, one of the criticisms that arises with some regularity in the secondary literature regards his rationalist approach to theology. It has been argued that postmodernism has called into question the validity of the very sort of rational inquiry that Pannenberg undertakes, and it is true that he does not incorporate an explicit response to the criticism of what might be characterized as his "enlightenment rationalism." However, a

---

469. I have argued that this ought not be exaggerated and have suggested that Pannenberg would be sympathetic to Wolterstorff's "permissions" oriented epistemology.

more useful criticism would be one that engages his proposals directly and shows why postmodernist critiques touch either his epistemic proposals or, more broadly, his doctrine of God.

In fact, in *The Post-Foundationalist Task of Theology*, F. LeRon Shults characterizes Pannenberg's method as postfoundationalist. Further, Pannenberg, in the foreword to Shults's work, seems sympathetic to Shults's claims. Pannenberg's epistemic commitments run more along coherentist than foundationalist lines. Additionally, the appropriation of Dilthey's philosophy and the characterization of truth claims as hypotheses are consistent with a central tenet of postfoundationalism: The indubitable foundation of knowledge sought at least since Descartes is simply not available. Consequently, Pannenberg's method must embrace the sort of epistemic humility implied by recognition of the provisional nature of Christian truth claims. One expression of this is the pervasive criticizability noted by Clayton. While postmoderns might not fully embrace all aspects of Pannenberg's work, surely this is one area of convergence between Pannenberg's theology and postmodernist concerns.

While those who find Pannenberg's work rationalistic are not without justification for their concern, it is worth considering his motivations. Without doubt, Pannenberg's fundamental concern with theology as it has been done during the course of most of the twentieth century is the damage done to the intellectual integrity of Christian doctrine. He argues that this has been a consequence of the fact that many (he believes most) Christian theologians have failed to take seriously the criticisms advanced against the various tenets of the faith. Instead of facing those criticisms head-on, he argues, Christian theologians have either simply ignored those objections, continuing to work in what Pannenberg calls a "pre-critical mode," or responded by a retreat to subjectivism. In either case, the atheistic critiques have gained plausibility because of the lack of direct response. One of the purposes Pannenberg sees for himself is the recovery of the intellectual integrity of the faith. He aims to accomplish this by demonstrating how the various objections raised to faith may be plausibly overcome. This goal suggests the rather rationalist methodology that Pannenberg employs. At the same time, one should recognize that claiming that a rationalist methodology is appropriate for Christian theology is not the same as saying that every individual believer must operate similarly, a step Pannenberg does not take.[470]

---

470. In fact, in private conversation in October 1999, Pannenberg said that it is the task of the systematic theologian to engage these questions and issues on behalf of the church and its individual believers. Those individual believers, then, may appeal to the work of theologians and philosophers rather than engaging these issues directly. In fact, it is not even necessary that the nonexpert be able to articulate the various defenses provided by the theological community.

By the same token, however, it is appropriate to set Pannenberg's rationalism within the broader set of methodological proposals competing for the theologian's embrace. In an age when the argument for the truth of Christian doctrine is often surrendered before the battle is even engaged, we should appreciate the commitment that Pannenberg has made to attempt to restore the intellectual credibility of the faith by participating in the public marketplace of ideas. Some have proposed alternate methodologies that essentially require a withdrawal from public debate, on the assumption that Christian truth claims are merely true for Christians. Pannenberg will not accept such an approach; to see something as "true for me" simply will not do. Whatever one finally concludes about Pannenberg's work, there can be no doubt but that he has taken with deep and passionate seriousness the assertion that Christian truth claims are about the way the world really is. For this, we should be grateful.

We considered a portion of the storied history of the arguments for God's existence in chapter 2, and these arguments highlight the debatability of God's existence. While one can present plausible arguments that God is, one can also raise plausible objections to each argument. Consequently, neither the atheist nor the theist decisively wins this argument, which means that the debatability of God's existence is a primary datum of human existence. The inability of reason to lead to a decisive answer concerning the existence of God (as well as concerning certain other fundamental philosophical issues) often leads to a form of skepticism that in turn easily ends in a variety of forms of relativism. The attitude seems to be that if these questions cannot be answered, perhaps there is no absolute answer and, therefore, any one answer is as good as another. I find Pannenberg's appropriation of Dilthey helpful on these issues. The way in which Pannenberg deploys Dilthey's insights allows him to say, in essence, even though we may not be able to decisively resolve these issues now, there is an objectively true resolution to each. In light of the eschaton, the truth of each and every one will become evident. Consequently, we need not give up on the concept of truth, even if we must admit that we exist in a world where the best we can do at any particular time is to advance provisional truth claims. Of course, this means that I am defending primarily an epistemic version of Dilthey's historical hermeneutic. As we have seen, however, Pannenberg often seems to propose a more ontological version in that he argues that the eschatological revelation of God's kingdom is determinative of essences, not just meanings.

To repeat one example, Pannenberg argues that the resurrection exerted retroactive power on the being of Christ so that the resurrection was determinative of Christ's deity. In essence, Pannenberg argues that if Jesus had not been raised, he would not have been the eternal Son. However, given Pannenberg's ontological construal of Dilthey, one has to recognize that he really means that the resurrection, in a very real sense, "made" Christ the eternal Son. Of course, one might just as easily claim that the relations run in the other direction. In other words, why not argue that instead of the resurrection having ontological significance for the being of Christ, it was the being of Christ that determined that a resurrection would occur? One could still deploy an epistemic interpretation of Dilthey, so that the resurrection made it clear, epistemically, that Jesus was the eternal Son. I suspect that before many will be willing to follow Pannenberg's ontological construal of Dilthey, he will need to say more about why it is necessary.

From Pannenberg's methodology, we move to what is clearly the linchpin of Pannenberg's entire proposal for rearticulating the doctrine of God: the concept of the true infinite. We saw the concept first in chapter 2 in our examination of Pannenberg's methodology. According to Pannenberg, the vague intuition of the infinite, mediated through the religious traditions, is what justifies God-talk. In chapter 3, we examined the concept of the infinite in some detail, in particular the concept of the true infinite, which must be understood as both transcendent to and immanent to the finite, and which Pannenberg learned from Hegel and would deploy in his doctrine of God. In chapter 4, we saw how this concept of the infinite drove Pannenberg's understanding of the divine eternity. In chapter 5, we saw that Pannenberg argues that the true infinite makes a concept of a divine essence that is a differentiated unity, as in the doctrine of the Trinity, essential to an adequate doctrine of God. In chapter 6, the concept was used in reconceptualizing God as an infinite field of power. Finally, in chapter 7, it became clear that the true infinite is the central concept in Pannenberg's understanding of the divine attributes. If the concept of the true infinite were withdrawn from Pannenberg's doctrine of God, it would seem to collapse.

Unfortunately, as we saw at the end of chapter 3, intuitions in either philosophy/theology or mathematics are deeply divided on the proper conceptualization of the infinite. Is it merely a mathematical concept? Or is it more accurately a metaphysical concept? Is it actual or potential? We have seen that these are the fundamental questions that would need to be resolved if we were to be able to decisively determine whether Pannenberg's deployment of the concept is correct or not, but such decisive resolution does not appear forthcoming. If Pannenberg's arguments are correct, it seems abundantly clear that the concept of the infinite in its metaphysical sense must be applied to God, and therefore, it must be deployed properly within the doctrine of God. On the other hand, if those are correct who, like Charles Hartshorne, argue that the idea of an actual infinite is incoherent,[471] Pannenberg's deployment is in error. However, if the infinite is primarily a metaphysical concept, I have argued that it provides very useful resources for resolving a number of disputed areas within theology and that Pannenberg's various proposals, absent other problems, should be accepted. It seems that, minimally, Pannenberg's proposed use of the concept is both coherent and plausible, and given the potential it has for resolving and clarifying certain problematic issues, it clearly has a high degree of attractiveness. In the final analysis, as one might expect, given Pannenberg's epistemic commitments, it is likely that he would argue that his proposal ought to be viewed sympathetically just to the extent it provides a way around difficulties within the doctrine of God.

Within Pannenberg's doctrine of the Trinity, there are several points that require our final attention. First, his proposal to inquire into the Trinitarian nature of God based upon the revelation of Christ seems entirely correct. While speculative ruminations based upon philosophical and theological analysis are useful, the primary reason Christians have for affirming a Trinity of Father, Son, and Holy Spirit is that this is what salvation history reveals. If this is correct, then it directly implies that beginning with the threeness of God and deriving the unity subsequently, as Pannenberg proposes, is the proper methodology. Additionally, Pannenberg gives us plausible reason to believe that derivations that begin with the unity and then attempt to derive subsequently the Trinity have historically led to either subordinationism or modalism. Finally, the general tenor of Trinitarian analysis in the latter half of the twentieth century demonstrated that there is widespread agreement on this point.

Of course, once one decides that the threeness of God is the proper point of departure for Trinitarian analysis, the next challenge one has to face is the question of how tritheism is to be avoided. As we have seen, perhaps the primary element of Pannenberg's effort to secure the unity of God, given that he antecedently has established God's triune nature, is the monarchy of the Father. The monarchy of the Father, which is mediated to him by the Son and the Spirit, serves as the mutual goal of the three Trinitarian persons. By sharing a single divine essence and sharing the common goal of establishing the kingdom of the Father, the three persons of the Trinity show themselves to be one. Those who are unsympathetic to social Trinitarianism will likely find Pannenberg's proposal disputable. Of course, Pannenberg is reluctant to consider his Trinitarian theology along the lines of a social model due to his view that the analogy is too weak. Neverthe-

---

471. Consider, for example, C. Hartshorne, *A Natural Theology for Our Time* (La Salle, IL: Open Court, 1967).

less, given his historical assessment of the difficulties that arise when starting Trinitarian theology from the unity of God, Pannenberg's proposal
seems to open up (recover?) a more fruitful path.

Perhaps the most innovative proposals of Pannenberg's Trinitarian theology are the concept of self-distinction and his understanding of the mutuality of the inner-Trinitarian relations. A primary intent of both concepts is
to do away with any hint of subordinationism. The former asserts that
each of the members of the Trinity distinguish themselves from each other.
These relationships based in self-distinction show that the persons are not
distinguished from the other by the other. In other words, the Father does
not distinguish the Son and the Spirit from himself, as if his deity is superior to that of the Son and the Spirit. Rather, the Son, the Spirit, and the
Father each distinguish themselves from each other.

Even more helpful is Pannenberg's argument for the mutuality of relations between Father, Son, and Spirit. In this case, the goal is to show that
the distinctive persons of the Trinity are, in fact, mutually dependent upon
each other for their deity. Pannenberg rejects the simple notion of the
Father as fount or source of the deity of the Son and Spirit. The important
point is that Pannenberg's proposal aims to overcome subordinationism by
making the individual members of the Trinity utterly dependent upon each
other for their deity. The dependence is different in each case; for example,
the Son is not the fount of the Father's deity and the Spirit is not the fount
of the Son's deity. While the dependencies are different, they are such that
the deity of each is mediated by the other two. Pannenberg presents his
argument from the standpoint of the evidence that can be adduced from
salvation history as well as from certain metaphysical principles. In both
cases, the arguments are, minimally, plausible and coherent with the other
proposals within Pannenberg's doctrine of God. Further, it seems clear that
the manner in which Pannenberg lays out the mutuality of relations
between the Trinitarian members makes a remarkable contribution to the
tradition's understanding of the equality of the divine persons. Specifically,
it does away with ontological subordination and shows how each Trinitarian person is God only in the fullness of the inner-Trinitarian relations. All
in all, Pannenberg's proposed Trinitarian doctrine, while not without some
difficulties (as suggested in chapter 5), seems to contain important improvements to the traditional doctrine.

Pannenberg's proposal to assign ontological priority to the future is
undoubtedly one of the most interesting and challenging of this raft of proposals relating to the Christian doctrine of God. Even a casual perusal of
the secondary literature exhibits the extent to which this has perplexed and
delighted his interlocutors. Our examination aimed first to clarify the content of the proposal and then to consider the sorts of problems Pannenberg

believes it resolves. There can be little doubt but that an epistemic version of the priority of the future flows directly from Pannenberg's appropriation of the work of Dilthey. To bridge the gap from epistemology to ontology, Pannenberg notes that when some future state of affairs is determinative for the meaning (which he takes to be equivalent to the essence) of some earlier state of affairs, the implication of that future state of affairs is not merely epistemic but is actually ontological. There may be some leeway in how one takes these terms, but it seems one can follow Pannenberg easily enough at this point.

One example of how this priority of the future (whether one sees it as epistemic or ontological) is played out within the doctrine of God is related to the divine eternity. In discussing this point, I observed how assigning priority to the eschatological future as regards God's knowledge opens a way around the alleged foreknowledge problem. It seems clear that if Pannenberg's analysis is correct, giving priority to the future provides a means for affirming God's knowledge of events that are future to humans while also preserving human free will. It would be helpful if Pannenberg expanded his presentation regarding the differences he perceives in affirming an epistemic priority of the future versus an ontological one. Either way, however, he has given us good reasons to consider the futurity of God as a mode of his being and, thus, to reflect upon how such a concept enhances our conception of God.

We come now to the most fascinating of Pannenberg's proposed modifications to the Christian doctrine of God: his proposal that the concept of an infinite field of power be used to give content to the claim that God is spirit. The ongoing challenge, at least for the foreseeable future, is likely to be how to preserve the personhood of God. Pannenberg concurs that this is essential to any adequate doctrine of God, and he provides a number of arguments aimed at showing that a field can be seen as personal. Further, at least for the sake of discussion, I contended that these arguments were plausible, even if rather speculative. However, I pointed out that it is likely that the "practical" issue is not whether a sophisticated metaphysical argument can be adduced that demonstrates the plausibility of conceiving a field of power as personal, but rather how the term "field of power" will be perceived. It seems we have to agree that it has an impersonal tone. Of course, Pannenberg argues that the divine essence as such is impersonal and is only personal in the concrete manifestation of the individual persons. However, the individual persons have to be conceived as personal instantiations of the divine "field of power," which still leaves us with the question of whether a field will be perceived as adequately personal. It is too early to make a final judgment on this matter, and further, even if the concept is likely to be perceived as impersonal, this is not adequate reason to dismiss this as a theological proposal. I concluded that Pannenberg's proposal that a field of power can be conceived as personal is clearly plausible.

We also considered the objections of those who argue that Pannenberg has inappropriately borrowed the field concept from the natural sciences. In the first place, Pannenberg believes that the work of Jammer has reasonably shown that this is not true. The more significant point to the objections raised by physicists is that Pannenberg does not really seem to recognize the status of the latest field theories. Their objection involves two primary points: (1) There are a number of fields within physics, and Pannenberg is not clear on which he means; and (2) the particular theory Pannenberg seems to have in mind (the vision of Faraday for a single overarching field) is the one currently thought to be the least likely to be true. These difficulties arise primarily because Pannenberg intends his appropriation of the concept of field to be taken literally. Since he claims the application is literal, he opens himself to these sorts of very technical and precise objections. I suggested in chapter 6 that Pannenberg would actually strengthen his proposal by admitting that he intends the application of the field concept to be either metaphorical or analogical. Some quotations seem to suggest that Pannenberg really intends something more metaphorical/analogical.[472] However, he needs to make the point more explicit and couple it with a more detailed analysis of the similarities and differences between the fields of physics and those he intends to deploy in theology.

This brings us to the last item of consideration: the overall relevance of Pannenberg's proposal. In a sense, this is the most difficult assessment to make, for it depends not so much upon our ability to read the coherence and plausibility of a given proposal, but rather upon our ability to assess accurately the mood of philosophy and theology in general. Here I will consider a pair of concerns. The first relates to the postmodernist situation in which theology currently finds itself, and the second relates to the metaphysics of Pannenberg's proposal.

The issues I have in mind under the first item are related to the sorts of concerns mentioned in a review of Pannenberg's *Systematic Theology* by William Placher.[473] In the course of his review, Placher suggests that Pannenberg's work is somewhat anachronistic and out of touch with modern concerns. There is, Placher writes, no attention to feminist concerns with masculine language, no real engagement with liberation theologies, and no meaningful interaction with those movements that question the very sort

---

472. W. Pannenberg, *Systematic Theology* (vol. 1; trans. G. W. Bromiley; Grand Rapids: Eerdmans, 1991), 412.

473. W. C. Placher, "Revealed to Reason: Theology as 'Normal Science,'" *Christian Century* 109, no.6 (1992): 192–95.

of rational project Pannenberg has undertaken. Pannenberg's work, some suggest, is a return to nineteenth-century metaphysics with a vengeance, the sort of metaphysics that has lost plausibility in the early days of the twenty-first century. The fundamental concern is whether Pannenberg's proposals will even get a fair hearing. It is possible that his overall proposals will be dismissed out of hand as "not the way we are doing theology today." Only time will tell whether such views as Placher's are correct or not. We can only hope that a number of theologians will undertake to pick up Pannenberg's baton and press the lines of thought he has opened to their conclusion.

The final issue has to do with the question of whether there is still a heart in theology today to undertake the rather complex and very sophisticated sort of metaphysics that underlies Pannenberg's theology. This suggests a range of issues from, for example, the deployment of the concept of the metaphysical infinite to the arguments in chapter 7 about the rejection and replacement of Aristotelian concepts of substance and accident. Many modern theologians have turned their attention away from such metaphysical speculations toward more "practical" matters. However, I have often said to students that there is nothing more practical that a theologian can do for his or her readers than to help them to think theologically, and the rigor of Pannenberg's work, if traced carefully, will make us all better at the critical task of engaging the world theologically. Of course, it is impossible to determine in advance how the tradition will respond; however, we must affirm that whatever final judgment is made, Pannenberg's proposals are too important to be dismissed before they receive a hearing.

What final word can I offer? First, there can be no doubt that Pannenberg's *Systematic Theology* contains one of the most significant articulations of the Christian doctrine of God that has come along in several years. We observed some difficulties that need to be resolved in order to strengthen the proposal, but the judgment concerning the significance of Pannenberg's work stands in spite of those. Second, my overall judgment concerning Pannenberg's proposal is that it is plausible and internally coherent. While this does not of itself demonstrate the truthfulness of Pannenberg's proposal, it is nonetheless a necessary condition that the proposal satisfies. Third, there are several historically problematic issues, outlined earlier, that Pannenberg's proposal has the potential to resolve. This amplifies the importance of seeing that Pannenberg's proposal gets a fair hearing. Finally, there can be little doubt regarding the depth of scholarship that underlies Pannenberg's work. While this does not prove anything as far as the viability of Pannenberg's proposal, there are few people who have his breadth and depth of knowledge. This means that Pannenberg has woven a virtually unmatched quantity of material together in his work, and this is important given his commitment to the concept of coherence as used in his methodology. The more material brought coherently together, according to Pannenberg, the more likely it is that the proposal is true.

In a day when "practical" concerns often obscure the importance of doing the really hard work of philosophy and theology, Pannenberg represents a return to the days when the importance of laying the proper metaphysical and philosophical foundations for theology were undertaken prior to moving on to the "practical" issues. However one finally views this, one has to respect the seriousness with which Pannenberg undertakes establishing this foundation. Since his mystical experience of Christ's call upon his life at age sixteen, Pannenberg has committed himself to fulfilling that call by dedicating himself to the furtherance of the kingdom of Christ. He has given us his best work; now we must appropriate it as best we can and attempt to carry the work forward. Time will tell whether we do justice to the gift Pannenberg has bestowed upon us.

BIBLIOGRAPHY

Works by Pannenberg

Anthropology in Theological Perspective. Translated by M. J. O'Connell. London: T&T Clark, 1985. (German: *Anthropologie in theologischer Perspektive*, 1983)

Basic Questions in Theology. 2 vols. Translated by G. H. Kehm. Philadelphia: Westminster, 1971. (German: *Grundfragen systematischer Theologie.* 3 vols., 1967)

Christian Spirituality. Philadelphia: Westminster, 1983.

"The Christian Vision of God: The New Discussion on the Trinitarian Doctrine," *Asbury Theological Journal* 46 (1991): 27–36.

The Idea of God and Human Freedom. Translated by R. A. Wilson. Philadelphia: Westminster, 1973. (German: *Gottesgedanke und menschliche Freiheit*, 1971; and an essay from *Terror und Spiel: Probleme der Mythenrezeption*, 1971)

An Introduction to Systematic Theology. Grand Rapids: Eerdmans, 1991.

Jesus: God and Man. 2nd ed. Translated by L. W. Wilkins and D. A. Priebe. Philadelphia: Westminster, 1977. (German: *Grundzüge der Christologie*, 1964)

Metaphysics and the Idea of God. Translated by P. Clayton. Grand Rapids: Eerdmans, 1990. (German: *Metaphysik und Gottesdanke,* 1988)

"Problems of a Trinitarian Doctrine of God." Translated by P. Clayton. *Dialog* 26 (1987): 250–57.

Revelation as History (with R. Rendtorff, T. Rendtorff, and U. Wilkins). Translated by D. Granskou. New York: Macmillan, 1968. (German: *Offenbarung als Geschichte,* 1961)

Systematic Theology. 3 vols. Translated by G. W. Bromiley. Grand Rapids: Eerdmans, 1991–1998. (German: *Systematische Theologie,* 1988–1992)

"Theological Appropriation of Scientific Understandings: Response to Hefner, Wicken, Eaves, and Tipler." *Zygon* 24 (June 1989): 255–71.

Theology and the Kingdom of God. Edited by R. J. Neuhaus. Philadelphia: Westminster, 1969.

Theology and the Philosophy of Science. Translated by F. McDonagh. Philadelphia: Westminster, 1976. (German: *Wissenschaftstheorie und Theologie,* 1973)

Toward a Theology of Nature. Edited by T. Peters. Louisville, KY: Westminster/ John Knox, 1993.

Works on Pannenberg

Braaten, C. E., and P. Clayton, ed. *The Theology of Wolfhart Pannenberg.* Minneapolis: Augsburg, 1988.

Buller, C. A. *The Unity of Nature and History in Pannenberg's Theology.* Lanham, MD: Littlefield Adams Books, 1996.

Burnhenn, H. "Pannenberg's Doctrine of God." *Scottish Journal of Theology* 28 (1975): 535–49.

Galloway, A. D. *Wolfhart Pannenberg.* London: George Allen & Unwin, 1973.

Grenz, S. *Reason for Hope.* New York: Oxford University Press, 1990.

Olive, D. H. *Wolfhart Pannenberg.* Waco, TX: Word, 1973.

Olson, R. E. "Trinity and Eschatology: The Historical Being of God in Jürgen Moltmann and Wolfhart Pannenberg." *Scottish Journal of Theology* 36 (1983): 213–27.

———. "Wolfhart Pannenberg's Doctrine of the Trinity." *Scottish Journal of Theology* 43 (1990): 175–206.

Polk, D. P. *On the Way to God*. Lanham, MD: University Press of America, 1989.

Tupper, E. F. *The Theology of Wolfhart Pannenberg*. Philadelphia: Westminster, 1973.

Worthing, M. W. *Foundations and Functions of Theology as Universal Science*. New York: Peter Lang, 1996.

Secondary Materials

Abraham, W. J. *Canon and Criterion*. Oxford: Clarendon, 1998.

Alston, W. P. *Perceiving God*. Ithaca, NY: Cornell University Press, 1991.

Aquinas, T. *Summa Theologica*. In *Basic Writings of Thomas Aquinas*. 2 vols. Edited by A. C. Pegis. New York: Random House, 1945.

Aristotle. *Metaphysics*. Translated by H. G. Apostle. Bloomington: Indiana University Press, 1966.

Athanasius. *The Letters of Saint Athanasius concerning the Holy Spirit*. Translated by C. R. B. Shapland. London: Epworth, 1951.

———. *On the Incarnation of the Word of God*. New York: Macmillan, 1947.

———. *Orations against the Arians*. Oxford: Clarendon, 1884.

Augustine. *Confessions*. Translated by A. C. Outler. Library of Christian Classics. Philadelphia: Westminster, 1955.

———. *The Trinity*. Translated by E. Hill. Brooklyn: New City Press, 1991.

Bainton, R. *Hunted Heretic: The Life and Death of Michael Servetus, 1511–1553*. Boston: Beacon, 1953.

Barbour, I. G. *Science and Religion*. New York: Harper & Row, 1968.

Barth, K. *Church Dogmatics*. Translated and edited by G. W. Bromiley and T. F. Torrance. Edinburgh: T&T Clark, 1956–1975.

Basinger, D., et al. *Reason and Religious Belief*. New York: Oxford University Press, 1991.

Berchman, R. *From Philo to Origen*. Chico, CA: Scholars Press, 1984.

Bernes, J., ed. and trans. *Early Greek Philosophy*. London: Penguin, 1987.

Braine, D. "God, Time, and Eternity: An Essay in Review of Alan G. Padgett, *God, Eternity, and the Nature of Time*." *Evangelical Quarterly* 66, no. 4 (1994): 334–37.

Cobb, J. B., and J. M. Robinson, eds. *Theology as History*. New York: Harper & Row, 1967.

Davis, C. F. *The Evidential Force of Religious Experience*. Oxford: Clarendon, 1989.

Descartes, R. *Meditations on First Philosophy*. 3rd edition. Translated by D. A. Cress. Indianapolis: Hackett, 1993.

Dilthey, W. *Der Aufbau der Welt in den Geisteswissenschaften*. Gasammelte Schriften 7. Göttingen: Vanderhoeck & Ruprecht, 1965.

Fackre, G. *The Doctrine of Revelation*. Grand Rapids: Eerdmans, 1997.

Feuerbach, L. *The Essence of Christianity*. Translated by G. Eliot. Buffalo: Prometheus, 1989.

Ford, L. "A Whiteheadian Basis for Pannenberg's Theology." *Encounter* 38 (Autumn 1977): 307–17.

Gregory of Nyssa. *Contra Eunomius*. Edited by P. Schaff. Nicene and Post-Nicene Fathers. Series 2. Vol. 5. Albany, NY: AGES Software, 1996–1997.

———. *The Life of Moses*. Translated by A. J. Malherbe. New York: Paulist Press, 1978.

———. *On Not Three Gods*. Edited by P. Schaff. Nicene and Post-Nicene Fathers. Series 2. Vol. 5. Albany, NY: AGES Software, 1996–1997.

Grenz, S. J., and R. E. Olson. *20th Century Theology*. Downers Grove, IL: Inter-Varsity Press, 1992.

Gunton, C. "Time, Eternity, and the Doctrine of the Incarnation." *Dialog* 21 (1982): 263–68.

Hanson, P. D. *The Dawn of Apocalyptic*. Philadelphia: Fortress, 1975.

Hanson, R. P. C. *The Search for the Christian Doctrine of God*. Edinburgh: T&T Clark, 1988.

Hartshorne, C. *A Natural Theology for Our Time*. La Salle, IL: Open Court, 1967.

Hegel, G. W. F. *Lectures on the Philosophy of Religion*. Translated by R. F. Brown et al. Berkeley: University of California Press, 1988.

———. *Science of Logic*. Translated by A. V. Miller. Atlantic Highlands, NJ: Humanities Press International, 1969.

Huffman, D., and E. Johnson. *God under Fire*. Grand Rapids: Zondervan, 2002.

Jammer, M. "Feld." *Historisches Wörterbuch der Philosophie*. Vol. 2. 1972.

Kant, I. *Critique of Pure Reason*. Translated by N. K. Smith. New York: St. Martin's Press, 1929.

———. *Religion within the Limits of Reason Alone*. Translated by T. M. Greene and H. H. Hudson. New York: Harper & Row, 1960.

Kittel, G., and G. Friedrich, eds. *Theological Dictionary of the New Testament*. Translated by G. W. Bromiley. Grand Rapids: Eerdmans, 1968.

Kuhn, T. *The Structure of Scientific Revolution*. Chicago: University of Chicago Press, 1970.

Lauer, Q. *Hegel's Concept of God*. Albany, NY: SUNY Press, 1982.

Mackie, J. L. *The Miracle of Theism*. Oxford: Clarendon, 1982.

McKenzie, D. "Pannenberg on God and Freedom." *Journal of Theology* 60 (1980): 307–29.

Moore, A. W. *The Infinite.* London: Routledge, 1990.

Muhlenberg, E. *Die Unendlichkeit Gottes bei Gregor von Nyssa.* Göttingen: Vandenhoeck & Ruprecht, 1966.

Munsch, R., and Sheila McGraw. *Love You Forever.* Willowsdale, Ont.: Firefly Books, 1991.

Neuhaus, R. J. "Reason Public and Private: The Pannenberg Project." *First Things* 21 (March 1992): 55–60.

Origen. *First Principles.* Translated by G. W. Butterworth. Gloucester: Peter Smith, 1973.

Padgett, A. *God, Eternity, and the Nature of Time.* New York: St. Martin's Press, 1992.

Pasquariello, R. D. "Pannenberg's Theological Foundations." *Journal of Religion* 56 (1976): 338–47.

Peacocke, A. *Creation and the World of Science.* Oxford: Clarendon, 1979.

Peters, T. "Trinity Talk." *Dialog* 26, no. 2 (1987): 133–38.

Pike, N. *God and Timelessness.* New York: Shocken, 1970.

Placher, W. C. "Revealed to Reason: Theology as 'Normal Science.'" *Christian Century* 109, no. 6 (1992): 192–95.

Plantinga, A. *Warrant and Proper Function.* New York: Oxford University Press, 1993.

———. *Warrant: The Current Debate.* New York: Oxford University Press, 1993.

Plantinga, A., and N. Wolterstorff, eds. *Faith and Rationality.* Notre Dame, IN: University of Notre Dame Press, 1983.

Plato. *Timaeus.* Translated by D. Lee. New York: Penguin, 1965.

Plotinus. *The Enneads*. Translated by S. Mackenna. New York: Penguin, 1991.

———. *The Six Enneads*. Translated by S. Mackenna and B. S. Page. Great Books of the Western World. Chicago: Encyclopedia Britannica, 1952.

Pojman, L. *Philosophy of Religion*. Belmont, CA: Wadsworth, 1987.

Polkinghorne, J. *Reason and Reality*. Valley Forge, PA: Trinity Press International, 1991.

Popper, K. *Conjectures and Refutations*. New York: Routledge, 1992.

Prenter, R. "Der Gott, der Liebe ist: Das Verhältnis der Gotteslehre zur Christologie." *Theologische Literaturzeitung* 96 (1971): 401–13.

Pseudo-Dionysius. *The Complete Works*. Translated by C. Luibheid. New York: Paulist Press, 1987.

Rahner, K. *The Trinity*. Translated by J. Donceel. New York: Herd & Herd, 1970.

Scharlemann, K. *The Being of God*. New York: Seabury, 1981.

Schleiermacher, F. D. E. *The Christian Faith*. Edited by H. R. Mackintosh and J. S. Stewart. Edinburgh: T&T Clark, 1989.

———. *On Religion*. Translated by J. Oman. New York: Harper, 1958.

Soskice-Martin, J. *Metaphor and Religious Language*. Oxford: Clarendon, 1985.

Stump, E., and N. Kretzmann. "Eternity, Awareness, and Action." *Faith and Philosophy* 9, no. 4 (October 1992): 463–82.

Swinburne, R. *The Coherence of Theism*. Oxford: Clarendon, 1993.

———. *The Existence of God*. Oxford: Clarendon, 1979.

Westphal, M. "Taking Suspicion Seriously: The Religious Uses of Modern Atheism." *Faith and Philosophy* 4, no. 1 (October 1987): 26–43.

Wood, L. W. "Pannenberg's Concept of 'Person.'" Unpublished paper.

Worthing, M. W. *God, Creation, and Contemporary Physics*. Minneapolis: Fortress, 1996.

INDEX